Romantic Re-Vision

Bryan Jay Wolf

Romantic Re-Vision

Culture and Consciousness
in Nineteenth-Century
American Painting and
Literature

The University of Chicago Press

Chicago and London

The University of Chicago Press, Chicago 60637
The University of Chicago Press, Ltd., London

This book was published with the assistance of
the Frederick W. Hilles Publication Fund of
Yale University.

In slightly different form, chapter 1 and the
epilogue of this book first appeared respectively in
the Summer 1980 (vol. 34) and Summer 1981 (vol.
35) issues of the *Georgia Review.*

Library of Congress Cataloging in Publication Data

Wolf, Bryan Jay.
    Romantic re-vision.

    Includes bibliographical references and index.
    1. Romanticism in art—United States.   2. Painting,
American.   3. Painting, Modern—19th century—United
States.   4. Ut pictura poesis (Aesthetics)   I. Title.
ND210.5.R6W6   759.13   82-2741
ISBN 0-226-90501-2 (cloth)   AACR2
ISBN 0-226-90502-0 (paper)

For Harriet

Contents

Illustrations

Preface

The following essays are experiments in a form of critical writing: explorations into the modernity of nineteenth-century American painting. As studies in the language and meaning of early Romanticism, they employ a critical vocabulary derived as much from contemporary literary theory and intellectual history as from the study of art. They are, as the title suggests, "re-visionary" in intent: they seek not only to revise our understanding of the nature of American Romantic painting—its remarkable complexity, modernity, and expressive power—but to help redefine the enterprise of criticism necessary to recapture that visual heritage. In a recent editorial in the *American Art Review*, Roger Stein argued persuasively for a form of art criticism geared to the cultural significance of visual "structure":

> To seek for the reintegration of form and meaning, to ask what any particular work tells us through its structure, its systems of forms, about American culture is thus an act of recovery: to repossess our past through its special visions . . . .[1]

This book is an exploration into some of the "special visions" animating the canvases, and occasionally the writings, of artists like Washington Allston, Thomas Cole, and John Quidor. It shares Stein's concern for the cultural expressiveness of a work of art, together with a sense of the integrity that any formal system of images and signs requires lest it be reduced to a merely "illustrative" level. Works of art are texts, and they are meant to be *read*, even when they record, as in the case of Allston, the collapse of their own intelligibility. The question is not *whether* a critic will choose to read the material he treats, but *how*. And here I confess some trepidation. Stein assumes that the act of cultural recovery is a benign one—that we come to understand the "past in its pastness" so that we can thereby "know its difference from and its likeness to our present." I am not so sure. In the very attempt to recover the past we come to alter it irrevocably. We bring to it the concerns of our own contemporary world, concerns built into the very language we employ. Our past resembles

Coleridge's "chameleon [that] darkens in the shade of him who bends over it to ascertain its colours." Coleridge's image in the *Aids to Reflection* might well serve as a motto for the present volume. Romantic re-vision is more than a twentieth-century activity: it is the story of a discovery in the nineteenth century—by artists for whom consciousness was becoming a mode of self-consciousness—that all vision eventuates in re-vision, an act of interpretation that alters what it beholds. No longer is perception an innocent act: the artist shapes as he sees, and in time, comes to see only what he shapes.

As the reader might infer, the essays that follow are studies in the peculiar modernity of American Romantic painting: its sense of loss and dispossession, its conservative fear of the artist's visionary powers, and its recurrent self-consciousness and self-referentiality. They seek, as Nathaniel Hawthorne sought a century earlier, to understand the present by first understanding the past, and they share with the author of the *Twice-Told Tales* the curse and blessing of double consciousness which characterizes so much of contemporary writing. In Janus-like fashion, they divide their attention between the objects they interrogate and the act of interrogation itself. Criticism in the modern world is an act of infinite hope. It gestures toward a past world it cannot help but re-constitute in its own image, while requiring from that past an explanation for its present. *Romantic Re-Vision* is no exception: it is as much a product of the world it describes as an account of the forces constituting, as early as the nineteenth century, an American mode of Romantic modernism.

The concern of the book is essentially interpretive. It seeks to construct from the artifacts and residues of the past—what Washington Irving would call the "flotsam and jetsam" of history—a narrative that renders both the reader and the critic active participants in the world they would understand. Hence the essayistic nature of the chapters that follow. *Romantic Re-Vision*, like all acts of reading, turns upon the textuality of its world. It understands the critic as a figure for whom the essay is perhaps the most congenial mode of writing, and it attempts, it *essays*, both a personal mode of vision and a larger moment of *contact* with a past that also represents its own intellectual origins. What is uniquely modern about all this is the inability of the contemporary critic—this critic at least—to remain within the boundaries of what might be termed the language of cultural intent. The effort of past historians to describe the culture they treat in its own terms—to recreate the past in a manner almost entirely congenial to the language and aspirations of that world— seems to me impossible today, in part because a past generation of schol- ars (I am thinking of figures like Perry Miller) have already written texts that cannot, in their own terms, be competed with, and in part because history will not allow the contemporary critic to write in the mode of his predecessors. I am not sure this is progress, but I am sure that it is change, and it makes a difference.

And the difference I would describe as Freud. What we have learned from Freud, whether we are interested in psychoanalysis or not, is that the language of conscious intention, the language in which a culture or artist explains himself, is only the tip of an intellectual iceberg. The responsibility of the critic, a responsibility that I take to be as much a doom as a destiny, is to provide a voice, a narrative, a saga, for those unstated and often unconscious structures that seem finally determinative for the whole. The critic then is a storyteller, a translator if you will, whose role is complementary to that of the historian and whose work begins where the latter's traditionally leaves off. It is his task, perhaps his vocation, to trace through the labyrinthine turnings of the texts he investigates that narrative thread which binds the writer to his culture and the reader to both. The thread is often an invisible one, present only in the silences and interstices of the text, and requires of the critic not only the tact to listen in silence but the courage to lend that silence a form and voice different from the text's own. The result can be disconcerting. In listening for resonances beyond those of the surface language, meanings in a work of art that operate at a level different from and occasionally subversive of its stated intent, we run the risk of rupturing the object into two separate and discontinuous halves: an artifact that we recognize—in its difference—as part of a past world, and an object that in its very modernity seems to betray the culture from which it once came.

Our dilemma is that of the Freudian reader of dreams, whose task it is to navigate between the "manifest dream content" and the "latent dream thoughts" in a manner that demonstrates how the latter speaks through the former. It is the latent dream thoughts that we seek: those meanings hidden or denied by the culture that produces them, and yet inscribed inevitably within the recesses and margins of the texts it creates. Until we have examined our objects for their deepest secrets, probing like the depth psychologist for those hints and adumbrations of a message behind the message, a covert operation within an overt object, we have not engaged the past in its peculiar and profound relation to the present.

Romantic Re-Vision may be interpreted as an argument for the role of mind in the shaping of American culture. As opposed to the more traditional readings of Romantic art as a celebration of nature in its vast and heterogeneous diversity, the essays that follow offer an alternative account. They focus on the tendency of the mind to substitute itself for the world around it, and suggest that, even in a painter as radical in his commitment to the American landscape as Thomas Cole, the role of nature is largely metaphoric, an extended battleground on which the aspiring painter wages a sublime struggle against the pressures and conventions of the past. It is not the reality of nature that is in question, nor the fidelity of the Romantic artist to the physical world around him. Rather, the American artist, as treated in these pages, is engaged in a dialectic of consciousness with itself. At times the struggle seems involuntary and in fact contrary to the artist's own deepest desires. Allston's aesthetic of parody, for example, grows out of the dissociation within his world between imaginative endeavor and moral aspiration. The self-referential quality of Allston's work, together with its parodic quotation from past styles, reflects a deeper language-boundedness in Allston, an incapacity to move beyond the mind's processes to a world unconfined by the limits of thought. Or again, we observe the usurping quality of consciousness in its *compulsion* to see in the works of John Quidor. The artist involuntarily inverts what he suspects to be the natural order of things by arrogating to himself the power of gods; he is compelled to see, and in the process he liberates psychic energies disruptive of the natural and social fabric. In time, the artist is displaced by his own imaginative and trespassing creations.

In drawing attention to the mediating role of consciousness in American Romanticism, I have tried not to lose sight of the grounding function of culture. However complex and tenuous the relation between art and the society that produces it, there still remains a pattern of reflection, criticism, and repetition by which the former maintains its echoing ties with the latter. We may take our cue here from Theodor Adorno. In his writings on Schoenberg, Adorno skirts a fine line between the fragile ties that link an art form to its culture on the one hand, and the deeply paradigmatic quality of those forms in both expressing and resisting the inner *telos* of society on the other. Despite the purely formal determinants that shape art according to criteria intrinsic to its medium, the artist remains for Adorno a barometer of social change. The task of the critic is to translate the seeming autonomy and social remove of the work of art back into the culturally laden language that surrounds it. The poignancy of the task lies in the difficulty of spanning both social and formal orbs. To live in the shadow of modernism is to undergo the breach, the separation, that divides the world of the mind and its form from the driving forces of history. Not that the two are ever finally asunder, but that the mediations between the two become ever more complex and difficult of resolution. *Romantic Re-Vision*, then, is both an insistence on the difficulty of deciphering the ties of art to society and an attempt to discern nonetheless the radical modernism undergirding American culture of the nineteenth century. It stresses with Adorno, not the ease, but the recalcitrance by which modern art yields up its cultural contents. And if, at moments, it seems to describe a world more present than past, then I must refer the reader to Coleridge's chameleon, and suggest perhaps that we are closer companions to the nineteenth century than we usually care to think.

A note on method. The choice of painters treated most prominently in this study—Allston, Quidor, and Cole—may appear somewhat idiosyncratic to the reader, a suspicion he or she no doubt will find confirmed by my tendency to discuss individual works not always associated with the central oeuvre of each artist. The reader's suspicion is not without foundation and deserves comment. I have chosen the painters I have for many reasons, not least of which is love. Each painter provides an individual, and to my mind, different instance of Romantic modernism. Together, they combine to form a vision of an American Romantic tradition that is larger than its separate parts. The story begins with Washington Allston and the revision of classical forms for modern ends, and it concludes a generation later with Thomas Cole and the creation of an American sublime.

Both Allston and Cole are relatively well known in American art historical circles. John Quidor is not. If Quidor appears at moments to be odd-man-out in this story—the "only kangaroo among the beauty," to borrow Emily Dickinson's apt description of herself[2]—then his presence in this book is an indication of how profoundly we need to rethink our understanding of the history of American painting. Quidor is a major figure who has only lately begun to receive the recognition he deserves. The problem, I suspect, is that we have not possessed until recently adequate critical tools for appreciating him. What appears initially as idiosyncracy on my part (or that of other similarly minded critics) in discussing Romantic art may really involve the continuing need for "canon revision": a reassessment of the forces and figures that populate the American visual landscape.

There are other points and procedures to be noted. The essays that constitute this book tend to focus on detailed analyses of individual works. The emphasis is on the text as much as the context, and, in particular, on the generation of visual texts from other texts (verbal or visual) over time. To readers familiar with literary criticism, this emphasis on close textual analysis will be recognized as a familiar legacy from the "New Criticism." However my readings may differ from those studies characteristic of the New Criticism, they share with the scholarship of the previous generation a deep commitment to the text itself. The essays that follow assume the "writerly" quality, as Rolandes Barthes has called it, of the works they treat. American paintings, like their literary counterparts, require the active presence and interpretation of the viewer. They are neither so simple nor so commodified as to fit neatly into the cultural categories we bring to them. On the contrary, they continually baffle and frustrate our everyday expectations, and require that we, like their makers, discard our habitual relation to the world in order to catch them in all their original dissonance and beauty.

I have tried in this effort of capturing to spread my net far. Literary texts are discussed on occasion at relatively great length because it has seemed appropriate to do so. Quidor, for instance, makes sense only in the context of Washington Irving, and both Irving and Quidor in turn appear with that much more precision and richness when placed within the purview of a tradition dating back to Milton. The same applies to Cole, who is indebted not only to John Martin's mezzotint engravings of *Paradise Lost* but to a tradition of sublime thinking that is at once Protestant and modern, and that is as rooted in a literary culture as it is in specific visual sources.

Had we world enough and time, as the poet says, this study might have moved to embrace eagerly other artists and additional objects of art. Lacking such leisure, I have chosen to work by a mode of critical condensation: to read individual works as intensely and as deeply as possible. I assume that the intellectually laden work of art carries within itself an abundance of meanings, some consistent, some not, and that every strong work of art condenses within itself the drama and concerns of its predecessors. Among its many different meanings, *revisionary* activity entails the effort of the artist to rewrite—to revise—his own history through the continual refiguration of past works (his own and those of the tradition from which he springs). Hence the discussion of Allston's landscapes in chapter 2 focuses on works not as well known, for example, as *Belshazzar's Feast*, but on works that possess a parallel integrity, narrating through their composition the drama of their development. So too with Thomas Cole and the Romantic sublime. In the years following his first recognition in 1825, Cole creates a visual idiom that is virtually complete by the time of his departure for Europe in 1829. Though his style changes significantly after his return from Europe, his influence *as sublime painter* upon other American painters dates from this initial period, and it is the story of his early years that I have chosen to tell. Together with Allston and Quidor, Cole brings to a conclusion that remarkable chapter in American art known as early Romanticism.

Bryan Jay Wolf
New Haven, Connecticut

Acknowledgments

First books, like first children, live many lives in the imagination before ever reaching the light of day. They owe their realization in large part to the encouragement provided by teachers and friends. Among the many individuals to whom I am indebted intellectually, I would like to thank especially Sydney Ahlstrom, Hans Frei, R. W. B. Lewis, David Minter, Niels C. Nielsen, Jr., Ronald Paulson, Elizabeth Reedy, Alan Trachtenberg, and Joseph A. Ward, Jr. Two people, colleagues and mentors both, have played special roles in the genesis of this book. Charles Feidelson, through his writing and later his teaching, first showed me the beauty and complexity of nineteenth-century American literature. From him I have learned the adventure that makes of literary criticism an exercise of perennial promise and excitement. Jules Prown opened my eyes to the power and possibilities of American painting. Under his tutelage I learned that art in the United States did not begin with Jackson Pollock, as I had once suspected, but instead, as Emerson wrote of Whitman, "must have a long foreground somewhere," for such an extraordinary "start."

There are others to whom I am indebted in a manner both formal and informal: Richard Brodhead, Robert Byer, Vincent Bynack, Harriet Chessman, Elizabeth Davis, Gerald Kleiner, Georgia and Russ Lyman, Ruth Nelson, Robert Weisbuch, and Patricia Yaeger. They were the angels with whom I wrestled, and I have partaken shamelessly of their influence, ideas, and support. One person in particular, John Elder, provided a combination of friendship, vision, and intellectual guidance for which no acknowledgment can suffice.

The manuscript was read with great care by a number of people whose advice I value and whose suggestions account for much that I hope is right with the book. In particular I am grateful to Wayne Franklin, Michael Fried, David Laurence, and John Riquelme. They may recognize many of their virtues in the text. The sins I reserve for myself. I am also grateful to Deedee Wigmore of Kennedy Galleries, New York, and Alexander Acevedo of Alexander Galleries, New York, for their generous assistance and information.

This book could not have been completed without assistance from Yale University. The concluding chapter on Thomas Cole was written while I was on leave of absence with a Morse Fellowship, 1978–79. Grants from both the A. Whitney Griswold Faculty Research Fund and the Frederick W. Hilles Publication Fund made possible the research and helped sub-sidize the publication of the book. Portions of *Romantic Re-Vision* ap-peared in altered version in *The Georgia Review* and are reproduced here with their permission.

And finally there are my students. Their many voices have blended into the larger cadence of the text, but their separate influences are very real and deeply felt. If writing is in any way a joint enterprise rather than an act of isolation, then they have been true partners, and I owe them more thanks than I can express.

Part One

Romanticism and
Self-Consciousness:
Washington Allston

1 Washington Allston and the Aesthetics of Parody

There is more work in interpreting interpretations
than in interpreting things; and more books about
books than on any other subject; we do nothing but
write glosses on one another.

MONTAIGNE, *Essays*

All day, I had wandered in the glittering
    metaphor
For which I could find no referent.

ROBERT PENN WARREN, *Or Else*

*A caveat to the reader
about a peculiarly
Romantic propensity*

*R*omanticism plays cunning games with us,
as contemporary criticism has come to discover. The Romantic text often harbors
within itself meanings subversive of its surface
intent, constituting through its various modes of
figuration a subtext that not only explicates its own metaphoric structure
but *criticizes* it as well. This rhetoric of self-criticism, implicit in the text
without actually dominating or defining it, exists, like the ancient god
Proteus, in many different forms. In proto-Romantic works like the
gothic novel, it tends to surface through the structure of discontinuity
which renders the empirical language of the novel inadequate to the
forces it must interpret. The narrative literalizes through its action the
vulnerability of its language to a world of subterranean currents outside
the range of its rhetoric. In the Romantic lyric, the effort of self-criticism
centers upon the nature and operation of tropes. The text becomes a
record of its own figurative evolution, exposing in the tension between
tenor and vehicle the larger patterns of dissimulation essential to the
making of fictions.

The pattern may be extended into the province of painting as well. For
figures like Washington Allston, America's first major Romantic painter,

the work of art is a complex and multilayered artifact, capable of sustaining a varied series of meanings at many levels of discourse. What occurs in the surface figuration of the work may be contradicted, or at least qualified, through alternative forms of signification implicit in its composition, structure, or sequence of allusions. Allston shares with individuals of his generation a double consciousness intent on the clarification—and occasional subversion—of its own modes of discourse. We see in the painted image an after-image, a qualifying rejoinder which the artist inscribes into his space as a means of commentary upon his work. Like Thoreau's experience at Walden Pond, "conscious of the presence and criticism of a part of me, which, as it were, is not a part of me, but a spectator, sharing no experience, but taking note of it," Allston too records not just the event, but the "I think" behind the event, the awareness of both the possibilities and the limitations of the shaping mind caught in the moment of self-reflection. Romanticism is inclined toward a rhetoric of disguise. It tends to view its symbols with distrust and to register within itself both signs of its discontent and hints for unraveling the duplicities of its language. Allston is no exception. His major works require that we treat him with the same respect we accord a magician: watching in fascination as we search for the sleight of hand. Where he differs from his contemporaries is in his method, not his madness. He offers us the pleasure of familiar recognitions, presenting us with images that we are certain we have seen before. We haven't, of course, and that is part of the game, but in that moment of recognition, that instant of a seeming familiarity, we encounter the language of parody and an aesthetic world shaped to the contours of the parodic imagination. Parody is Allston's mode of self-criticism, his means of commenting not on the weaknesses of the painter, but on the deeper limitations inherent in human vision. To discover among the conventions of Romantic portraiture an undertone and echo of the parodic is to encounter that "certain doubleness" which renders the Romantic text its own best critic.

I

Wherein the painter and writer creates images of exile of a peculiar sort

Washington Allston creates a curious portrait of his friend and sometime banker Samuel Williams prior to Allston's departure for Boston in 1818 after a seven-year sojourn in England (fig. 1).[1] Boston-born Williams sits casually, though somewhat stiffly, in a high-back wooden chair whose projecting dolphin-shaped arm rests resemble, however faintly, an ancient chariot arrested in its forward motion. Williams's posture places him at a slight angle to the picture plane. His right arm borders a small writing table to his side,

1. WASHINGTON ALLSTON, *Portrait of Samuel Williams*, before 1818. Cleveland Museum of Art, purchase, Mr. and Mrs. William H. Marlatt Fund.

his hand draping the arm rest and carrying the viewer's gaze from his downward-pointing index finger to the sinuous curve of the dolphin head. His left hand holds open a book that rests on his lap. Williams is not reading; he seems instead self-absorbed, maintaining no direct eye-contact with the viewer. His startling white cravat, exaggerated in size and prominence even for the fashions of the day, together with the luminous flesh tones of forehead and face, draw the viewer's attention to his abstracted stare in a setting otherwise solemn and colorless. But Williams offers no response. His oblique gaze fails to communicate to the viewer any inkling of his thoughts, and we are confronted instead with a revery that seems oblivious to our efforts to penetrate it. Behind Williams in the left-hand quarter of the painting appears a world curiously in contrast to the drab interior in which Williams sits. Animated by rich swirls of Venetian color—blues, pinks, and creams—an antique landscape complete with river, castle, and distant mountain hovers between two Doric columns that separate the architectural foreground from the distant landscape. Before the massive archway which frames this exterior view stands Williams's writing table. Two pages of manuscript, an inkwell with quills, and several books—in short, the materials by which human vision is recorded and communicated—lie upon the table. The tip of a quill visible to the side of Williams's elbow suggests that Williams has been writing. The top book of the three on the table points back into the landscape, as does the tall feathery quill that spans foreground and background in its diagonal placement, the only explicit visual link between architectural interior and background. Together quill and book provide a clue, however indirect, to the revery that absorbs Williams's attention. They carry the viewer outside the confining interior, with its dark browns and blacks, to the energy and brilliance of the background world. The animating whites and pinks of Williams's face seem similarly linked with the creams and reds on the other side of the threshold pillars. By line and by color the viewer moves from the painting's primary focus on Williams's likeness to a secondary focal point in the antique landscape, the latter an "objective correlative" for the former.[2] To penetrate Williams's revery we must comprehend the significance of the Baroque backdrop; the world of his thoughts has been transcribed, as the apparatus of the writing table suggests, in the picture emerging on the other side of the columns.

A similar situation occurs in the opening scene of Allston's gothic novel of 1821, *Monaldi,* written three years after the *Portrait of Samuel Williams* was painted. Allston frames his tale of a young painter—deceived by his innocence and his overactive imagination into the attempted murder of his dulcet wife—with the curious adventure of an American traveler whose singular accident in the Italian countryside leads him to the manuscript containing Monaldi's history. The novel begins at dusk one autumn.

> There is sometimes so striking a resemblance between the autumnal sky of Italy and that of New England at the same season, that when the peculiar features of the scenery are obscured by the twilight it needs but little aid of the imagination in an American traveller to fancy himself in his own country; the bright orange of the horizon, fading into a low yellow, and here and there broken by a slender bar of molten gold, with the broad mass of pale applegreen blending above, and the sheet of deep azure over these, gradually darkening to the zenith—all carry him back to his dearer home. It was at such a time as this, and beneath such a sky, that (in the year 17—) while my vetturra was slowly toiling up one of the mountains of Abruzzo, I had thrown myself back in the carriage, to enjoy one of those mental illusions which the resemblance between past and present objects is wont to call forth. Italy seemed for the time forgotten; I was journeying homeward, and a vision of beaming, affectionate faces passed before me; I crossed the threshold, and heard—oh, how touching is that soundless voice of welcoming in a day-dream of home—I heard the joyful cry of recognition, and a painful fulness in my throat made me struggle for words—when, at a sudden turn in the road, my carriage was brought to the ground.
>
> Fortunately I received no injury in the fall; but my spell of happiness was broken, and I felt again that I was in Italy.[3]

Allston's American narrator contrasts Italy with his "day-dream of home" as if both were regions of the mind: the former, Italy, an image of exile comprised of pilgrimage and the toil of ascent ("my vetturra was slowly toiling up one of the mountains of Abruzzo"), the latter, America, a region both past and anticipated, lost home and aspired-to goal. What is unclear is the relation between these two worlds. The narrator's mountain ascent, no matter how arduous the journey or how diligent the climber, can never issue in the "dearer home" the pilgrim-traveler yearns to find. It is always on the other side of a visionary "threshold" whose crossing entails inevitably a "sudden" and metaphysical "turn in the road," bringing "carriage . . . to the ground" and the traveler back to Italy. No route but an imaginative one—a "day-dream of home"—can return to the wanderer those "beaming, affectionate faces" now lost. The process by which this imaginative transformation occurs is especially noteworthy: "the peculiar features of the scenery are obscured by twilight" until the present world, Italy, becomes no more than a vehicle for the vision it has called forth. The traveler must blur the world around him, rendering what is literal more suggestive, in order to create "mental illusions" of home. By a progression of darknesses, a subtle veiling of reality, the features that once individuated the landscape and proclaimed one's exile serve instead as the material and language of imaginative vision, allowing through their blurring, "an American traveller to fancy himself in his own country."

Samuel Williams shares with the revery-prone narrator of *Monaldi* a situation of exile. His dolphin-armed chair, like the narrator's coach, seems a vehicle of imaginative fancy, more quiet and less passionate than the imaginative transport of the poet William Butler Yeats, "Astraddle on the dolphin's mire and blood" a century later.[4] Like the anonymous narrator of *Monaldi*, Williams dwells in a world whose spatial articulation reflects a persisting epistemological dilemma in Allston at this period. Both figures inhabit confining interior spaces, whether a carriage in the case of Monaldi's narrator or a castellated Baroque chamber; the somber hues of Williams's room suit the mood of the narrator's coach. Juxtaposed against these brown worlds, though confined to the background, is a vista of resplendent color whose attainment seems, however indirectly, the object of the subject's revery. Could the coach fly or the dolphins take wing, they would surely carry their voyaging subjects across the threshold that separates present from past, real from ideal. Nor is each work without its appropriate "threshold" images. In *Samuel Williams* the middleground columns both introduce and interdict the background landscape; they allow visual access to a visionary world at the same time as they distinguish foreground from background, denying the sitter any access but that of the imagination. The writing table at the base of the columns plays a similar role, sealing off the space between Williams and the background landscape at the same time as it provides, through the implements upon it, access of a different sort. The tools of the writer are a visual correlate for the presence of the painter, whose imagination must provide the wings that the dolphins lack. Midway between interior enclosure and exterior freedom, the writer-artist translates escape and revery into vision. In *Monaldi* the narrator visualizes this process in domestic rather than baroque imagery. Where Williams conjures antique landscapes, the narrator of *Monaldi* seeks his "dearer home," here literalized into a house and threshold that the wandering pilgrim must cross in order to embrace the "affectionate faces" within. So too the "autumnal sky of Italy," like the columns enclosing Williams, introduces a "resemblance," a visionary world, which we may partake of only by forgetting the real Italy that is always before us. In both works, a similar spatial imagination seems to convey a single epistemological stance: each finds the self entrapped within an imprisoning environment and seeks to break the bondage by an imaginative flight. The containment of the present, which exiles the self from its sense of home, can be overcome not by actual return, but by the mind's mediation, which transforms time and place into timeless, visionary regions. Our real prison is at the same time a threshold to imaginative freedom; one navigates between the two on the wings of the imagination.

II

On the nature of leaps and bounds

Yet something is wrong—the threshold once crossed dissolves, the "voice of welcoming" is "soundless," and the "joyful cry of recognition" never passes beyond "a painful fulness." The narrator "struggle[s] for words" that will not materialize, and the moment of consummation brings "recognition" other than that sought: instead of "home" he is returned to Italy. His dreams are all too literally brought back to earth. The dualism implicit in the spatial worlds of *Samuel Williams* and the narrator of *Monaldi*, that disjunction which separates subject from his vision, had initially seemed bridgeable in the powers of the imagination to transform reality into the materials of vision. Yet the recognition that greets the narrator by such a process is ironic; his discovery that thresholds return one not to the home one seeks but to the ground we would escape suggests a world more contained and confined than even the imagination can transfigure. Each individual is caught in a dialectic of bondage and escape, and for each figure escape is a correlative of vision. Yet vision requires language—not the spoken word, necessarily, but those deeper vocabularies by which the mind constructs a world: image, gesture, syntax, and convention. In *Monaldi*, the narrator employs a domesticated vocabulary of the past to suggest that which is not Italy and not to be found by further travel, however extensive, through the Abruzzo mountains. In the *Portrait of Samuel Williams* the backdrop landscape uses a vocabulary of time—a winding river receding into the landscape, a castle in ruins, and a charged and turbulent sky—to suggest a world wholly outside the sitter's time.[5] What Allston seeks in these works is not the past *per se* but the unutterable; whether sublime or domestic, the past is itself only a metaphor for that which is not present. In its irrecoverability, its disjunction and distance from the present, the past provides Allston with a language for that which is "soundless." It is the "voice" of the unvoiced and unvoiceable, that which is outside language brought to articulation.

To be recalled to earth, however, to encounter that "sudden turn in the road" which is the fate of *Monaldi*'s narrator, is to be reminded that we are creatures of language after all. In our very efforts to express the inexpressible—to be translated to visionary realms outside the confines of the real and the present—we can travel only as far as our imagination will carry us. And that imagination is itself bound by the very language it would transcend. Hence in *Samuel Williams*, the backdrop landscape that can suggest a world outside time and language only through images of temporality. Hence too the quotidian quills, ink, and manuscript leaves to Williams's right: they are surrogates for the artist's tools, and they remind us that all visionary endeavors, whether visual or verbal, paintings or prose, arise from and must return to their origins in language, place, and time. Such tools dissolve art into its constituent elements, lest we forget that visionary transcendence, like all acts of magic, is a sleight-of-hand that conceals the very artifice that makes it possible. No matter how high or far the balloon of vision ascends, to borrow a phrase from Henry James, it is bound to the earth by a thread so finely spun as to seem at times invisible. The higher the flight of the imagination, the more seamless-seeming the thread that binds it to the earth, but it remains a thread throughout, its fineness masking the web-like manner by which it surrounds and encloses the dreamer. We are language-bound, earth-mired, and our feet, like our occasional leaps (we call them "bounds"), return continually to the brown earth from which we departed.

III

A caution: Dualism is not what it would appear to be

But the irony—the truly grand irony buried most deeply in the compositional space of *Samuel Williams* and *Monaldi*—is not that of our servitude, our language-boundedness, but that of our freedom. Freedom becomes for Allston our proudest fiction, and dualism the means by which we maintain it. Return for a moment to the *Portrait of Samuel Williams*: its style differs significantly from the mode of portraiture fashionable in London of the early nineteenth century. The brilliant, fluent brushwork that Gainsborough had introduced to portrait painting of the late eighteenth century, bringing to the surface of the canvas an energy and elegance that later artists like Henry Raeburn and Thomas Lawrence would assume, finds little counterpart in the much more solidly modeled *Samuel Williams*. Allston's concern for light, though characteristically Romantic, lacks the more radical experimentation occurring in much portraiture around him. He uses light conservatively to shape a three-dimensional figure in space, and, in the tradition of Rembrandt, to draw attention to the mental energy and inner illumination that locate the center of personality in consciousness. British portraitists like William Beechey, John Hoppner, and Thomas Lawrence conceived and expressed human character in far different terms; where Allston perceived a centered self whose focus was interior and introspective, his

British counterparts were busy dissolving the self as a discrete and conscious unit. The tendency of Romantic British portraiture to lose the "solidity and personality" of its sitters in its "obsession with light" was not a flaw, as critics have sometimes maintained,[6] but instead the inner logic by which light and surface brilliance came to express an altered sense of personality. The self was understood less as character or consciousness than as energy linked to a world of natural forces. The bravura style of Allston's contemporaries programmatically flattened the canvas, deemphasized realistic three-dimensional modeling, frustrated the viewer's desire to read interior character, and drew his attention instead to the brushwork and surface brilliance of the canvas. Technique and brushstroke were not only central to this mode of portraiture, but became in fact the unstated subject of the painting. They did so not simply as a protomodern concern for the painting as a two-dimensional object, but in order to break out of the traditional concept of the self as a container of individual properties, and to replace it with a self less centered, less defined by character and consciousness, and more a confluence of unbound energies.[7] There thus exists an enormous epistemological gap between Romantic British portraiture of the period and Allston's painting; whatever else is occurring in Allston, his sense of the self is still private and centered. Allston has more to do with a traditional Protestant emphasis on interior consciousness than he does with the diffused sense of selfhood and corresponding revolution in style and handling in British art.[8]

Yet Allston is not as traditional as he might seem. He shares with his British contemporaries, however else he may differ, a compositional format that consciously postures as an older style. Robert Wark has noted the recurrent antiquarianism of British portraiture:

> This exploitation of the art of the past takes on considerable emphasis in the late eighteenth century.... Clearly the late eighteenth-century artist understood and was prepared to exploit the power of images, forms and styles derived from other times and places to strike the spectator's imagination through association. And the willingness of the artists to play on these associations certainly contributes to the stylistic variety present in the art of that period.[9]

Despite his warnings that allusions to Van Dyck often transformed "ordinary pictures" into "better pictures than they really were," Reynolds borrowed freely from the seventeenth-century master, as did his contemporary and rival Thomas Gainsborough.[10] The more somber *Samuel Williams* derives not from the flamboyance of Van Dyck but from the technique of Baroque portrait composition, which Americans had assimilated through the influence of Sir Godfrey Kneller, the German-born portraitist who dominated British painting in the opening decades of the eighteenth century.[11] In an American *Self-Portrait* (fig. 2) as early as that of Captain Thomas Smith, painted around 1699, one can see the influence of Kneller and Sir Peter Lely in the "solid forms and convincing space" that lead the viewer "diagonally upwards" into the receding pictorial space:

> The background is no longer simply an abstract plane setting off the figure, but contains a window punched through the wall that allows the eye to proceed deeper into space to a scene of a harbor, fortress and battling ships.[12]

Though Allston's background "window" opens to a world that is interior rather than external and social, his compositional format springs directly from the same vocabulary of Baroque portraiture that influenced Smith. Smith, however, in the closing years of the seventeenth century, was *au courant* in his efforts (or at least as much so as an American artist could be). Allston is not; his style is not merely antiquated in *Samuel Williams*, but dated, lacking even the excuse of provincial isolation that an artist like Copley might have advanced a generation or two earlier.[13] The effect upon the viewer cannot help but resemble Thomas Cole's pointed observation on Allston's landscapes:

> His taste was pure and elevated far above that of most of his contemporaries ... [but his admiration for the Old Masters] led him somewhat astray .... His pictures, beautiful as they are, always reminded me of some work or school of art.[14]

That Allston's *Portrait of Samuel Williams* should remind the viewer "of some work or school of art," deriving its individuality from conscious imitation of a prior and outmoded style, introduces us to the paradox of Allston's modernity: the painter for Allston is most free when most imitative, for only then does he acknowledge fully the extent of his language-bound vision. What Cole perceived as a weakness may be interpreted instead as the key to Allston's genius. Allston paints according to an aesthetic of quotation, establishing a world in which parody, the mind in the process of continual self-quotation, serves as the ultimate achievement as well as the final limitation of human vision. The *Portrait of Samuel Williams* is a parodic image; its background landscape alludes not to nature and the natural world but to a tradition of past art (to be other than antinaturalistic would in fact defeat its purpose). So too with the overall pictorial space—its neo-Baroque qualities, like the exaggerations of a Mannerist painting, are designed to undercut the illusionistic claims of

2. THOMAS SMITH, *Self-Portrait,* ca. 1699. Worcester Art Museum, Worcester, Massachusetts.

much Renaissance and post-Renaissance art. For realism and fidelity to nature, Allston substitutes quotation and an awarenesss of the mind's enclosure within its own conventions and artifices. Allston seems to ask that his viewer respond as Cole did: to sense in his work the beauty *and* the imitation, as a step ultimately toward understanding the beauty *of* imitation. If embarrassed—as Cole was—that such high aspiration should be coupled with derivative formulation, then the viewer should not feel ashamed at the apparent limitations of the painter, for ultimately they are not his, but for limitations inherent in the human mind itself, whose noblest flights are always restatements of past thoughts. What Allston

3. RENÉ MAGRITTE, *The Field Glass (La Lunette d'Approche)*, 1963. Menil Collection, Houston.

acknowledges in his self-consciously antiquated and imitative style are the boundaries of the imagination—the inability of the mind, at the very moment of imaginative flight, to escape the language and conventions that inevitably confine it.[15]

IV

From allusion to illusion

Samuel Williams is perhaps better understood when juxtaposed with a very different but equally unsettling work of René Magritte, *The Field Glass* (1963; fig. 3). Magritte shows an interior wall space, flat, brown, and conventionally divided along its bottom third by a horizontal band of molding. Centered in the upper two-thirds of the painting is a large, double-paned window, the right-hand side of which is partially ajar. What disturbs the viewer in this otherwise banal and familiar image is that the background skyscape seems similarly ajar, as if attached to the window rather than independent of it. The innocent ice-blue skies and fluffy white cumulus clouds that fill the left-hand pane stop at its border; they reappear in the angled surface of the right-hand pane, but the space separating the two—the one area where one would most expect to find an unobstructed view of the heavens—is instead a long black void. To heighten the problematic nature of the painting even further, Magritte has allowed the window frame to show through the upper left corner of the right pane. The artist has painted an entirely domesticated and con-ventional set of images, only the more strongly to unsettle the viewer by the failure of his common-sense expectations. The distinction between interior and exterior space, together with one's implicit faith in the reality of objects external to the mind, collapse here in the presence of a threshold—the window—that fails to have two sides. The Renaissance concept of painting as a "window onto the world," extended in Baroque portraiture into the device of the painting (or window) within a painting, is revealed here for the "agreeable cheat" that it is.[16] Unlike Renaissance art, however, where the creation of an illusionistic picture space in no way threatened the reality of a three-dimensional world, Magritte's painting not only questions the illusionism of the painter's craft, but the very nature of our everyday experience. All space becomes potentially interior space in *The Field Glass*, and heaven, the realm of that which is most transcendent and most aspired for, merely the illusion with which we dress our windows to prevent claustrophobia. All else is blackness and unknowledge.

Though a century and a half separates the visionary yearning of *Samuel Williams* from the startling playfulness of *The Field Glass*, the two

weave their tales upon a common loom. Magritte's haunting window, ajar
only as an expression of its deeper closedness—or the mind's deeper
closedness—expresses dramatically and self-consciously what is implicit
in the melancholy dualism of *Williams*. The landscape to Williams's right
is not an opening into a world that carries Williams beyond the confines
of his surrounding space; on the contrary, it is the completion of that
enclosure, an extension of the wall space at Williams's back (note for
instance the manner in which the molding running along the walls extends visually into the architrave of the colonnade). Columns become cell
windows in *Samuel Williams*, relieving the claustrophobia of Williams's
confinement by the illusion of freedom that they create. Williams, however, is no more free than the viewer of Magritte's painting; he is simply
less happy with his situation. Magritte's work achieves its effect by the
starkness and power of its visual pun; illusion and reality are jumbled
together with a classical clarity that belies the painting's problematic nature. Allston's procedure is somewhat different. Where Magritte had
used *illusion*, Allston employs *allusion*. His antiquated landscape refers the
viewer not outside itself to a real nature, but alludes instead to a stylized
convention of Baroque nature painting. The effect is similar to Magritte's
illusionism: the viewer is referred to an unreal landscape, an artifice of
the mind, which offers no real egress from the picture plane even as it
sustains the illusion of escape. The dualistic space of Allston's painting is
thus a myth promising nature and referentiality where there is none.
Dualism is not an evil to be avoided, but a necessary fiction that sustains
man in his myth of freedom and his belief in worlds beyond the mind's
making. To live in a world where parody is the measure of human
achievement—to know external reality only as a creation of the human
mind and art as the self-quotation by which the mind knows itself—is to
discover the grand illusion at the heart of both *Samuel Williams* and *The
Field Glass*: that reality is a wall that we paint ourselves, adding windows,
like freedoms, whenever the claustrophobia becomes too great. Parody,
the reversion to an art form grounded in quotation, is the means by
which we acknowledge the mental walls around us, just as dualism is the
memory—or our creation of the myth of a memory—of a referential
world outside the self no longer available. Such dualism refers us in the
midst of our deepest yearnings to a world beyond the mind, which we
flatter ourselves by calling commonsensical and real, while parody reminds us that windows, like pictures, were made to be hung upon *walls*,
their efficacy limited only by our willingness to believe. The stylized,
baroque nature of the *Portrait of Samuel Williams*, with its allusive background and outmoded composition, thus serves the same purpose as the
"sudden turn in the road" and ensuing "fall" in *Monaldi*. While *Monaldi*

brings us unceremoniously back to earth, *Samuel Williams* reminds us, through its dated imagery, that we are locked in the prison house of language. Human existence involves of necessity bondage within the mind's gilded cage that allows us to conjure a world beyond the bars—on the other side of the threshold—as if it were real.

V

The aesthetics of parody

We may put it this way. Parody for Allston is more than a matter of quotation. The parodic imagination transforms the act of allusion from a simple quotation at the level of content into a complex system of meaning elaborated within the formal organization of a work and concerned with the very possibilities and limits of language itself. For an artist like Allston working in the opening decades of the nineteenth century, parody provided a means for transcending the boundaries of prevailing aesthetic theory. It allowed the artist a self-referential level of discourse implicit in his formal organization that extended beyond the range of articulated content and occurred at a point prior to any specific act of thematization. The parodic imagination invested the work of art with an awareness of its status within a signifying system, using that status as a means of qualifying and often contradicting those meanings traditionally associated with the content. In a painting like *Samuel Williams*, for example, the themes of bondage and escape commit Allston to a world dichotomous in structure and reliant upon the imagination as a source of liberation. With the introduction of a parodic framework, however, the painting's ostensible meaning is reversed, and the freedom promised by the imagination proves instead to be illusory, a self-conscious fiction devised for the ego's survival. Semantic liberation—the promise of meanings beyond language—and syntactic enclosure collide in a moment of reversal that we may take to be the true center of all parody: a turning that inverts the ostensible meaning of a work of art through a level of discourse implicit in the aesthetics of the work though often unvoiced in its content. The success of parody depends historically upon the paradox on which it is founded, that it remain a subtext submerged within a host text, a silent parasite calling attention through its forms to the limitations inherent in any signifying chain in a manner determinative for the meaning of the whole.

For the artist at the beginning of the nineteenth century, the significance of parody as a mode of aesthetics hinged on its capacity to subvert the images and canons of meaning that constituted it. Parody liberated nineteenth-century Romanticism from the assumptions and biases of more referential modes of discourse, providing it instead with a thrust toward modernism that emphasized syntactic enclosure over referential intent. It transformed the artist-philosopher from a builder of systems to a manipulator of signs, a consummate gamesman with the rhetoric and "metaphors of Occidental metaphysics."[17] The power of the parodic imagination lay in its ability to transform a formal rhetorical structure—*parōdia*—into a vehicle for a larger concern with the nature and limitations of semiotic systems. By shifting the burden of meaning in a work of art from the ostensible subject to its organizing principles, it wed literary or visual formalism with linguistic self-awareness. The result was a work uniquely modern in character organized around a central tension or turning (*peripeteia*) that instructed the viewer by virtue of its formal implications not to trust the claims of its content. This self-conscious and self-subversive mode of aesthetics linked Allston to the Kantian revolution of the late eighteenth century, a development that he probably imbibed secondhand through the auspices of his friend and mentor, Samuel Taylor Coleridge. *Samuel Williams* is an examination into the very foundations and possibilities of knowledge in a world defined by the limits of language. The work's awareness of its own formal and syntactic limitations is Allston's means of limning the boundaries of knowledge at the moment when semantic and referential systems of discourse were on the brink of historical collapse. Not until the twentieth century would painters like Magritte restore to the subject of the painting an order of discourse at least as strong as its formal meaning. Magritte's paintings thematize the contradictions, absurdity, and silence implicit in the parodic *peripeteia*. They invoke a body of imagery whose purpose as signifiers is to dramatize and render explicit the character of their own formal structure. The difference between Allston's allusionism and Magritte's illusionism is simply the difference that history makes between a parodic formalism that subverts its chosen signifiers and one that has learned to thematize at the level of the signifier the message of its forms.

VI

Wherein consciousness appears as a mode of self-consciousness

Lest Allston sound at this point so remarkably modern that we seem to have wrenched him bodily from the nineteenth century and a world we usually assume to be noticeably less self-conscious than our present age, we need to examine two paintings by Allston's German contemporary, Caspar David Friedrich (1774–1840).[18] Friedrich's affinities to Allston bear examination, for they reveal a recurrent self-consciousness in early nineteenth-

4. CASPAR DAVID FRIEDRICH, *Woman at the Window,* ca. 1818 or 1822. Nationalgalerie, Staatliche Museen Preussischer Kulturbesitz, Berlin.

century Romanticism that deserves attention. In *Woman at the Window* (1818 or 1822; fig. 4), Friedrich suggests a form of intellectual closure not unlike the parodic visual entrapment at work in Allston. Friedrich's wife Caroline leans against the sill of a recessed window, her back to the viewer and her dress a loosely brushed brown that blends into the various browns of the surrounding interior (Friedrich's studio).[19] Her posture, together with the oppressive height and presence of the studio walls, bespeaks her entrapment and belies the apparent freedom gained from the opened casement before her. The uniform blue of the sky and the splotched green poplar stand on the opposite bank of the River Elbe, both visible on the other side of the imprisoning window, provide the only bright color masses in the painting.[20] Like the curiously menacing innocence of Magritte's blue skies and fluffy clouds in *The Field Glass*, Friedrich's blue heavens are seen only as framed and measured by window and casement. They divide the sky and snatches of exterior space available to the viewer, and thereby explicate in miniature the dilemma of the picture as a whole. Vision is available in the world of this painting only as mediated by the mind. As Vermeer a century and a half earlier had used the lattice work on windows to suggest visually the presence of the artist's mind, ordering and measuring the world as it passes across the threshold dividing exterior from interior space, so Friedrich repeats the motif of windows, not to suggest the availability of freedom, but to depict instead the mediated quality of all vision.[21] The theme of mediation (or mensuration) as an image for the mind occurs not only in the rectilinear division of the windows and panes but in the cropped ship masts and lines that intrude upon the window space like the elements of a jigsaw puzzle or an unexplained geometric proof. Though one may *infer* a three-dimensional world of river and boats beyond the studio walls, the viewer *sees* only a flattened and disjointed series of planes which by force of habit we may take to represent a whole world. The placement of planes is itself significant, for in its irregularity (the room tilts to the right, the woman leans to the left, the visual center of the painting is somewhat to the right of the otherwise symmetric-seeming interior), Friedrich creates a space somewhat "out of joint," a comment upon the limitations inherent in human vision. Man sees only as the mind arranges, a world somewhat askew, and vision has become for Friedrich an affair of elegiac loss.

In a painting of the same period, *Chalk Cliffs at Rügen* (ca. 1818; fig. 5), Friedrich juxtaposes a heart-shaped foreground frame of trees and grasses with a semiabstracted color plane of water and jagged white chalk cliffs. The radical discontinuity between foreground and background is reinforced by the gestures of the three observing figures, each of whom braces himself by hands or feet against the vertiginous abyss before him

5. CASPAR DAVID FRIEDRICH, *Chalk Cliffs at Rügen*, ca. 1818. Stiftung Oskar Reinhart, Winterthur, Switzerland.

or her. Yet the peculiarity of the abyss lies not in the potential sense of terror or annihilation that it evokes, but in its visual beauty. It is in fact stunning. Friedrich has chosen to transform the ocean from an image of power and sublimity to an expanse of decorative space. Like Emerson's nature, the infinitude of space, though latently threatening, is present as an arena of rich visual possibility whose attainment depends solely upon the direct and unmediated encounter of foreground figures and background vista.[22] There is no *actual* traversing between precipice and ocean, no ascending road or vetturra to guide the pilgrim to the background realm. Instead foreground and background are separate planes, contiguous but discontinuous realms, where contact occurs as a visionary activity or not at all.

In *Chalk Cliffs at Rügen*, the stylized pattern of sea and sky, flat and abstracted, plays a role similar to the window world of *Woman at the Window*. The measured, geometric frames of the latter are replaced by decorative patterns in *Chalk Cliffs*; what remains constant in both is the mediated, artificial quality of each work. In *Women at the Window* Friedrich teases the viewer with the paradox of a world whose three-dimensional reality is only an inference from a set of two-dimensional planes. The flat and disjointed planes of "reality" must be extrapolated by the viewer into a three-dimensional world. The task of interpolation and the illusionistic quality of vision that it implies form the central tension of the painting. In the *Chalk Cliffs*, the decorative rather than natural quality to the landscape, its pointedly artificial nature, subverts our sense of a naturalistic space and reminds us instead—through its stylization—that the scene has been shaped by a creating mind, a mind whose presence is as embedded within the painting as are the chalk cliffs themselves. This self-reflexive aspect of the painting is further emphasized by a compositional technique of framing common to both *Chalk Cliffs* and *Woman at the Window*. In each a background world of blue and green is framed by a middleground border, in *Woman at the Window* the lower window and frame, in *Chalk Cliffs* the exaggerated chalk cliffs themselves. This middleground frame, which tends coloristically to bridge foreground and background palettes, is itself framed in turn by the foreground space, predominantly brown or green. Though foreground, middleground, and background are all flattened into an apparently dualistic space and radically juxtaposed as if without mediating transitions, they are in fact bound together by a process of sequential framing whose very flattening masks the technique employed.

This tension between framing technique on the one hand and the viewer's sense of direct contact with a background world on the other, resembles the dualistic play in Allston's *Samuel Williams* between interior space and backdrop landscape. In Allston the classical landscape exists as a curious form of closure. Referentiality is revealed as a myth, and dualism its vehicle, the illusion by which a language-bound world sustains itself through dreams of a larger reality. In Friedrich we see a similar recognition. The turquoise-tinted sea and voyaging vessels in the *Chalk Cliffs at Rügen* are as mythic in their decorative and stylized patterns as the pale blue sky and erect poplars of *Woman at the Window*. They are products of the mind's mediating vision, not only *constructed* with varying degrees of mimetic fidelity but "deconstructed" into the imaginative acts that they are. Their self-referentiality—the visible sketch lines below the woman's dress, the bottles of studio chemicals to the right, the angular and off-centered nature of the *Woman*, the mediating panes/planes of reality, the attenuated framing technique that suggests a dualistic space even as it reduces that space to a never-ending sequence of mental frames, the decorative and geometric motifs—this continual inscription of the presence of the painter in the process of creation into the work itself expresses the act of self-quotation that has come to characterize in Friedrich and Allston the essence of visionary activity.[23] Sight has become *in*-sight, a continual introspective inquiry into the mind's own powers and limitations. For both painters, referential intent—the desire to make contact with a world external to the self—has been subverted by self-referential enclosure. For Friedrich as for Allston, our grand illusion and greatest freedom is the myth of dualism—our faith in a referential world—by which we deny, even as we must eventually recognize, the self-enclosed parody of the modern mind.

2   The Collapse of Intelligibility: Allston's Classical Landscapes

By our own spirits are we deified:
We poets in our youth begin in gladness;
But thereof come in the end despondency
    and madness.
WILLIAM WORDSWORTH, "Resolution and Independence"

I only said the Syntax—
And left the Verb and the pronoun out—
    EMILY DICKINSON, "Going to Him! Happy Letter!"

*U*nitarian Boston in the early decades of the nineteenth century resembled in its worldview nothing so much as the magical isle of Shakespeare's *The Tempest*. The magic was less noticeable by the nineteenth century, the penchant for fancy more subdued and reasonable, and the air, one suspects, no longer sustained a world as rich and ritual-laden as late Elizabethan England. But whatever differences in tone and temper distinguished the two worlds, they shared with each other bonds of a deeper nature. Common to both was a single animating energy that drew its strength from the "anthropocentric revolution" that had arisen in Renaissance England and crossed the Atlantic aboard the merchant ships of prosperous Boston businessmen.[1] Elizabethan England shared with Boston Unitarianism a sense of culture as an autonomous enterprise; for each the energies and providences once attributed to God seemed increasingly the province of society. Puritan America had understood man as radically limited—culpable before God and incapable of effecting his own salvation. Grace was that source of healing power external to the self by which man and God were reconciled, not by actions of the former but by love of the latter. The drama of the soul was compounded in the seventeenth century by a social contract implicit in the "covenant theology." The relation of man and God—while intensely private for Puritan New England—was never without important social im-

24

plications: the fate of the state was dependent upon the fate of the individual, and both rested ultimately upon the gracious love of a righteous God.

The sustaining force of *The Tempest* is neither God nor nature, but the combination of human intellect and natural force that transforms thunder into music and chaos into community. *The Tempest* is a peculiarly auditory play: it begins with a clap of thunder (a reminder that nature in its raw power is no respecter of human station—"What care these roarers for the name of king?") and concludes with music and a masque ("the isle is full of noises, / Sounds and sweet airs that give delight and hurt not"). That the masque is interrupted by the quixotic attempts of Stephano and Trinculo to overthrow Prospero's kingdom only serves to reinforce the sense of fragile balance by which nature's potential treachery is transmuted into the magic of society. As Leo Marx has noted:

> Prospero directs the movement toward redemption, not by renouncing power, but by exercising it to the full . . . . Prospero's experience represents a denial of the idea, expressed by Gonzalo, that we should emulate the spontaneous, uncalculated ways of mindless nature . . . . Prospero's success, finally, is the result not of submission to nature, but of action—of change that stems from intellect.[2]

Marx goes on to note that Prospero's island world, not unlike Thoreau's Walden, "offers the chance of a temporary return to first things," thereby regaining for the self "access to sources of vitality and truth." In its pattern of symbolic movement from "corrupt city" to "raw wilderness" and then finally "back toward the city," it anticipates many later "American fables" and therefore may be read as a "prologue to American literature."[3] It is also a prologue for reasons other than the pastoral pattern Marx describes. By locating the resources by which society sustains and heals itself within the social process, or at least a particular moment within that process, *The Tempest* harbingers a revolution in comparison with which the Protestant Reformation appears to be "a negligible theological performance."[4] The magic of Prospero—flawed and furious human intellect directing the forces of nature—has come to replace the grace of God. Ariel's music is a metaphoric condensation of society's own magical capacity to renew and restore itself—to achieve through "nurture" what "nature," untouched, could never fashion of its own. The process is mysterious and unaccountable, "invisible" and "enchanting" as the music which accompanies it:

> Full fathom five thy father lies;
>   Of his bones are coral made;
> Those are pearls that were his eyes;

> Nothing of him that doth fade
> But doth suffer a sea-change
> Into something rich and strange.
> Sea nymphs hourly ring his knell.
> [1.2.397–403]

The haunting combination of death and transfiguration in Ariel's song, like the imagery of sleep and vision woven throughout the play, suggests the magic and artifice by which natural facts are absorbed into the social fabric even as they are transformed (for otherwise they could not be absorbed). The "sea-change / Into something rich and strange" is the process of culture itself analogically distilled in the play in the image of art. Ariel, Prospero, Shakespeare are all artificers whose skills answer the demands of the Boatswain in the opening confusion of *The Tempest* for an "authority" who "can command these elements to silence and work the peace of the present." Music possesses such command, and with it language and culture, capable of "allaying," as Gonzalo was not, "the waters...fury and my passion / With its sweet air." Caliban's warning to Stephano about Prospero is largely correct:

> Remember
> First to possess his books; for without them
> He's but a sot, as I am, nor hath not
> One spirit to command.
> [3.2.88–91]

Divested of his books, of the learning, culture, and discipline that go into the magic of civilization, Prospero is as naked as the elements he conjures. His abjuration of his powers at the close of the play is not a renunciation of forces external to society, but an acknowledgment that the process of healing and restoration is completed.[5] Like a dream whose course is run, whose death-like silence has been the scene of profoundest vision and restoration, *The Tempest* returns us to a world again balanced and whole. Its magic is the music of its own invisible process.

Shakespeare's magic reappears as organic metaphor in the language of William Ellery Channing, minister and spokesman for Boston Unitarianism and brother-in-law of Washington Allston. Channing inherits from and shares with Elizabethan England a sense of reality as analogic, comprised, like the great Chain of Being, of hierarchically arranged levels of order, each bearing an analogy in pattern, structure, or meaning to every other level of the "chain." Michel Foucault has described "the sixteenth century *episteme*," the manner in which a culture measures and reconciles its experiences against its norms, as a network of parallel and interchangeable patterns whose reversibility and . . . polyvalency endow analogy with a universal field of application. Through it, all the figures in the whole universe can be drawn together. There does exist, however, in this space, furrowed in every direction, one particularly privileged point: it is saturated with analogies . . . and as they pass through it, their relations may be inverted without losing any of their force. This point is man: he stands in proportion to the heavens, just as he does to animals and plants, and as he does also to the earth, to metals, to stalactites or storms.[6]

Channing echoes the world Foucault describes as if nineteenth-century Boston were a later and somewhat rationalized analogue of sixteenth-century Europe. In "The Essence of the Christian Religion" he writes:

We think, perhaps, that nature has a beauty of its own, in which we can delight, without reference to any reality above it. But natural beauty is an image or emblem of harmonious qualities of the mind. It is a type of spiritual beauty.[7]

Anticipating Emerson at the same time as he reflects an older Puritan, even medieval, worldview, Channing presumes upon the analogic order of the universe in order to affirm a radically anthropocentric Christianity, "having but one purpose, the perfection of human nature, the elevation of men into nobler beings."[8] According to Channing's "perfectibilitarianism," man represents that "privileged point" of Foucault's analogic world not simply as the single term around which all the others revolve ("all analogies can find one of their necessary terms there"), but as the center point of a world created solely to sustain the individual in his quest for "moral perfection." There exists "no true good which has not its spring in the improvement of our highest nature."[9] Foucault's sixteenth-century epistemological center has been reworked by Channing into a teleological endpoint—human perfection—and religion in turn is harnessed to the service of man's moral advancement:

Men will yield their faith to no system which does not bear the plain marks of being adapted to the highest principles and powers of human nature, and which does not open to it a career of *endless improvement*.[10]

Yet Channing is no easy Arminian, leaving to man's free will the perfection of his nature. His language is deliberately ambiguous. Were man wholly capable of his own salvation, then God would be nothing more than a heuristic device, the vestige of an older worldview in which grace alone could overcome man's radical sin. Man knows no radical sin according to Channing, but neither is he the engine of his own salvation:

But I need a more direct, immediate, explicit testimony to the purpose of God. And such a witness is Christianity. This religion is not a deduc-

tion of philosophy, resting on obscure truths, and intelligible but to a
few. It is a solemn annunciation from heaven of human immortality,
and of a diviner life than this . . . . We want that truth, which gives worth
and grandeur to our whole existence; which alone inspires perfect trust
in God; which alone teaches us respect for man . . .and which can carry
us forward against the strength of passion, temptation and all forms of
evil.[11]

The regeneration of self and culture that Shakespeare described as magic
even as he circumscribed it within the recuperative processes of society
itself, Channing leaves to the power of a God who has been domesticated
to the terms and potential of human nature. His God, like Shakespeare's
music, remains an unaccountable and irreducible sum only within a
world itself wholly naturalized. Though Alonso may protest to Prospero
that "These are not natural events," and "there is in this business more
than nature / Was ever conduct of," his complaint betrays the poverty of
his imagination more than it illuminates the nature of reality. It is the
magic of the natural world, a magic distilled from nurture's transformation of nature, which *The Tempest* celebrates. Channing rescues his God
from an extraneous supernaturalism, as Shakespeare preserves the ir-
reducibility of his magic, by infusing what is most real and human with
music so fine and invisible that it may after all be only appearance and the
airy labor of a dream. However great the spell of Prospero's enchantment
or sublime the moral stature of Channing's God, the real revolution they
represent resides elsewhere: in the rhetoric of culture that confines *The
Tempest* to a world of social processes, however unnameable, for Shakespeare, and in the rhetoric of perfection that renders cosmic teleology a
human enterprise for Channing. For both, the world has become man's,
and all the magic therein.

I

In the years 1800–1801, as Allston was graduating from Harvard and
preparing to depart for Europe, Unitarianism in Boston was still more
a sentiment than a formalized denomination. The battle between liberals
and more traditional Calvinists that would erupt over the vacancy of the
Hollis Chair of Divinity at Harvard, precipitating what has come to be
known as the "Unitarian Controversy," was still two years in the offing.[12]
Moderate Calvinists continued to hold sway over Harvard and Boston (at
least formally), and only King's Chapel boasted an explicitly Unitarian
and independently ordained minister.[13] But what appeared on the surface of events as isolated phenomena reflected deep-running currents
in the cultural mainstream. King's Chapel was symptomatic of an ongo-

6. WASHINGTON ALLSTON, *Romantic Landscape,* 1801–3. Concord Free Public Library, Concord, Massachusetts.

ing liberal revolution in the eighteenth century that Sydney Ahlstrom has characterized as self-consciously "Arminian," "maritime," literate, and firmly opposed "to revivalism and the . . . pietistic emphasis on a religion of the heart." Partially under the influence of "Anglican latitudinarianism . . . the century's harsher forms of religious radicalism were transmuted into a benign, optimistic, and utterly respectable Christian rationalism."[14]

Allston no doubt imbibed, as if by osmosis, this religion of reasonable men, first while a classmate of William Ellery Channing at Robert Rogers's private school at Newport, Rhode Island, from 1787 to 1796, and then while a student at Harvard.[15] His first known major landscape, the *Romantic Landscape* of 1801–3 (fig. 6), painted in London under the influence of Claude or his mid-eighteenth-century British followers, reveals a pastoral imagination subordinated significantly to a Unitarian sensibility. The conventional elements of Claudian landscape are present in the Allston painting: a foreground composition consisting of rustics (three lounging men on a hillock and a back-turned peasant woman supporting a covered basket on her head), roads, rocks, and shrubbery; an asymmetrically framed landscape with a large tree defining the border of the canvas on the left and smaller clusters of vegetation to the right; a placid body of water in the painting's middleground; and distant mountain and sky in the back. Though essentially quiet and reposeful like a Claudian pastoral, *Romantic Landscape* lacks the suffused atmospheric glow often associated with landscapes of Claude and Richard Wilson. It also lacks an iconography of ruins, which Deborah Howard has noted distinguishes the mood of a Wilson landscape from that of Claude. "Wilson's pictures encourage an openly sentimental nostalgia for the past, using the simplest visual symbols—antique fragments, ruins and classical figures."[16] Allston's landscape is more pastoral than past, a vision of moral order rather than a lament for a lost world. His differences from Claude are significant. Two Claude paintings from his series *Landscape with the Rest on the Flight into Egypt,* the first painted around 1638, and the second variantly titled *Pastoral Landscape with the Flight into Egypt,* 1647, highlight the distinctions.

In the earlier *Landscape* (fig. 7), Claude positions his central figures, Mary with the Christ child, an attending angel, and Joseph unsaddling their donkey, in a tightly knit foreground tableau set in a wooded clearing of uncertain relation to the middleground road behind them. Between foreground figures and middleground highway stands a dense and dominating grove of trees, obscuring the passage from foreground to middleground and isolating the pastoral tableau. The pilgrims are thus distinguished from their pilgrimage; they inhabit a foreground space with no direct or visually explicit passage returning them to the main road, and in their repose seem to define "flight" by the necessity of "rest." They are pictured at a moment of hiatus when motion has stopped, bearing greater affinity to the misty, slumbering mountain of the deep background than to the middleground road that defines them as travelers. The result of this compositional paradox—which pictures flight by rest and plays the stasis of the foreground and background against the process of bridge, stream, and pilgrims in the middleground—is to unsettle the distinctions implicit within the picture between life as eternal flight and life as significant repose. Claude's concern seems to lie less with the integration of time and eternity and more with the assertion of a rightful place for the still and timeless within a world desacralized and temporal. The background mountain slope, distant, hazy, and slumbering like death itself, serves as an analogue to the foreground tableau, similarly still and removed from the brisk businessing of life. The mountain validates the repose of the figures, suggesting their repose may be less a flight from flight and more a moment of contact with the truer, because more abiding, stillness of

7. CLAUDE LORRAIN, *Landscape with the Rest on the Flight into Egypt,* ca. 1638. Galleria Doria Pamphilj, Rome.

sleep, death, and eternity. The validation of the figures is at the same time a justification of the painter, whose work of art, like the tableau he paints, is a creation of stillness in a world of time.

That human nature should be understood as time-bound is for Claude a profound loss, and an inevitable and ironic correlate of the secularization of man that is the height of Renaissance achievement. Man in time is the creature who inhabits Renaissance space, modeled, weighted, naturalized, and removed forever from the timeless gold-leaf backgrounds that once linked him with the angels in God's empyreum. Visual realities now measure canvases once defined by moral perspective, for as Benjamin Franklin was to notice a century and a half later, a secular world runs best on time. He might have added that it has no choice, for once man is naturalized—incorporated into the landscape as one creature among others—he is accountable to the laws of nature and may deny his temporality only in acts of madness or art. Claude's New England contemporary, Ann Bradstreet, added a third term to this sequence: God. In the closing stanza of "Contemplations," perhaps the single finest poem of seventeenth-century America, she concludes her extended foray into human mortality with an ending midway between the Renaissance and Puritan theodicy:

> O Time, the fatal wrack of mortal things,
> That draws oblivion's curtains over kings,
> Their sumptuous monuments, men know them not,
> Their names without a record are forgot,
> Their parts, their ports, their pomp's all laid in
>   th' dust,
> Nor wit nor gold nor buildings 'scape time's rust;
> But he whose name is graved in the white stone
> Shall last and shine when all of these are gone.[17]

Human nature is understood as temporal, a common enough Renaissance theme but an especially poignant one in Bradstreet, whose Puritan dogma is severely tested by her overwhelming sense of human mortality. The curiously prescient and haunting irony of the stanza lies in its two closing lines, where immortality is granted only to those whose names are "graved in the white stone." Revelation 2:17 mentions such a stone as a pledge of eternal life: "I will give him a white stone, with a new name written on the stone which no one knows except him who receives it." The image suggests a gravestone, which for the Christian marks the entrance into life divine, but it also sounds intriguingly close to the image of the artist whose immortality remains attached to the graven images he leaves behind. The ambiguity of the phrase allows for either interpretation; he "whose name is graved in the white stone" (and oh how heavy is the weight of that word "graved") may be artist or Christian. What concerns us here is that the poem assumes as its reality man in a state of nature, which is to say man as finite and temporal, and proposes to redeem that state by forces external to nature, be they from God or the imagination.

Claude, one suspects, can no longer invoke God except, perhaps, as a naturalized image of stasis. The restfulness of his painting, especially as expressed in the stillness of foreground and background, is the closest he comes to Bradstreet's Revelation, and unlike Bradstreet, who can play linguistically with death while believing, at least consciously, in eternal life, Claude has only the comfort of silence, that stillness which may be either life or death. What he insists upon is his right to the stillness, that in a world desacralized and shorn of its gold-leaf, respite is still available. Claude's desire does not appear to be nostalgic: he seems to insist only that "rest"—that moments of imaginative stasis that are as much a part of time as its flow—should be as valid as flight. It is Claude's equivalent to the magic of Shakespeare and the mystery of Channing. Lost, however, in the translation of God into the language of timeless repose is the assurance that death and rest are not the same. One needs Bradstreet's God for that.

With the painting of the *Pastoral Landscape with the Flight into Egypt* (1647; fig. 8), approximately nine years after the earlier *Landscape with the Rest on the Flight into Egypt,* major changes have occurred in Claude's style. The Holy Family is no longer recognizable as such: they appear instead as rustics, indistinguishable from the swains and fellow travelers who share the space around them. The frieze-like tableau in the foreground of the earlier painting has been dissolved here into a more active series of gestures, which in turn better integrate figures with the surrounding landscape (one figure clings to a sapling while kneeling on the river ledge to obtain water, another sits in a chair-like configuration of rocks at the water's edge while a large boulder supports her basket and child). The integration of figures and landscape is repeated in the harmony of the landscape as a whole. The centerground cluster of trees that distinguished the foreground from the receding planes of space behind it in the earlier *Landscape* has been thinned and removed to the side in the later work. The effect is to open the landscape into one broad, continuous plain. Balancing the grove of trees to the painting's left is a distant promontory in the background right that rises abruptly from the hazy plain. Between the grove and the mountain a ribbon of road, river, and green pasturage winds maze-like from the foreground figures back to the distant horizon. Cattle sup from the river on the left, goats on the right, and man, like the beasts that surround him, draws sustenance from the flowing river in the painting's center. What has happened since the earlier *Landscape?* Man has been integrated into the natural world around him; the distinctions that separated the Holy Family from a pilgriming mankind, lending the former a measure of repose and eternal stillness that the latter lacked, no longer obtain. All are pilgrims now, indistinguishable from each other, just as nature itself no longer divides into separable planes. The mazy, almost monotonous continuity of the central plain is unbroken until one reaches the abutting promontory, which does not so much arrest the space in its progress as it frames the central plain and sends it on its way. The figures inhabit the plain world, they are denizens of time and the river. The mountain is no longer their analogue, a validation of their repose, but a backdrop to their drama, deriving its power from the contrast it provides in its steep and sudden ascent from the level plain. The promontory is present as other, not-man,

8. CLAUDE LORRAIN, *Pastoral Landscape with the Flight into Egypt,* 1647. Staatliche Kunstsammlungen Dresden, Gemäldegalerie Alte Meister.

its stillness contrasted with the world of human history passing endlessly by.

Almost two centuries of history separate Allston from Claude. For the earlier painter the secularization of history entails a naturalization of man and a subsequent tendency to lose the divine as a distinguishing dimension of natural process. In Allston the opposite occurs. Natural history is understood, as with Claude, as a form of pilgrimage, but where Claude tends to turn pilgrimage into flight, and then arrest flight with stasis (or dissolve stasis itself into prolonged and endless wandering), Allston integrates the two into a single process. Claude's flight becomes in Allston a moral voyage that commences in the lowlands of the painting's foreground and proceeds by vertical ascent to the dominating mountain in the center background. In the *Romantic Landscape* the mountain is neither an analogue to the painting's foreground figures nor a contrasting backdrop to their historicity; it represents instead the endpoint of their journey, visible, massive, and *attainable* as Claude's summits were never meant to be. Where Claude's landscapes are hilly at best, and in the case of the 1647 *Pastoral* painfully flat—so much so that motion into the picture proceeds horizontally and usually at eye-level back to the horizon—Allston's composition ascends as it recedes. Motion back through pictorial space is accompanied by a vertical progression that carries the viewer from the upright form of the foreground basketed woman, to the middleground travelers directly above her, to the heaven-pointing peak and circular opening in the skies. This vertical thrust is in turn reinforced by a movement from dark to light, and from green and brown to blue, as one ascends from the bottom to the top of the canvas. Mountain mists turn into skyborne clouds, lush green yields to pale blue, and earth itself reaches through the white mountain peak toward heaven. By a combination of accessible mountain, cooling color scheme, and vertical visual ascension, the language of Claude is thus brought into the service of a moral "perfectibilitarianism," a dubious distinction indeed when one considers that Claude understood the newly won human freedom of the Renaissance as a desacralization of the self and an enthrallment to time. For the young Allston, human freedom lies in the perfection to be attained at the end of the process—life's voyage— where mountain reaches into the sky, and the clouds themselves seem to dissolve into a pale blue circle of transcendent heaven.

"Have you faith in your souls, as capable of ascending to sinless purity?" Channing asks of his congregation. "The purpose of God to raise the soul from the power of moral evil to perfection—this is the beginning and end of Christianity."[18] Allston's painting is hardly a study in Christian ethics; like Shakespeare's *Tempest* world, it assumes human nature to be secular, and the processes of culture self-sufficient to the moral transformation of man. Yet it shares with Channing a sensibility that is distinctly Unitarian: it employs a grammar of ascent to suggest a vision of human perfectibility; it understands that perfection as a triumph of spiritual nature over the material world; and it images the struggle and discipline by which Channing's inner "darkness" is transformed into "moral perfection" by use of chiaroscuro and a diagonally advancing path to reinforce the in-direction of the journey (as Gonzalo concludes at the end of *The Tempest*, "Here's a maze trod indeed / Through forthrights and mean-ders"). Shakespeare had reconceived individual conversion as a form of cultural regeneration. What the Puritan experienced in a moment of overwhelming conviction, no matter how long the period of "prepara-tion" prior to conversion, Shakespeare had diffused into the temporal operations of society itself. Channing would recast Shakespeare's lan-guage, conceiving of religion as a form of education and acculturation whose purpose is to "watch over, educate and guide . . . [human] nature to perfect development."[19] He shared with Unitarian Boston "a deep-seated disinclination to regard a specific experience of conversion as essential to the Christian life. The liberals . . . affirmed rather that the Christian life was a continuous rational process of self-dedication."[20] Though Allston's *Romantic Landscape* is perhaps a little less "rational" than certain Unitarians might have desired—it is visually quite lush and sensual, sharing with late eighteenth-century paintings like West's *Death on a Pale Horse* (1802, Philadelphia, Pennsylvania Museum of Art) and Copley's *Watson and the Shark* (1778; fig. 35) an attempt to engage man's emotive nature as well as his moral capacities—it assumes a moral space where maturation rather than conversion defines the soul's progress. Hence the prominence of the road in Allston's painting. Where Claude normally provides little or no explicit passage from a painting's foreground to its background, or sets the viewer instead within an open, endless plain, Allston very carefully navigates his figures through a visually distinct roadway. The drama, which occurs for Claude in the foreground and relies on the background only as it qualifies the more immediate scene, either by validating it or by ironically undercutting it, would be meaningless for Allston unless related integrally to the background endpoint. Claude is not concerned, as was Allston, for moral perfection; stasis is something different from regeneration and bears greater resemblance to death than to spiritual ascent. His paintings suggest that the temporalization of man entails a loss of divinity, while Allston invokes temporality as a means of sanctification.

Allston's late eighteenth-century faith in culture as a process of temporal regeneration—the capacity of a society to renew itself in time through its own processes—commits him, as it does the Unitarian world from which it derives, to a reality that is wholly mediated. For Allston, as for Shakespeare and Channing, the perfection of the self occurs as a series of cultural performances—social processes that acculturate the naked self and assimilate it into a larger sociomoral fabric. The perfection achieved in this idealized scheme is profoundly different from that envisioned in the Emersonian "ego" three decades later. Emerson's cry for "transparency" is an attempt to disentangle the self from the mediating structures of society and history; the relation of man to nature is understood by Emerson as a form of disencumberment in which the self is disclosed to itself in a dialectic of consciousness that may or may not extend beyond the perceiving mind. What is most important to Emerson is neither nature as image of the natural world, nor nature as figure for the human mind, nor even nature as figure for the divine mind, but the essential aloneness of the self as it confronts without intervention or mediation the sources of its sustaining power. As Perry Miller noted many years ago, the bond that links Edwards to Emerson is the "Puritan's effort to confront, face to face" the "physical universe . . . without the intermediacy of ritual, of ceremony, of the Mass and the confessional."[21] Emerson invoked his Puritan heritage as a defense against the mediating vision of Unitarianism with its insistence on a self defined by social processes. He reconceived conversion as a moment of transparency and sought thereby to explode the logic of social transformation implicit in the Enlightenment worldview. In Allston the logic is reversed. Presocial origins are important, not, as for Emerson, as points of return, but as points of departure where significance is to be gained only in the transformation of one's origins into culturally determined end-products. The viewer enters the *Romantic Landscape* (fig. 9), as he enters life, an instinctual creature on the route to moral identity. The lush, dark colors of the painting's foreground, the country path directly accessible to the viewer, and the gesture of the reclining centerground shepherd, pointing as if to direct the sideward glancing woman—and, by implication, the viewer—to the ascending path before her, all combine to create a point of origins for spectator and figures: a moment of emotive and empathetic appeal that draws the viewer into the sensual foreground world and launches him on the sky-ascending route of moral and spiritual perfection. The interplay of diagonally winding road with the chiaroscuro of light and shadow, however, renders the recession into pictorial space a process of profound indirection. The viewer's direct visual access to a focal point in the mountain peak is counterpointed by the undulating road that makes us voyage, to traverse and ultimately to transform; like the mists that Allston localizes from Claude's generalized atmospheres to a specific stage of the journey, the process through time is transfigured into a progress into eternity. Romanticism is generally thought to share with certain forms of Protestantism a logic of conversion: the supernatural erupts into the temporal, validating time from a moment outside it and retaining its informing vitality through the powers of memory. For Allston this moment of unmediated vision is replaced by a process of continual mediation. The self is most authentic when least "natural"; it requires that acculturation which Emerson will later consider death, and achieves through time what Emerson sought by arresting temporality.

Allston's world in *Romantic Landscape* shares more with Enlightenment Boston than it does with the Transcendentalism of Concord. Thirty years earlier, John Singleton Copley had expressed in the spare iconography of his portrait of *Paul Revere* (1768–1770; fig. 10), an image of social mediation that the *Romantic Landscape* would elaborate and transpose to a pastoral setting, but would not essentially alter. In *Paul Revere,* Copley fills the picture space with a series of reflective surfaces: a brightly polished

9. WASHINGTON ALLSTON, detail of fig. 6, *Romantic Landscape* (foreground figures).

10. JOHN SINGLETON COPLEY, *Paul Revere*, 1768–70. Courtesy, Museum of Fine Arts, Boston. Gift of Joseph W., William B., and Edward H. R. Revere.

mahogany table on which appear the images of Revere's engraving tools as well as a reflection of Revere himself; and a flawless teapot, polished as brightly as a mirror and reflecting in magical detail the undersides of the fingers clasping it. If the pun on "reflection" may be carried one step further, Revere himself appears in the act of reflection, head resting on hand, meditating on the nature of the crafted object before him in a manner that in turn mirrors Copley's own self-reflexive relation to the painting.[22] Reflection is Copley's metaphor for transformation, serving a purpose similar to Allston's imagery of ascent. By means of a visual synecdoche, the activity of reflection comes to summarize the transformation of raw nature—its cultivation and refinement—into finished (polished) products of civilization. Such mediation occurs at all levels of the social structure: it is present in the craftsman's transformation of coarsely planed lumber into the immaculately polished surface of Revere's table; it is repeated in Revere's own shaping activities as silversmith; and it is implicit in Copley's relation as artist and creator to the canvas before him. To lend form—to transform reality—is to bring the luster of civilization to the raw materials of life. For Copley, as for Allston in the *Romantic Landscape*, mediation is a form of creation and the heart of culture itself. Allston thus commences his career within the context of late eighteenth-century thought, and shares with the incipient Unitarianism of his age a sensibility that consistently privileges mediatory processes over other forms of experience.

II

What early Romanticism inherits from the Enlightenment is not only a habit of mediation, but an allegorical style. Paul de Man has noted the use of allegorical language in early Romantic texts as a rhetoric of restraint against the more "mystical" claims of Romantic symbolism: where symbolic language presumes a unity between subject and object, signifier and signified, allegory draws upon the discontinuity between language and its referent to suggest the deeper discontinuities in the subject's experience of the world and time.[23] In the *Italian Landscape* of 1805–8 (Andover, Massachusetts; fig. 11), Allston creates a severely rational space to replace the Claudian rusticity of the *Romantic Landscape*. The painterly modeling of figures from pigment and occasional use of impasto in the earlier work yield to a more neoclassical sense of form in the *Italian Landscape*: line predominates over color, the palette cools from the warmly sensual colors of the *Romantic Landscape* to pale blues and muted greens, the light becomes uniform and crisp, and the space is planimetrically arranged. If a *genius loci* may be said to preside over Allston's altered imaginative world

11. WASHINGTON ALLSTON, *Italian Landscape,* 1805–8. Addison Gallery of American Art, Phillips Academy, Andover, Massachusetts.

(especially in the middleground architectural sequence), it is Nicolas Poussin rather than Claude Lorrain. Allston shares with Poussin an impulse toward allegorization centering in the desire for organizational clarity and the rationalization of form. Poussin's comment, "My nature forces me to search for and to love well-ordered things, fleeing confusion, which is as contrary and inimical to me as deep darkness is to light,"[24] expresses Allston's own tendency in the *Italian Landscape* to dispel shadows, eliminate chiaroscuro, and substitute for nature as perceived a more rigorously conceived world of classical order.[25] Both painters were inclined toward an ever increasing intellectualization in their works: drawings were often more naturalistic and free-form than the paintings that followed them, and repetitions of earlier paintings or themes were almost without exception more tightly knit condensations or rearrangements of the earlier works.[26]

In the *Italian Landscape*, the disposition of space along cerebral rather than affective lines enhances the allegorical dimensions of the work and suggests, like the background landscape in *Samuel Williams*, the artist's distance from the natural world. Nature is employed for antinaturalistic ends, alluding in its stylization to Poussin and an art-historical tradition that privileges the mind as the center of moral order over any mimetic fidelity to an external world. Rather than pursue that strain of Romanticism engaged in an almost systematic recovery and reassertion of the emotive self, Allston turns his back on more emotionally encoded forms of art and directs his energies instead toward works that might be termed, following Friedlaender, "classicistic" in nature:

> The difference between "classic" and "classicistic" in art corresponds to the contrast in late eighteenth century terminology between "naive" and "sentimental" poetry. Raphael's approach to Antiquty was naive and direct, as in a different way, was that of Rubens. Poussin's was colored by sentiment and reflection.[27]

Transposing Friedlaender's categories to Allston's art, ony might say that nature in Allston is present only as it has been stylized "by sentiment and reflection" and passed through the crucible of consciousness (or as Emerson might term it, "nature passed through the alembic of man"). With the painting of the *Italian Landscape*, Allston's vision is confirmed in its classicistic direction toward increasing mediation and reflective distance. The attempt at psychological or emotional expression in works like the *Romantic Landscape* or *Rising of a Thunderstorm at Sea* of the following year is deferred if not altogether suppressed.[28]

Allston's pursuit of mediated vision rather than a language of immediacy is not a result of personal preference, but the consequence of a habit of mediation common to Unitarian Boston and the Enlightenment culture of which it was a part. The turn to Poussin is a means of rationalizing experience—abstracting and distancing oneself from nature-as-given in order to conceive a world more imaginatively perfect. In the *Italian Landscape* moral transformation comes to be expressed through forms of aesthetic distance. The central pilgriming figure, who represented in the *Romantic Landscape* an Everyman, the embodiment of human nature in its sensual reality and spiritual capacity, reappears in altered guise in the *Italian Landscape* as both quester and observer figure, a wandering youth with staff in hand who gazes over his shoulder and across a body of water to the idealized forms of a classical city. The various stages of the youth's life have been schematized and abstracted in a triad of vignettes that occupy the left foreground of the painting (fig. 12), each linked to the other by the motif of the staff, an emblem of voyaging. In

12. WASHINGTON ALLSTON, detail of fig. 11, *Italian Landscape* (foreground figures).

the center foreground, in a vignette that suggests youth and fecundity, two stylized peasant women in resplendent costume gather grapes in their baskets while a young child clutching a staff and his mother's robes looks on. The quizzical glance of the child as he watches the kneeling woman calls attention to the process of observation already present in childhood—here hesitant and directed toward an external world maternally defined. The second vignette of the triad contains the figure of the bare-footed youth, contemplating like a character out of Poussin the city to his right. His back-turned stance in the act of observation resembles that of the artist or viewer in the presence of the canvas. As we behold in looking at the painting an idealized pictorial space, he too seems to gaze upon a rationalized image whose status as imaginary or real is uncertain.[29] The empirical curiosity of the child in the center-ground tableau venturing his first hesitant steps toward autonomy has developed here into the youth's visionary quest. That the youth has not yet reached his destination, that it is present and accessible only in the visionary background, suggests the subtle and terrible tension between vision and consummation that divides, like the lake between city and youth, the ideal from the real. Vision is possible as the product of distance. It is that which is aspired to while always remaining in the future.

The future itself becomes past in the third figure of the triad, a barefooted old man in a toga, alone like the voyaging youth, but now immobile. Seated on a mound of boulders at the base of a gently undulating tree, his staff clasped to his bosom, he seems to muse, indifferent to his surroundings, upon a landscape that can only be interior and past. Allston's elderly pilgrim exists proleptically within the painting; he not only adumbrates the direction of Allston's art in the revery studies of his later years, but he also suggests the inevitable outcome of Allston's classicizing imagination within the *Italian Landscape* itself. The passage of transcendence that concludes the imagery of ascent in the *Romantic Landscape* finds its equivalent in the *Italian Landscape* in the image of the brooding old man, rather than in the distant and inaccessible mountains that fill the right background. In the earlier *Landscape* the visual recession brought viewer and voyager from foreground to mountain peak, coalescing there in a moment of transcendence that was both spiritual and moral. In the *Italian Landscape* voyage and vision *diverge* as the pilgrim remains alone with his memories on the opposite shore from the mountain background. He bounds a diagonal that commences in the left foreground, spans the voyaging youth, center tree trunk, and architectural stairway, and concludes in the distant mountain range of the painting's right. His stationary and revery-bound figure marks an alternative to the mountains' visionary distance, and provides the youth, who stands as a fulcrum between the old man and the peaks, with a metaphysical end point very different from the one he aspires to with his glance. The division between foreground and background, old man and visionary mountains, suggests that the ethics of ascent and the aesthetics of mediation are not necessarily compatible. Memory and introspection conspire in the foreground figure to substitute their own powers for the moral landscape the younger pilgrim seeks. As a consequence, what was essentially an act of spiritual attainment in the earlier painting results instead in the later one in an activity of consciousness alone with itself: an old man seated with his memories upon a rock. Ethically defined behavior is thus reconceived in the *Italian Landscape* in visionary and aesthetic terms, and pilgrimage, which had earlier been an act of sociomoral significance, now seems a form of protoartistic activity whose culmination is interior, just as its style is classicistic. It is the mind of man rather than the power of moral perfection that the painting deals with.

It was Poussin's achievement, as Friedlaender notes, to create not only a rational landscape, but a moral one. "Poussin, for the first time in the history of landscape painting, had effectively invested the beauty of nature with didactic significance."[30] Allston presumably discovered in Poussin a precursor whose distinction lay in his capacity to forge ethics and aesthetics into a single visual idiom. In a more Claudian vein, Allston had achieved similar results as early as the *Romantic Landscape*. His later preference in the *Italian Landscape* for the intellectualized classicism of Poussin over Claude's more evocative style reflects his faith in the capacity of the mind to arrange and transform reality into a significant order. To the young Allston, aesthetic beauty and moral truth are one; their common source is the mind's power to mediate and thereby shape the world surrounding it. A little over a decade after the *Italian Landscape*, the British poet John Keats would announce to the world that "Beauty is truth, truth beauty." Keats's visionary rhetoric, however, shares little of Allston's intellectual faith. His apothegm masks a greater doubt that all history is "sylvan history," the making of fictions, and especially the fashioning of the greatest of fictions, that "Beauty is truth, truth beauty." Allston too produces a "sylvan history" of "leaf-fring'd legend," not, like Keats, to relieve "A burning forehead, and a parching tongue," but to relive a classical unity where mind and nature intersect.

Reliving, however, inevitably entails revision, and in the very process of reconceiving Poussin's moral-aesthetic order Allston has altered it irrecoverably. What is implicit in the triad of foreground vignettes, as it is implicit in the compositional space of the whole, is a logic of displacement. The diagonally circling path that denies the pilgrim direct access to his visionary destination even as it renders possible, by its distancing, a view of the whole; the center-ground body of water that reproduces on its placid surface the visionary prospect of the city at the same time as it alters that which it mimics, providing an image of vision that is revision, rearranging as it sees (the semicircular bridge-trestles become, in conjunction with the water, slightly pointed ovals, the direction of the extended classical steps is reversed, etc.); the visionary city itself, conspicuously elevated on foundations above the ground, accessible only by bridge and ascending stairs;[31] the distant and barren blue mountains that are no longer accessible to the pilgrim except as entertained in the imagination or retained by memory; and the introspective old man, the real end point of the journey, a visionary whose sight has turned inward and who no longer understands transcendence as anything other than acts of memory and consciousness; each of these elements expresses in however divergent form the displacement implicit in the process of mediation. To mediate is not simply to transform—whether by the processes of culture as in the *Romantic Landscape* or by an act of the mind as in the *Italian Landscape*—but to establish a distance between vision and origin that propels one further and further from original contact with any primary reality. The more the world is construed as mediate—the larger one's sense of an intervening process between the initial reception of "sense data" and their eventuation in knowledge—the more reality becomes a form of mental activity and the subject of thought the processes of the mind itself. Art ceases to be naive in Schiller's terms when its subject is itself, when classicistic vision replaces classicism, and all reflection is a form of self-reflection.

Return for a moment to Ariel's magical song of transfiguration in *The Tempest*:

> Full fathom five thy father lies;
>   Of his bones are coral made;
> Those are pearls that were his eyes;
>   Nothing of him that doth fade
> But doth suffer a sea-change
> Into something rich and strange.
>   [1.2.397–402]

The "sea change" Ariel describes is strangely undergirded by death. Ferdinand, who hears the song, mistakes it as a confirmation of his father's loss ("This ditty does remember my drowned father"), though he acknowledges in Ariel's music a consolation that assuages his grief:

> Sitting on a bank,
> Weeping again the King my father's wrack,
> This music crept by me upon the waters,
> Allaying both their fury and my passion
> With its sweet air.
>   [1.2.390–94]

Music springs from death and loss like flowers from a grave, the loss a secondary presence attendant upon the process of creation and transformation. In *The Tempest* the whole is clothed in a garb of gaiety and magic. The audience knows Ferdinand's father to be alive and subject to a "sea-change" far more profound than the one Ferdinand fears. The process of transformation is thus bound by a promise of return: its consummation is the reintegration of self and society in a renewed whole. This possibility of return insures that transformation will not result in any form of displacement. The death in Ariel's song—the loss essential to creation and implicit in all modes of transformation—is bound by the analogical context in which it occurs. Analogy insures the congruence of levels of being; the pattern of one level is repeated with variation at other levels, such that a process of transformation which carries the individual from one stage to another (innocence to maturity) still returns him to a familiar and habitable context. Displacement occurs when analogical structure breaks down and can no longer return one to an origin similar to the origin-al. Then the loss of origins implicit in the process of transformation becomes absolute and irrevocable. Origins are experienced as a form of loss born of creation and retained in memory; they are inscribed in consciousness as that which is no longer present. In an analogical environment, the promise that the world is a continuous text—that the transformation required for acculturation, and of art, its synecdochic paradigm, will return one to a familiar space, similar in pattern if not in substance to one's point of departure—guarantees the boundedness of transformation, its accountability to a familiar world, and its refusal to pass over into displacement.

Synecdoche is the trope that expresses the quality of analogical bounds. It derives from a world congruent in its entirety and concentric in its relation of parts. Even as one passes from level to level—from part to whole and then to further whole *ad infinitum*—one is engaged in a constant drama of return. In Ariel's song, grounded in the synecdochic progression of music, art, and culture, the presence of death threatens to turn into the pressure of displacement and dissolution ("him that doth fade . . . that doth suffer a sea-change"); loss essential to transformation is acknowledged at the same time as it is contained by the promise of "something rich and strange," and this promise in turn provides the limits of the transformation. Synecdoche, as the essential metaphoric structure of the play, guarantees that the strangeness of transformation, whether from bone to coral, from innocence to maturity, from nature to nurture, will not result in estrangement. The playful magic of Ariel's tune assures us of the beneficence of Shakespeare's transfigurations. What is thus achieved by the end of the play is the power of analogy itself, the capacity of a congruent and concentric world to receive change as a mode of restoration.[32]

In Allston the power of return is lost. The habit of mediation that grounds both the *Romantic Landscape* and the *Italian Landscape* begins to miscarry in the latter into a form of involuted self-referentiality, where displacement comes to stand for transformation, and the process of dispossession is inscribed into the aesthetics of the painting. The presence of the introspective old man, together with the repeated formalizations of distance and deferral within the composition of the painting itself, mark the eruption of a new and highly intellectualized order of discourse into the coherent moral world of the *Romantic Landscape*. Allston appropriates the model of Poussin in the *Italian Landscape* to create a visual idiom expressive of the mind's capacity for moral transformation, but soon discovers in the abstractive tendencies of his space, and the segregation of pilgrim from his visionary destination, the rapacious tendency of the mind to substitute its own processes for social reality. Though the *Italian Landscape* subordinates its formalizing instincts to the larger demands of a classical order, its recourse to tropes of distance and spatial separation hints at an opening hiatus between thought and reality, vision and origin, and suggests, as if in an undertone, that darker alliance between creation and death which undergirds Ariel's song of transfiguration. To conclude one's journey with the introspective figure of an old man seated in the foreground of the canvas is to experience the impossible gap between desire and consummation—the absence and void—that memory alone attempts to alleviate.

Allston painted few landscapes in the decade following the *Italian Landscape* (1805–8).[33] His return to Boston in the years 1808–1811 seems to have been occupied with portraits of family and intimate friends and with occasional historical works. When he next resumed serious landscape art in the *Italian Landscape* of 1814 (Toledo, Ohio; fig. 13), Allston introduced for the first time in his work a golden mist-like light and a vocabulary of ruins that together create a tone wholly elegiac in effect. The displacement implicit in the Andover *Italian Landscape* of 1805, where the artist's visionary activity appeared to carry with it a secondary awareness of its own potential dislocation, no longer seems to be only an undertone accompanying the rational aspirations of the work, but becomes instead the shaping metaphor of the painting itself. Theme, tone, and composition in the Toledo *Italian Landscape* all revolve around the fact of loss, while loss itself serves as the occasion for recording the price of creation within the work created. What the Toledo *Italian Landscape* proclaims is that mediation has become distance and distance its own story. As mediation engages the self within the language of its own processes and absorbs mimetic or moral intent within self-referential enclosure, the memory (or the myth of the memory) of its now absent origin comes to be inscribed into the recessional composition of the visual space. The *background* of the Toledo *Italian Landscape* retains the narrative imagery that had earlier constituted the foreground and middleground of the Andover painting. A central body of water disperses to either side of the painting the avenues of access to the architectural focal point at its center: a peasant with burro parades over a simple footpath to the viewer's left, a bridge with horse, wagon, and travelers appears to the right. Allston's concern for pilgrimage as a mode of visionary activity—his thematics of voyaging—persists in the Toledo painting only as a memory, as distant within the background and the dissolving haze as it is buried within an irretrievable past. The architectural imagery expressing human possibility in the earlier work has here developed into a more somber image of human des-

13. WASHINGTON ALLSTON, *Italian Landscape,* 1814. Toledo Museum of Art, Toledo, Ohio. Gift of Florence Scott Libbey.

tiny: death, loss, and desolation replace the vision that had once characterized imaginative activity. Allston's dream of visionary progress has been arrested in the stasis of the foreground figures and is retained in the painting's background only as a "trace," a secondary reminder of a world once primary but now dispossessed.

The Toledo *Italian Landscape* belongs to that tradition of Arcadian pastorals which Erwin Panofsky has identified as arising for the first time in the seventeenth century in Guercino's *Et in Arcadia Ego* (1621–23, Rome, Galleria Corsini), a theme deriving from Virgil's eclogues:

> In Virgil's ideal Arcady human suffering and superhumanly perfect surrounding create a dissonance. This dissonance, once felt, had to be resolved, and it was resolved in that vespertinal mixture of sadness and tranquility which is perhaps Virgil's most personal contribution to poetry.[34]

Poussin pursues Guercino's initiative in his two versions of *The Arcadian Shepherds* (the Chatsworth painting of 1629–30 [fig. 14], and the Louvre version of 1639–40 or 1642–43). In the Chatsworth picture, shepherds and shepherdess trace out the words *Et in Arcadia Ego* on the urn-shaped sarcophagus while a recumbent river god spills a vessel of water onto the

14. NICOLAS POUSSIN, *The Arcadian Shepherds* (*Et in Arcadia Ego*), 1629–30. The Devonshire Collection. Chatsworth. Reproduced by Permission of the Chatsworth Settlement Trustees.

ground. The attention of the swains to the writing on the sarcophagus rather than to the skull that rests upon it is more than a "telling symptom of Poussin's intellectualistic inclinations."[35] It reflects instead the potential tension between different modes of discourse within the painting. The natural imagery of the death's head and sarcophagus is not self-evident to the shepherds. They seek explanation in the writing that adorns the tomb for the meaning of the signs before them. What Poussin paints is the potential dissociation of language from an analogical world that once contained it. As Foucault notes, prior to the seventeenth century "the sign and its likeness," "nature and the word," could "intertwine with one another to infinity, forming, for those who can read it, one vast single text."[36] In *The Arcadian Shepherds* the "text" of natural imagery is no longer accessible except as interpreted by the *written* text on the sarcophagus surface. Language will become in the seventeenth and eighteenth centuries, according to Foucault, a value-neutral and "arbitrary" system of significations, secondary to the primary reality of things. In the Chatsworth *Arcadian Shepherds* one begins to see this process occurring in the conflict of texts whose differences potentially overshadow their unified meaning within the painting, namely, death. The presence of the foreground recumbent river god, who receives scant attention from Panofsky, Friedlaender, and Blunt, is in fact crucial to the significance of the painting.[37] His identification as Alpheus is less important than his presence as an emblem of time, the water spilling from his pitcher even as life flows silently by the careless shepherds. Coming between the viewer and the midground action, he serves as a frame to the painting, providing a perspective for the viewer that is more than visual. Because we understand the gesture of the spilled vessel as an image of time, we are distinguished from the Arcadian rustics whose ability to read emblematically is in doubt. Again, his mature adult body, as opposed to their youthful figures, distinguishes the youthful quality of the swains, wholly oblivious to the significance of time's passage, from the greater—and by implication more mature—knowledge of the viewer. Poussin has used the river god to highlight the immature world of the shepherds and to confine the tension between natural and rhetorical imagery to a particular stage in the process of maturation. The dissociation of word from thing noted by Foucault is not a generalized cultural malaise in Poussin but a particular form of immaturity whose passing marks one's entrance into adulthood. The painting may be understood as ironically undercutting the idea of "natural" symbols by suggesting instead the deeply textual and social nature of all discourse, verbal or visual. Like the young lovers in certain Shakespearean comedies, Poussin's youths fail to read coherently the text of the world, not through any fault of the cosmic order, but as a blindness inherent in the youth they must outgrow. The seed of a more general dissociation, which Foucault notes in the following centuries, is present in Poussin, but in the Chatsworth *Arcadian Shepherds* it is still held well within the bounds of a socially coherent order.

The themes of youth and death are transformed into a modern idiom of somewhat different effect in the fountain/tomb imagery of Allston's Toledo *Italian Landscape* of 1814 (fig. 15). Allston's foreground is peopled by three rustics, the central figure a fruit-bearing woman in classical garb whose simplicity and abstraction resemble the classical features of Poussin's statuesque maiden in the Louvre version of *The Arcadian Shepherds*. Behind her and to the right sits another maiden, a pitcher at her feet, next to whom stands a country swain who rests on his staff while gazing at the seated woman. Though shepherd and seated woman form an integral pair, they share with the central standing figure profiled faces all directed to the painting's right. There the viewer finds a rectangular block of masonry that is apparently part of a larger, though largely hidden, fountain, its most salient visible feature being a vertical slab with a sculpted lion's head in the center. From the head flows a continuous stream of water that fills the hollow rectangular block beneath it. Both by length and shape the unadorned block resembles a sarcophagus and suggests, in its relation to the youths, the intrusion of death within their world of courtship. One might well apply to it the words visible on the gabled, though otherwise plain, rectangular monument in the center of Poussin's painting: *Et in Arcadia Ego*. Though much scholarly controversy surrounds the meaning and interpretation of the Latin motto in Poussin's words, its absence in Allston in no way mitigates its implied presence.[38] What in fact appears on the fountain/tomb are the epitaph-like words "W. Allston 1814." The void of the hollow sarcophagus, however, is filled by an unending supply of water, transforming the place of death—particularly the artist's death—into a source of life. The process assumes sexual overtones through the iconography of the seated woman: the vessel at her side is, by analogy, an image of her own sexuality, a paradigm of the presence and absence that is the source of her creativity. This association of absence and death with the processes of creation is repeated in the vegetation of the painting, where the central foreground tree grows next to the trunk of a tree once larger but now destroyed. The juxtaposition of living plant with stunted remains, a traditional convention of pastoral art, had appeared earlier in the Andover *Italian Landscape*, a reminder not only of mortality, but of the sacrifice and dislocation accompanying mediated vision. In the Toledo painting, where the vegetation is generally more sparse and attenuated, tree and stump occupy a greater portion of the visual space. The luxuriant growth of the center-ground Andover

15. WASHINGTON ALLSTON, detail of fig. 13, *Italian Landscape* (fountain and signature).

tree is here superseded by the ravaged appearance of a plant whose survival has been at much greater cost than could possibly have been anticipated by the earlier painting.

What we see occurring in the Toledo *Italian Landscape* is a division of foreground and background that reverses the priorities of the Andover painting and substitutes for the visionary aspirations of the earlier work a self-referential account of the latter's own intellectual genesis. In the Andover *Italian Landscape* of 1805–8 imagery of pilgrimage had been primary, dislocation secondary, and visionary activity had served as the fulcrum balancing the two in uneasy equilibrium. The relation between foreground and background had been that of present to a visionary future. In the Toledo *Italian Landscape* the sequence is reversed. The movement from foreground to background, rather than detailing the artist's desires for the *future*, records instead his remembrances of a *past* distinguished by its visionary aspirations. A process of displacement comes to absorb the picture's energy, and the yearning of the earlier painting is now preserved in the later picture's background only as a memory of the now lost origin. Pilgrimage has become an affair of the past and memory the surrogate for vision.

This process of reversal by which the present of the Andover *Italian Landscape* appears as the background and distant past in the Toledo painting reflects a deeper spatial imagination in Allston that underlies his writing as well as his painting. In a letter to John F. Cogdell prior to Cogdell's departure for Rome, Allston describes the contemporary world of 1842 as a "present foreground" from which he can "look back into the past" "as if reversing a telescope":

> As to the glowing works of art by which you will be surrounded in Rome—they will breathe new life into you. Even at this distance of time I live upon them in memory. In that "Silent City," as my friend Coleridge used to call it, were some of my happiest dreams; for they were the dreams of youth, to which even *the then gorgeous present was but a dark foreground to the beautiful and dazzling distance of the future*. And though my approaches to that future have uniformly caused it to fade more and more into the common daylight, laying bare to the senses the illusions of the mind, yet I do not regret that I once so dreamed of it; *since I have only, as if reversing a telescope, to look back into the past, even from my present foreground*, matter of fact as it is, to see the same delightful, though imaginary distance—dimmed, indeed, because diminished, but still the same. The visions of the past are not always lost to us; they may become less defined, but they do not vanish.[39] [Emphasis mine.]

Allston's prose suggests two possibilities in the relation of the "present foreground" to the background. The first, associated with the "dreams of

youth," identifies the "future" with a visionary background and understands the "dark foreground" as nothing more than a place of origins. We
see this mode of composition in the Andover *Italian Landscape*. The second possibility—that of the Toledo painting—recasts the background
world into a lost but visionary *past* accessible by "reversing a telescope . . . from my present foreground." By a compositional inversion in
which temporal concerns are translated into spatial terms, Allston traces
the diminishment distinguishing the "dreams of youth" from the "illusions" of later life. The aspirations of the past are inscribed into the background of the painter's vision, and the structure undergirding Allston's
work, whether in prose or pigment, reveals in its retrospection that
deeper reversal of the painter's dreams which one finds in the Toledo
Italian Landscape.

The paradox of the painting, proclaimed through the stasis of the foreground figures, the inscription of a visionary past in the background composition, and the conjunction of sexual-creative imagery with that of
death, is that visionary activity, because self-displacing, results inevitably
in intellectual death. To create is to undergo the separation that distinguishes vision from origin, the mediation that displaces as it transforms.
Death permeates the canvas in the tomb-like form of the fountain, the
truncated tree stump, and the classical ruins of the painting's middleground. Poussin's *Arcadian Shepherds* encounter death as a larger process
of growth; their vitality and sexual energy stand in contrast to the hollow
stare of the death's head even as they must assimilate its lesson as part of
their own history. Poussin foregoes sadness for the excitement of moral
discovery, while Allston abandons moral aspiration in the Toledo *Italian
Landscape* for the knowledge of loss implicit in all creation. Moral intent is
replaced by aesthetic self-awareness, as mediatory activity comes to distance itself from its ostensible sociomoral origins, preserved now only in
memory as a background inscription; and the subject of the painting becomes the process of its own loss and displacement. The right middleground temple, fragmented and decayed, serves as a signature for the
painting as a whole; its disfigured façade and fragmented Doric column
remind us not only of life's transience and the *vanitas* of human endeavor, but of the absence and decay at the very heart of human
achievement.

But death may function for the artist in a manner analogous to a two-
way street. It represents at one level the language of loss and displacement, a metaphor for the gap that arises when mediation fails to achieve
its synecdochic return and becomes instead endlessly self-referential, as
occurs in the stasis and haze of the Toledo *Italian Landscape*. At this level
death is the language by which the artist expresses his own awareness of

the implications of his art.[40] At a second level, however, death is a source of renewed life—not a renewal of the origin, that impulse to visionary moralism preserved only in the painting's background, but the birth of a new mode of art: parodic, classicistic, and beautiful in the pathos with which it transforms death and dislocation into a new aesthetic. We may call this aesthetic modern, for it is an art self-consciously language-bound and built upon a sequence of self-referential allusions. The beauty of the Toledo *Italian Landscape* is the beauty of an art form aware of its own secondariness and capable of transforming that awareness into a modern voice. That this loss is beautiful—that the displacement implicit in all acts of mediation bears aesthetic fruit even as it buries moral aspiration—is the unsounded meaning borne in the phrase *Et in Arcadia Ego*. The moral import of the words is less important to modern ears than the aesthetics they inaugurate: all art born of mediatory vision is doomed by a cruel and beautiful necessity to continual displacement, eventual death. At this level death is the language of the parodic self proclaiming its perpetual secondariness.

Death had been present all along as the ally of artistic activity in a work as early as Claude's *Landscape with the Rest on the Flight into Egypt* (ca. 1638), where the stillness of the foreground tableau, together with the death-like repose of the background mountain, had been asserted over and against the narrative present of the middleground bridge, roadway, and river. In the bifurcated visual language of the *Landscape with the Rest on the Flight into Egypt*, Claude had in effect created a modern idiom directed against the temporalization of the world and the secularization of man by positing a mode of stillness, whether through art or through death, incommensurate with historical time. Claude presents two forms of what might be termed "visual synecdoche" in unresolved and incompatible juxtaposition. Stasis and process, foreground tableau and middleground bridge, are each parts competing to represent the whole, voices claiming by analogy an identity with the larger work, even as they betray by the fact of their competition their deeper fragmentation. In Allston, Claude's dual synecdoches miscarry into a form of synecdochic parody, where a landscape of dislocation accounts for its lost origins at the same time as it acknowledges its incapacity to return. Allston draws to a close the cycle of Claudian pastoral as a mode of antinarrative by rendering it a parody of itself—synecdoche miscarries into displacement, and displacement finds its voice in parody, the "classicistic" imagination of the modern world. It is *parodic* because it is both self-quoting on the one hand, incorporating its past origins as present loss, and self-conscious and classicistic on the other, subverting any mimetic intent by subsuming itself within a stylized tradition of pastoral art (a tradition itself present not as direct quotation but only in the memory and irony of its loss). It is *synecdochic* in its inversion of the traditional bases of synecdoche—a world analogically bound, congruent in its entirety, concentric in its parts, and capable of return (whether to origins or an accommodating analogue of the origin)—into an off-centered, disphasic pattern of allusions and repetitions whose common center is present only as a mythic past, now lost, incorporated into the memory of the work as a mode of accounting for its present dispossessed state. One might term this mode of synecdoche-manqué "parody," understanding the latter as the end point of a particular historical and linguistic process that begins in symmetries and ends, by the close of the eighteenth century, in dissociation bearing traces of the earlier state. From this point of view, parody is a mode of modern discourse born of the failure of analogical return. It stems from a habit of mediation and culturally conceived autonomy that one can trace from Shakespearean England of the late sixteenth century to Unitarian Boston of the early nineteenth century,[41] and it results when the displacement and self-referentiality implicit in all mediated discourse produce in turn an aesthetic of their own. It is a bittersweet fruit harvested from an eighteenth-century faith in the mind and its powers of mediation—a form of modernism bequeathed to us by the world of Enlightenment thought.

Synecdoche, as a visual rather than a literary trope, is a form of completion, a figure of mimetic intent that the artist uses to conjure the whole of reality by the presence of several of its parts. In Friedrich's *Woman at a Window* (fig. 4), synecdoche is played upon as a habit of mind by which abstract and two-dimensional pictorial units are invested with the referential qualities of an external reality. Friedrich's window images awaken expectations of a referential world, even though their self-consciously abstract nature draws attention away from that world to their own mediatory presence. In thus painting his window images in a manner subversive of their mimetic function and instead drawing attention to their formal characteristics, Friedrich exposes the assumptions and habits of referential inference much as the Scottish philosopher David Hume half a century earlier scrutinized and then dismantled the notion of causality. According to Hume's account,

> Philosophers, who carry their Scrutiny a little farther [than average Men], immediately perceive, that, even in the most familiar Events, the Energy of the Cause is as unintelligible as in the most extraordinary and unusual, and that we only learn by Experience the frequent CON-JUNCTION of Objects, without being ever able to comprehend any thing like CONNEXION betwixt them . . . . So that upon the whole, there appears not, thro' all Nature, any one Instance of Connexion, that is con-

ceivable by us. All Events seem entirely loose and separate. One Event follows another; but we never can observe any Tye betwixt them. They seem *conjoin'd*, but never *connected*. And as we can have no Idea of any Thing, that never appear'd to our outwards Sense or inward Sentiment, the necessary Conclusion *seems* to be, that we have no Idea of Connexion or Power at all, and that these Words are absolutely without any Meaning, when employ'd either in philosophical Reasonings, or common Life.[42]

Hume's general conclusion is that "All Inferences from Experience, therefore, are Effects of Custom, not of Reasoning."[43] Were one to substitute a concern for "mimesis" for that of "causality," as Friedrich in effect does through his window imagery, he would discover referential thinking to be a habit of "constant conjunction," a tendency implicit in the association of the human mind rather than a law of natural relations. This habit of referential thought we denote synecdoche. No longer the expression of an analogical world, synecdochic thought becomes for Friedrich a self-conscious and problematic process by which referentiality is *posited* rather than assumed.[44] The claustrophobia of *Woman at the Window* is the fear that all referential inference from parts to whole is an illusion of the mind; the hope of Friedrich's work—like that of Allston—is the awareness that within the enclosure of human language lie the possibilities of new beauties, new fictions, equal to the splendor of the old.

III

This story, like all good stories, has a moral and denouement. The moral concerns the gilded quality of Allston's linguistically bound world, while the denouement traces within Allston the collapse of systems of intelligibility in works increasingly nonreferential in nature. A comparison will help to make the point. Referentiality—already problematic in Allston and Friedrich—becomes a game played with great skill and even greater audacity by Samuel Taylor Coleridge, Allston's friend and perhaps the single greatest intellectual influence in Allston's life.[45] The *Biographia Literaria* may be read as a study in the limitations and possibilities of referential discourse: it appears to progress by a strategy of indirection, mystifying where it would explain, eluding all self-accounting, and generally substituting a studied incoherence—anecdotal and disjointed—for the philosophical insight it promises. The issue at stake in the *Biographia* may not be, as critics have been prone to argue, whether Coleridge was as great a philosopher as he was a plagiarist, but that he was a profound literary innovator, pursuing by voice and tone what could no longer be achieved by serious philosophical discussion.[46] The true subject of chapter 13, famed for Coleridge's definition of the "Imagination," is not the series of definitions blurted out in the closing lines of the section as if Kant, Fichte, Schelling, and the whole of German Idealism had imploded into a single paragraph, but the persona who narrates the chapter, displaying his erudition as a child assembles his blocks—not for any intrinsic order or relation but for the sheer joy of construction. Extended epigraphs by Milton in English, Leibnitz in Latin, and "Synesii *Hymn*." in Greek are followed by three paragraphs of ostensible philosophical discourse that threaten to break into anecdote and vocabulary that does break into Latin; the whole is then itself interrupted by the insertion of a "letter from a friend" that comments on the text in progress, thereby blurring completely the distinction between text and audience, and recapitulating, in the dislocation it describes, the reader's own sense of narrative intrusion and the utter failure of the discursive progress of the chapter.[47] The letter is as effusive, and alludes as continually, as the style of the persona, from which it is ultimately indistinguishable. It is followed by the author's complete concurrence with the writer's sentiment on the inadvisability for philosophic and economic reasons of continuing the chapter, and the swift condensation of the author's ideas into two brief paragraphs on the "IMAGINATION" and "FANCY." A concluding sentence refers the reader back to the preface of "The Ancient Mariner," a reference, perhaps, to a style of mock-heroic epic that seems to burlesque the description of an ordered universe intelligible to man in the chapter's opening lines from book 5 of *Paradise Lost* (where the angel Raphael explains to Adam the unity and *telos* governing creation). The chapter thus appears to be a carefully constructed anticlimax, deferring and then deflating its central argument even as it puns and plays with the initial inadvisability and ultimate impossibility of achieving its objectives. The pattern of anticlimax in chapter 13 itself repeats the organization governing the earlier chapters of the book, and especially the relation between chapters 12 and 13, where an extended "Chapter of requests and premonitions concerning the perusal or omission of the chapter that follows" precedes the comic anticlimax of chapter 13 with a series of ten prefatory "THESES" apparently designed to confound the very process of enlightenment they ostensibly pursue. Thus by a complex and marvelous literary strategy, replete with neologisms, pseudo-erudition, and mock-rhetorical excursions, Coleridge manages to defeat, subvert, and traduce the philosophy he supposedly propounds. His method anticipates Kierkegaard on the Continent and Poe across the ocean, both of whom are engaged in the exercise of irony and parody to create a literary strategy subversive of philosophical claims. The *Biographia* seems to pursue in prose what "The Ancient Mariner" effects in verse: an exploration of the limits of language, first in its radical incapacity actually to utter truth (that which Coleridge would call "living" and locate beyond the bounds of discursive language); second, in those modes of literary indirection (parody, puns, irony, self-subversion, gamesmanship, posturing, and role-playing) that seem to deny the enclosure of language and our reliance upon it even as they engage in a consummate form of language play; and third, in the possibilities of new aesthetics, new modes of literary voice, constructed from the debris of the old and welded into wholly transformed figurations. The dream-like tone of "The Ancient Mariner" expresses a world where referential signals are no longer intelligible, where the signposts of a once coherent order have dissolved into obscure hints that no longer seem capable of directing the reader to a world recognizable as home. Referentiality has become a game, an *a priori* characteristic of language in search of its own aesthetic.

Allston, too, will play Coleridge's game, for he is one of its authors. In works like *Coast Scene on the Mediterranean* (1811; fig. 16) and *Moonlit Landscape* (1819; fig. 17), elements of genre painting, seascape, and nightscape coalesce into images of haunting beauty and unaccountable mystery. Barbara Novak has noted the "proto-luminist" quality of Allston's *Coast Scene:*

> The painting itself is "smooth as glass." The ships are "almost stationary" against a cool but brilliant sunset. The smooth containment of the image, the curiously flattened and ambiguous space in which light radiates outward yet remains firm—establishing a wall-like plane—make it one of the earliest proto-luminist landscapes in American art. It shares with the luminism of the 1850's and 1860's the ultra-clarity of foreground detail (as in the shadows of the cart wheels), while the background blinds and dazzles.[48]

She goes on, however, to distinguish the more imaginative nature of Allston's canvases from those of the luminists:

> An ultimate distinction between Allston and the luminists is that the latter give the quality of dream to the scene perceived in reality, while Allston's images seem to derive more directly from the imagination, untempered by immediate confrontation with fact.[49]

By what appears to be a process of arrested narrativity—gestures and events frozen *in medias res*, shadows exaggerated, distorted, and cropped unaccountably by the picture frame, events that demand readability even as their mute silence denies it, objects unaccountable within the space they inhabit (a vessel of rowing galley slaves drifts quietly through the *Coast Scene*, while the abandoned sailboats in *Moonlit Landscape* appear

16. WASHINGTON ALLSTON, *Coast Scene on the Mediterranean,* 1811. Columbia Museums of Art and Science, Columbia, South Carolina. Bequest of Robert W. Gibbes.

disproportioned to the nearby bridge and supporting body of water)—Allston seems to suspend time and space and to reduce referentiality to a lingering dream. What Allston has achieved is a form of voice, what Richardson terms "mood," whose enchantment is the play of the imagination in the midst of its disquietude. By distending reality, narrative dissolves into magic, and the filament linking fact and fancy is beat into a substance so fine and airy that all that remains is the infinite suggestability of an echo without source.[50]

Allston shies away, however, from an aesthetic that transforms the problematics of referentiality into a self-perpetuating game. He seems uncomfortable with the voice that handles dislocation as if it were a form of magic, and dwells instead on the terror and displacement that accom-

17. WASHINGTON ALLSTON, *Moonlit Landscape,* 1819. Courtesy, Museum of Fine Arts, Boston. Gift of William Sturgis Bigelow.

pany a world shorn of its "readability."[51] In two earlier landscapes of the Andover period, *Landscape with Lake* (1804) and *Diana in the Chase* (1805), Allston's gradual transposition of foreground vegetation into imagery of death anticipates the virtual breakdown in many of his later works of all systems of natural communication. In the *Landscape with Lake* (fig. 18), a chasmed and rutted left foreground provides the border of a road that carries the viewer to a centerground lake and background palisades abutting the distant shore. A fallen tree straddles the winding chasm at one point, resting in an abundant bed of vegetation that receives it in a manner wholly naturalistic in appearance and appropriate to the cycles of death and life by which nature operates. In *Diana in the Chase* (fig. 19), painted only a year later while the artist was in Rome, a similar format masks deep-seated changes in tone and detail. The leafy abundance of the foreground tree dominating the rutted space of *Landscape with Lake* is replaced by the bifurcated trunk of a tree whose surviving half resembles the struggling and attenuated pine of the Toledo *Italian Landscape*. The chasm, which in *Landscape with Lake* was explicable, its crevices illuminated by sunlight and darkening only with shade and distance, has been transformed into a dark and undefined void in *Diana in the Chase*: its sides are steep, mysterious, and beyond the capacity of the viewer to measure. The fallen trunk which again spans the chasm hangs precariously against the walls of the abyss; it seems not so much to bridge the sunken space as to highlight its nature as unfathomable void. There is no hint in this painting of a naturalist assimilation of death into the larger processes of nature. There is only mystery, absence, and the refusal of nature to account for its own phenomena. The surface of the lake is less placid than in the earlier work, the colors of land and sky darker and more turgid, and the background peak more craggy, lacking entirely the softening tufts of vegetation that rendered the palisades familiar and accessible in the older version. The road, which was distinct and bounded in the former, has virtually dissolved into a maze of vegetation and clearings in the latter. Even the narrative interlude of the right foreground reinforces the sense of death and

18. WASHINGTON ALLSTON, *Landscape with Lake*, 1804. Courtesy, Museum of Fine Arts, Boston, M. and M. Karolik Collection.

19. WASHINGTON ALLSTON, *Diana in the Chase,* 1805. Courtesy of the Fogg Art Museum, Harvard University. Gift of Mrs. Edward W. Moore.

incongruity by reminding the viewer that he is observing a *lost* arcadian landscape: Diana and her consorts are not attainable or accessible to us.

What has happened between the painting of the two works is that Allston has lost his intellectual innocence. Nature is no longer natural: its boundaries are less distinct, its meanings less accessible, and its mysteries—chief among them death—are more ominous and less susceptible of conventional resolution than Allston might once have thought. In Poussin natural imagery in the early period of the Chatsworth *Arcadian Shepherds* accounted for itself contextually, and the implicit disjunction of language systems was characterized—and thereby contained—as a stage of immaturity for which the resolution was *growth*. Allston, however, grows only by way of loss. Maturation proceeds as a process of radical doubt, dismantling the signposts of an intelligible reality while acknowledging that true vision consists of a blurred reality beheld clearly.

The process is even further exaggerated in *Saul and the Witch of Endor* (1820–21), where Allston transfigures Benjamin West's earlier treatment of the subject, *Saul and the Witch of Endor* (1777; fig. 20), in a manner parallel to the British painter John Mortimer's restatement of what Robert Rosenblum has called the "Neoclassic Horrific."[52] In *Sextus the*

Son of Pompey Applying to Erictho to Know the Fate of the Battle of Pharsalia (1771) Mortimer

replaces reason by conjury, beauty by ugliness, an architectural background by a mysterious cave, and measured gestures by terrified reflexes. Moreover, the horrific qualities of this Roman subject are underscored by the febrile figure style and the murky, erratic light, visual elements borrowed from that most unclassical of artists, Salvator Rosa.[53]

Both West and Allston arrange their compositions around diagonal forms that meet in the center foreground to form a "V." This apex of witch's rod and Saul's supplicating hands is bound in West's work by the classical architectural setting that defines the space, stabilizing the disruptive potential of the diagonal forms at the same time as it translates the potential energy of those forms into the closed circular rhythm that

20. BENJAMIN WEST, *Saul and the Witch of Endor*, 1777. Wadsworth Atheneum, Hartford, Connecticut.

joins Saul's bowed form to the gesticulating figure of the witch and the ringlets of smoke surrounding the conjured ghost. The magic of the painting (the low crescent moon is an image and witness of that magic) is thus bound by the rational space that defines it; if not itself rational, the magic is still commensurate with the mind's capacity to conceive and understand. The integrated transition from Saul's extended arms to the witch and centerground ghost bespeak the adequacy of the language of gesture and response to the phenomena of the natural world. Even the horror of the observing soldiers to the right remains well within a vocabulary of psychological postures dating back at least to Poussin.[54] West's painting provides a study in the inability of eighteenth-century culture to embrace ideologically forces perceived as foreign and intrusive.

In Allston's version a quarter of a century later (fig. 21), the tight compositional reins by which West controlled his space have distended and erupted into a work unbalanced, off-centered, and without stabilizing forms. West's architectural interior has become a cavernous and undefined enclosure; the space is no longer habitable but instead empty, barren, and alienating. The softly contoured "V" implicit in West's forms has hardened into an awkward and exaggerated set of diagonals in Allston. Saul's implausible and unstable posture (he is supported by a background rock) and his gesticulating right hand, which points neither to the witch nor ghost but, like an electrical ground, seems to dissipate its energy on the cavern floor, suggest the rupture that has occurred between natural phenomena, defined here as unnatural, and human response. West's magical crescent moon is in Allston a diffuse and largely hidden field of light; the circle of smoke enclosing West's ghost, confining its energy within an incantatory formula, spreads from its circular base in Allston to fill the upper left half of the canvas with a void of smoke and haze. Interior space is less distinguishable in Allston from exterior, just as West's ability to discriminate rational forms from magical ones seems to blur in Allston into a space uniformly mysterious and unaccountable. Allston appears either to have lost control or to have abjured it altogether. West's faith in the intelligibility of his world—its capacity to cohere in the face of the unknown and to assimilate mystery into culturally recognizable forms—has collapsed in Allston. Language is not the master of mystery but its victim, as incommensurate to its world as Coleridge's philosophical accounts appear to have been to a nondiscursive reality. But the freedom Coleridge felt to play with this insufficiency—his apparent willingness to transform linguistic enclosure into the mind's joke upon itself and to create in the process a new form of narrative voice—Allston seems reluctant to follow. The formidable figure of the witch of Endor, whose solid and columnar form and magisterial pose contrast sharply with West's

21. WASHINGTON ALLSTON, *Saul and the Witch of Endor*, 1820–21. Mead Art Museum, Amherst College, Amherst, Massachusetts.

witch, a conventional mountebank exercising her power, suggest in Allston a deeper seriousness attached to the act of conjuration. West's painting carries one back to the shallow centerground ghost, while Allston's canvas confines the viewer as if by physical spell to the foreground relation of Saul and witch. She becomes in Allston's work a creator, embodying in her figure that concern for creative power, that moment repeated in almost all of Allston's historical works when energies unaccountable to the rational mind break through the natural world and transform conduits into oracles and vessels into voices.[55] The paradox of the painting is not that the witch should command such power, but that Allston's concern with creation—and with the energies of the artist—should intensify even as the reality narrated is dismantled and rendered unintelligible. Creation bears an inverse relation to knowledge. The breakdown of semiotic structures, the failure of sign systems to communicate meanings other than the imagery of their own collapse, derives from an act of creation too powerful for the circuits of language to contain without injury. Knowledge eventuates in the impossibility of knowledge, and creation, dispossessed of a language adequate to its mystery, engages in an act of continual subversion on the one hand and ultimate self-referentiality on the other. The lesson of *Saul and the Witch of Endor* is not one that Coleridge might have drawn: that creation shapes an aesthetic playpen out of the boundaries that confine it. Rather, the painting suggests Allston's more somber fear that vision distends and distorts the space in which it is realized. There can be no return, for the mind is alone with its own power.

In *Monaldi*, composed contemporaneously with *Saul and the Witch of Endor* in 1821, the consequences of this logic of disintegration are given narrative voice and shape. The story unfolds as an inverse conversion experience, a *Bildungsroman* gone mad. Monaldi, the artist-hero, dwells in a post-Kantian "noumenal" world where vision has been torn from its roots in "phenomenal" reality and sustains itself instead by the intuitive powers of moral Reason in alliance with the heart. Monaldi's vulnerability to Maldura, an artist-impostor associated with "phenomenal" and therefore material realities, reflects a deeper division of the self into two conflicting, and in the course of the novel, unreconciled, personae: the inner man of vision and the external worldly self. The strife between the two carries Monaldi from innocence to madness, the latter a form of knowledge-as-catastrophe. His inability to navigate through the external world without misreading its signs and overreacting to their significances is a tragic and inevitable consequence of both the disjunction of mind and world and the cleavage of personality, which together leave the artist isolated with the "ever-multiplying phantoms of the imagination." Monaldi's incapacity to read correctly is linked to the language-bound quality of his world. Communication occurs not by a simple act of expression, but by repeated forms of indirection: eyes meeting in mirrors, snatches of overheard music, and tales told within tales. The process at points becomes almost Proustian in its reliance upon accident and trifles for revelations of unexpected significance:

> Hence it is that some women may even love long before they are aware of it. For in that place of mystery [the heart] is born, if we mistake not, a pure woman's love; and hence too it may be, as if partaking of the nature of its birthplace, that it is so long shadowy to the everyday eye . . . till some magic accident—a word, a look, the merest trifle—gives it a name and substance.[56]

For Allston art ideally is that "magic accident," the "merest trifle," which lends an unvoiced reality "a name and substance." *Monaldi* ultimately is a tale of the breakdown of integrated selfhood in a world itself semiotically disrupted.[57]

The final step in the collapse of epistemological processes seems almost predictable. Visionary activity in the earlier Allston (*Italian Landscape*, 1805–8) was accompanied by a secondary awareness of distance, and distance itself found expression in the imagery of loss and modes of self-accounting that occur in works of the middle period (*Italian Landscape*, 1814). This classicistic dimension to Allston's work, its tendency to express its self-referential and displaced status with a parodic voice, reflects a deeper language-boundedness that Allston could on occasion parlay into an aesthetic idiom in its own right, but that more often than not results in an ironic mode of vision more debilitating than empowering. Emerson, who appreciated Allston's person and character more than he did his painting, saw in Allston a "feminine" sensibility that he thought "receptive, and not masculine and creative." He sought from Allston, as he did from all his countrymen, a "charged cloud" overflowing with "terrible beauty" and emitting "lightnings on all beholders."[58] Though it is unclear whether Emerson ever actually appreciated such qualities when he found them, his judgment of Allston bears a deep kernel of truth. Allston's ironic vision does not allow him to be the oracular artist Emerson sought.[59] Even when his beauty is "terrible" and prophetic, as in *Elijah in the Desert* (1818; fig. 22), his work seems as much a warning against the isolation and power of the imagination—its aridity when self-sustained—as it is a gesture toward new worlds and new visions. As Doreen Hunter has pointed out, Allston's later theoretical writings represent a careful effort "to circumscribe the vaulting ambitions of romantic idealism." In the *Lectures on Art*, composed in the decade before his death, Allston "was determined to fix the imagination into a context of permanent, uniform, and public truths":

> When one studies these *Lectures* in the light of Allston's career...it seems more likely that...[his] ambiguity reflects, not a forward movement into unexplored realms of romanticism, but a half-concealed retreat into the security offered by common-sense philosophy. Allston qualified his enthusiasm for the romantic values of feeling and originality. He constrained the imagination within the rules and impediments of a correspondence theory of knowledge and confined it to the "construction" of forms and ideas verifiable by all men.[60]

This conservative bias in Allston seems allied with the role of memory in his painting. Memory is the language of mediation in early Romanticism, a metaphor for expressing the pattern of displacement that accompanies the process of vision. It lends coherence to a present perceived as fragmented and disjointed, only, paradoxically, by distancing that present, rendering it meaningful only when rendering it inaccessible.[61] Memory is

22. WASHINGTON ALLSTON, *Elijah in the Desert*, 1818. Courtesy, Museum of Fine Arts, Boston. Gift of Mrs. Samuel Hooper and Miss Alice Hooper.

thus a metaphor for origins, expressing the hope for a (remembered) point outside the mediatory field even as it acknowledges by distancing that point the enclosing embrace of language. Its irony is the dispossession it expresses: in search for the familiar and the known, one lands anew elsewhere. In Allston one suspects that memory becomes more than a trope describing the pains of displacement, more than a means even of gilding linguistic enclosure with referential discourse. By conceiving the ideal as past and expressing referential loss as a mode of temporal discontinuity, Allston commits himself to a rhetoric of loss and nostalgia incompatible with the sustained game-playing of a voice like Coleridge's. The apparent freedom of the latter to invent and subvert is denied Allston by his reification of memory into a mode of permanent stasis. Where Coleridge seems to end in irony and laughter,[62] Allston concludes with death.

That is his final metaphor. The dislocation and loss of the earlier landscapes resolves itself into a deeper death instinct, a mode of counter-consciousness, recurring in works of Allston's final American period from 1819 until his death in the summer of 1843. Geoffrey Hartman has noted that Romantic "consciousness is accompanied by an increase in self-consciousness" and a fear of the intellect as a "corrosive power of analysis . . . that 'murders to dissect.'" In response to this phenomenon, Romantic poetry

> begins to be valued in contradistinction to directly analytic or purely conceptual modes of thought. The intelligence is seen as a perverse though necessary specialization of the whole soul of man, and art as a means to resist the intelligence intelligently.[63]

For a writer like Hawthorne, art is not so much antidote to the prying intellect as accomplice; contrary to what Hartman describes for the British Romantics, Hawthorne links the visionary powers of the artist with the rapacious intellect of figures often described as scientists, occasionally as voyeurs, whose appetite for knowledge outstrips the constraining admonitions of the heart. Allston proceeds by a somewhat different, though related, mode. Concerned like Hawthorne for the apparent schism between heart and intellect, he resorts to a form of visual energy not only nonverbal but preverbal. For Hartman "anti-self-consciousness" "is non-limiting with respect to the mind":

> It seeks to draw the antidote to self-consciousness from consciousness itself. A way is to be found not to escape from or limit knowledge, but to convert it into an energy finer than intellectual.[64]

Though one senses in Allston's images of revery "an energy finer than intellectual," there is no corresponding affirmation that the "antidote to self-consciousness" resides within "consciousness itself." Allston lacks that Germanic sense of a progressive and dialectic resolution to the dilemma of consciousness from within the cycle of alienation and return common to much of nineteenth-century Idealism. Instead, revery provides Allston with a mode of stasis deriving its power from its preverbal, metalinguistic imagery. Consciousness is not so much transcended as dismantled. In *Beatrice* (1819; fig. 23), Allston constructs an image of pre-Victorian sentimentality—a virginal girl with side-turned head in a moment of devotional pause—to express, ostensibly, a state of innocence "primeval" and unarticulable. Her thoughts, were they expressible, would probably parallel those of a maiden Allston describes in his brief poem "Rosalie":

> "O, pour upon my soul again
>   That sad, unearthly strain,
> That seems from other worlds to plain;
> Thus falling, falling from afar,
> As if some melancholy star
> Had mingled with her light her sighs,
>   And dropped them from the skies!

23. WASHINGTON ALLSTON, *Beatrice,* 1819. Courtesy, Museum of Fine Arts, Boston. Anonymous gift.

"No,—never came from aught below
   This melody of woe,
That makes my heart to overflow,
As from a thousand gushing springs,
Unknown before; that with it brings
This nameless light,—if light it be,—
   That veils the world I see.

"For all I see around me wears
   The hue of other spheres;
And something blent of smiles and tears
Comes from the very air I breathe.
O, nothing, sure, the stars beneath
Can mould a sadness like to this,—
   So like angelic bliss."

Like Beatrice, Rosalie seems bound in a spell of unearthly sorrow and tenderness that bathes the world with "hue of other spheres." Beatrice shares with Rosalie not only a common mood, but probably a common destiny, as related in the poem's concluding stanza:

So, at that dreamy hour of day
   When the last lingering ray
Stops on the highest cloud to play,—
So thought the gentle Rosalie,
As on her maiden reverie
First fell the strain of him who stole
   In music to her soul.

The poem is not so much a paean to innocence as a tale of seduction, where yearning maidenhood results in sexual initiation. The fascination of the poem lies in the tone of poignance that acknowledges the confusion of spiritual plaint with sexual interlude by underscoring the vulnerability of the former to the latter. The energy of the first three stanzas is deeply erotic, though it fails to understand itself as such, and only in the last stanza does the moment of recognition arrive. With the recognition comes the end of the poem, for it can no longer sustain a poignance based on the confusion of spirituality with erotic energy. Innocence is measured by the failure of self-understanding. In *Beatrice* the viewer is treated to visual clues not unlike the suppressed moments of doubt that surface in "Rosalie" and betray her confusion of earthly and divine passions ("No,—*never came from aught below* / This melody of woe"; "This nameless light,—*if light it be*"). The cross cradled and half-hidden in Beatrice's hand; the sinuous interweaving of gold chain and rounded fingers; the gesture of hand to heart; the delicate net of gold that loosely binds her flowing auburn hair; the velour-like drapery of her rich, dark costume, emphasizing in its fullness the figure beneath; all suggest an erotic energy woven into the spell of spiritual devotion though unrecognized by the sitter. In *Beatrice* Allston retrieves a stage of consciousness prior to the plunge into identity and individuation, pregnant with possibility, and poignant because suspended between innocence and self-awareness. The semiotic disruption of *Saul and the Witch of Endor*—the failure of unknown and creative power to translate itself into an adequate linguistic structure—is here expressed more gently as a mode of prepubescent confusion between religious and sexual energies (imagery of the former serving as an uneasy vehicle for the latter). When examined in the context of Allston's other works from the period, *Beatrice* suggests a counter-linguistic mode of consciousness—a state prior to language rather than an alternative to it—and the sentimental, though unstated, equation of sexuality and loss in the painting in turn suggests limitations inherent in Beatrice's revery: it is proleptic of its own loss and therefore doomed by that which renders it valuable.

In two paintings entitled *Italian Shepherd Boy* (1819, Detroit [fig. 24], and 1821–23, Brooklyn [fig. 25]), Allston translates revery from a historical stage of consciousness prior to language to a classical state unbound by time and conventional cognitive awareness. Allston's androgynous youths—presexual, preverbal, unindividualized—participate in a stasis far more profound than the silent meditation of Beatrice. They dwell as Pan figures, pipes in hand, in a densely foliated forest world, enclosed by vegetation that opens only onto itself and relegates the blue sky to a small and unimportant patch of upper canvas. They repeat compositionally earlier works of youths posed in pastoral settings. Sir Joshua Reynolds's *Lady Gertrude Fitzpatrick as "Sylvia"* (1787; fig. 26), similarly centers a young child amidst imaginative glens in rustic costume. Reynolds's painting, however, disports itself as a high cultural joke: the child plays at being a peasant as she does at being an adult, and her play is but a variation on the deeper forms of cultural posturing and historical quotation that for Reynolds and his generation are hallmarks of an advanced and culturally aware society. In Allston the opposite has occurred: rusticity is a mode of return. Allston's shepherds are linked to their pastoral environment not as youths in rural garb—aristocracy playing with its pastoral conceits—but as figures of stasis, images that in the larger context of Allston's art seem to slow to a stop the process of language and replace it by reversing it, unraveling the web of language until all that is left is an energy of repose and the silence of unsung songs (notice the pipes at the sides of the figures, unvoiced, and if played, unvoiceable, for their music is always without words). Death is Allston's final conceit, and like all "conceits" it is

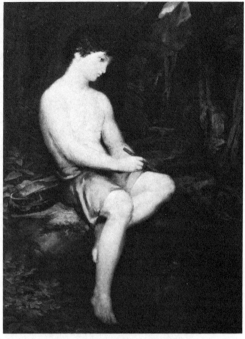

24. WASHINGTON ALLSTON. *Italian Shepherd Boy*, 1819. Detroit Institute of Arts. Gift of D. M. Ferry, Jr.

25. WASHINGTON ALLSTON. *Italian Shepherd Boy*, 1821–23. Brooklyn Museum, Dick S. Ramsay Fund.

a figuration, conceived, composed, and elaborated in the imagination. It is Allston's mode of return, a surrogate for the dolphin-crested chair of *Samuel Williams* and the mountain-climbing coach of *Monaldi*'s narrator. Through revery, its vehicle, and stasis, its analogue, death promises that final symmetry which binds one once again to the soil of one's origins. Keats, in the "Ode to a Nightingale," creates a dense bower world of indolent and brooding unrest not unlike Allston's dark forest of the *Italian Shepherd Boy*. Similarly, Keats's half-insensate persona divests himself of sight, as Allston's figures of voice, in order to accommodate himself to a world without vision's analytic powers. Unlike Keats, however, Allston does not fear the death implicit in repose and in the abdication of cognitive processes. Stasis is for Allston only another figurative window on the façade of the world permitting an egress from language and an imagined return to prelinguistic origins.

For in Allston all return is a conceit, as are all windows. Venture back for a last glance at the two paintings of the *Italian Shepherd Boy*. Their stasis seems misplaced: though demigods of a protean realm, they preside over no visionary pilgrimage, and possess neither the impulse to

26. JOSHUA REYNOLDS, *Lady Gertrude Fitzpatrick as "Sylvia,"* 1787. Courtesy, Museum of Fine Arts, Boston. Given in memory of Governor Alvin Fuller by the Fuller Foundation.

journey nor the vision that accrues with experience. If saved from history, they are robbed of youth. Against the claustrophobia of language Allston had attempted to "strike the reason dumb,"[65] dissolving language into mood and both into death. But death too in Allston is its own ironic parody. The dualism of *Samuel Williams* has been preserved here in the creamy tones that distinguish the shepherds' figures from the dark labyrinthine energy of the backgrounds. Planes of flesh and forest meet by juxtaposition and maintain their separate identities: Allston's pastoral world will not permit a final return. Pastoral is a figured form of language, and offers at most a *fiction* of death. In the brooding figures of Allston's faun-like heroes, as in the stylized nature of the image itself, Allston can achieve no more than the illusion of a moment's respite from the damning process of self-referentiality. In *Samuel Williams* a dualistic space provided the fiction of worlds elsewhere; linguistic enclosure was transformed into imaginative freedom, as walls sprouted windows and views hung like pictures from barren surfaces. In the two versions of the *Italian Shepherd Boy*, Allston closes the window, seeking in death not the myth of freedom but the illusion of return. That is Allston's final conceit: death is the fiction of a world where language has ceased. To dismantle the burden of consciousness Allston must ungild the cage, peel blue skies off faceless walls until all life and all vision are stilled in a great unrest. But the final joke—parody's last irony—is that the echoes won't stop. The windows don't disappear—they cannot. Even death is a figured image, another fiction on the wall, and stasis the *image* for that which is un*imag*inable. We start where we began: the cage, you see, will not be ungilded.

Part Two

Romanticism and
the Imagination:
Thomas Cole,
Washington Irving, and
John Quidor

3 Knowledge as Narcissism: Milton, Cole, and the Myth of the Fall

> I shuddered as I stood upon the edge of this abyss, and feared for a moment that the crumbling earth would slide from beneath me. I have often mused upon the brink of a rocky precipice, without a thought of its destructibility; but here the great mass, bearing marks of rapid and continual decay, awakened the instantaneous thought that it was as perishable as a cloud.
>
> THOMAS COLE, Journal entry, 24 August 1831

The myth of the Adamic man looms large in the American past. As pursued by R. W. B. Lewis in *The American Adam*, it is the focus of a "native American mythology" that understood the "authentic American as a figure of heroic innocence and vast potentialities, poised at the start of a new history."[1] As a historical narrative, the myth of the American Adam comes to us with uncertain credentials. Is prelapsarian Adam necessarily doomed to repeat the Fall, or does the American Eden possess some quality that distinguishes it from its earlier counterpart, protecting the latter against the failure of an earlier innocence? For Thomas Cole, the answer seemed as inevitable as the course of empire itself. In a series of five canvases by that name, Cole depicted the triumph of human will over nature as a conflict that dooms even as it regenerates. As savagery yields to the pastoral state and both result in civilization and the "Consummation of Empire," so empire itself is fated to destruction and desolation. The moral of Cole's canvases for mid-nineteenth-century America, as Perry Miller has noted, was a lesson that "society instinctively strove to repress...an ineluctable cycle of rise and fall" that doomed the American experiment, like all great visionary adventures before it, to failure and repetition.[2] There was another moral to Cole's story, which he pursued separately in a earlier work titled *Expulsion from the Garden of Eden* (ca. 1827–28). Eden, like empire, seemed bound by a logic and

81

history of its own; to understand the possibilities of Adamic man, the artist had first to remove him from his prelapsarian world and set him on the other side of Eden's walls. Let Adam's potential be weighed against the extent of his loss—measure his possibilities by his knowledge and his future by his past—and then, perhaps, we will know what is new in man. Cole's Adam is not Lewis's ingenue with a "preadolescent ignorance of the convulsive undertow of human behavior," but a creature of over-abundant knowledge for whom consciousness has become a mode of self-consciousness. A century and a half earlier, the English Puritan poet John Milton, blind and visionary, had chiseled the outlines of man's fall to consciousness into the mind and memory of the post-Renaissance world. *Paradise Lost* harbored within it an implicit caveat to a modern age Milton foresaw and then forswore on the horizon of Restoration England. Too great a concern with the human mind, too deep a plunge into the abyss of self, could only catapult man into a narcissism too strong to be appeased. Like many of his Romantic contemporaries, Cole had read Milton and perceived in the myth of the Fall a metaphor for the modern world, a means of accounting simultaneously for the vast power and profound limitation of the American Adam. With Milton he pursued the agony of knowledge, and in *Expulsion from the Garden of Eden* he explored the process of displacement that accompanies the mind in the travail of self-awareness. To understand Cole's *Expulsion*, therefore, let us first inquire into Milton's primal Parents.

I

Milton has Adam react in *Paradise Lost* to Eve's revelation of her "fatal Trespass" with stunned silence, "amaz'd" and "Astonied," his capacity for speech virtually lost, until

> thus at length
> First to himself he inward silence broke.
> [9.894–95][3]

Addressing Eve, whose physical presence belies her spiritual absence, he cries to her in the silence of his thoughts:

> O fairest of Creation, last and best
> Of all God's works, Creature in whom excell'd
> Whatever can to sight or thought be form'd,
> Holy, divine, good, amiable, or sweet!
> How art thou lost, how on a sudden lost,
> Defac'd, deflow'r'd, and now to Death devote?
> [9.896–901]

That Adam should initially lose his capacity for speech and subsequently recover it through an extended interior monologue, a form itself paradoxical since addressed to Eve though contained entirely within his mind, provides a measure of the dimensions of Eve's act. Adam's capacity for language, paralyzed at first, returns only in distorted form from its original high purpose as the voice and instrument of Reason. Speech had been granted to Adam as a mode of understanding. Through the process of "naming" the creatures of God's creation, Adam had transformed his perception of the world into knowledge of it. Understanding for Adam is an activity of the imagination: a capacity to transfigure what is seen into an emblem of powers and relations unseen, the metamorphosis of vision into the visionary. It requires, as Geoffrey Hartman has noted, that the sign should become "symbol so proleptically, [that] imagination so imposes on nature, that an intrinsic discontinuity appears."[4]

> I nam'd them, as they pass'd, and understood
> Thir Nature, with such knowledge God endu'd
> My sudden apprehension: but in these
> I found not what methought I wanted still;
> And to the Heav'nly vision thus presumed.
>   [8.352–56]

What is lacking is Eve, a figure to confirm Adam in his "happy consciousness," knowing himself through knowledge of the creation around him. Eve is Adam's own self and "consort," an externalization born from his ribs who literalizes through her creation the necessity for otherness intrinsic to all knowing. To know oneself, the self must extend beyond itself. God responds to Adam's plea for a helpmate:

> Thus far to try thee, Adam, I was pleas'd,
> And find thee *knowing* not of Beasts alone,
> Which thou has rightly *nam'd*, but of thyself,
> Expressing well the spirit within thee free,
> My image . . . .
>   [8.437–41; emphases mine]

Adam's identity depends upon his teleological awareness: self-knowledge arises from a process of naming that confirms the namer in his rightful relation to creation.[5] But Eve is more than other. She is also Adam's "sole partner," not only a spiritual companion but, as the pun suggests, a temptation to privacy and aloneness. Her presence makes real both the appetitive possibilities of language—that knowledge should be linked with the enlargement of desire—and a new type of spiritual rapaciousness, a greedy engorging "without restraint" that fails to transform desire into vision or to sanction as *symbol* what it consumes as food for eye or mouth.

Adam's interior monologue, sandwiched between the "Speechless" silence that follows Eve's revelation and his subsequent resumption of public language, chronicles his mental journey from an innocent to fallen state. What occurs is a deformation of language: Adam subverts the public nature of "discourse" and transgresses the proper function of Reason by casting his lot solely with the unredeemed because unvalorized "link of Nature":

> Flesh of Flesh,
> Bone of my Bone thou art, and from thy State
> Mine never shall be parted, bliss or woe.
>   [9.914–16]

Language turns in upon itself. No longer a "discourse" opening onto a world beyond the mind of man, it confirms Adam instead in the self-centeredness of his thoughts. His decision to follow Eve parallels in its rhetorical construction his earlier vow to God:

> I now see
> Bone of my Bone, Flesh of my Flesh, my Self
> Before me; Woman is her Name, of Man
> Extracted; for this cause he shall forgo
> Father and Mother, and to his Wife adhere;
> And they shall be one Flesh, one Heart, one Soul.
>   [8.495–99]

The Miltonic formulation of the biblical injunction that man should "cleave unto his wife" involves, as does the original, two moments: (1) the sundering of past ties ("for this cause he shall forgo Father and Mother") (2) in the name of a new order ("And they shall be one Flesh"). The two are linked in a sequence of growth: the self steps outside the early matrix of influences constituting its home in order to establish a new center beyond the circumference of the old. This process of self-transcendence, where growth arises out of loss, is an essential feature of the Miltonic world.

It can be traced back to Milton's early pendant pieces of his Cambridge days, *L'Allegro* and *Il Penseroso*, in which Milton reveals the antithetical implications of his imagination by premising sublime vision upon the renunication of pastoral dalliance.[6] The "heart-easing Mirth" of *L'Allegro*—a world of plentitude and happiness—is renounced in *Il Penseroso* ("Hence vain deluding joys") for the larger discontinuity essential to Miltonic visionary experience. As Stuart Ende notes,

> Milton is a poet who is intensely aware of proper relationship, of mutual discourse between self and other; but surmise silences that

hoped for dialogue because it represents a self-involvement that denies otherness, which to the poet is the only life, however antithetical. In Milton one cannot compensate for "mortal fraility," one can only oppose it.[7]

Or to express the point psychoanalytically: "The difference between the satisfaction of *L'Allegro* and *Il Penseroso* is from one view the difference between sublimation and repression."[8] The tradition of *L'Allegro* assuages loss by restoring natural pleasures, while that of *Il Penseroso* seeks for deeper visions in the rejection (or at least the ultimate rejection—there is dalliance along the way) of earthly pleasure.

Adam's failure to make the transition from the pleasures of the *L'Allegro* tradition to the demands of *Il Penseroso* can be seen in his reversal of the injunction by which man should "adhere" to woman. The loyalty of each to each, when pursued under divine sanction, expands and liberates; an older self is put by and a new self put on as the poetics of pastoral yield before the enlarged demands of epic verse. The pattern parallels Christ's injunction to his disciples:

> I came not to send peace, but a sword. For I am come to set a man at variance against his father, and the daughter against her mother . . . .[9]

Adam, however, turns the command to cling to woman into an occasion of self-limitation. The irony of his commitment to Eve is that it occurs, as the model of an interior monologue would suggest, as a regression of the self upon itself, a movement inward instead of outward, made all the more tragic by being couched in the language of growth.

The stillborn nature of Adam's thought can best be understood when contrasted with an earlier scene in which Eve, confronting a similar dilemma, grows beyond her childlike fascination with herself into a more mature relation with the surrounding world. Awaking from the sleep of Creation, Eve wanders down to a "liquid Plain . . . Pure as th' expanse of Heav'n." Staring with "unexperienc't thought" into "the clear / Smooth Lake, that to me seem'd another Sky," she encounters, like Narcissus, her own entrancing image:

> As I bent down to look, just opposite,
> A shape within the wat'ry gleam appear'd
> Bending to look on me, I started back,
> It started back, but pleas'd I soon return'd,
> Pleas'd it return'd as soon with answering looks
> Of sympathy and love . . . .
>
> [4.460–65]

The danger of Eve's situation is the narcissism it promises. Eve not only mistakes herself for another, but finds her mirror image at the center of her perceptions. In misconstruing the surface of the waters for "another Sky," she confuses the lake for Heaven, perceives herself as the focus of this "wat'ry" Paradise, and seems thereby to invert the proper order of creation. The consequences are profound, for the Miltonic world, by a logic inherent in the Protestant imagination, links inversion with personal and poetic collapse. Milton conceives of creation, as did an American Puritan of the following century, Jonathan Edwards, as a series of "emanations and remanations" from a single sustaining force, Godhead:

> one Almighty is, from whom
> All things proceed, and up to him return . . . .
> Indu'd with various forms, various degrees
> Of substance, and in things that live, of life;
> But more refin'd, more spiritous, and pure,
> As nearer to him plac't or nearer tending
> Each in thir several active Spheres assign'd,
> Till body up to spirit work, in bounds
> Proportion'd to each kind.
> [5.469–70, 473–79]

For Milton the failure of the visionary imagination lies in an arrest and reversal of this expansionary pattern. Reality is confined within narcissistic boundaries and reduced to a trope for the observing mind. Eve's danger, like that of all young poets, consists in just such a reversal. Captured by her own self-love, she is in danger of substituting herself as a surrogate center for a universe properly defined through the recognition of otherness. If sublimation provides the pattern for pastoral experience, then Eve's narcissistic dalliance on the liquid plain reveals sublimation, contrary to Freud's understanding of it as the process of civilization-making, as nothing more than a counterfeit, a ruse for implementing an essentially self-aggrandizing economy. Gazing into the "liquid Plain" (an allusion in part to the "burning Lake" of Hell, scene of another anti-Heaven), Eve risks not only mistaking herself for the whole of reality but, in so doing, construing herself as the center of a new Heaven.

The narcissism implicit in Eve's situation is a natural consequence of her uninstructed humanity: a reminder that true vision is, as Ende notes, an "intellectual and anti-natural state." Like a child, she lacks experience ("I thither went / With unexperienc't thought") and exhibits before the "smooth wat'ry" surface the instinctive propensities of an untutored and uninformed mind. What occurs next is what distinguishes Milton from his later, and religion-lost, successors:

> there I had fixt
> Mine eyes till now, and pin'd with vain desire,

> Had not a voice thus warn'd me, What thou seest,
> What there thou seest fair Creature is thyself,
> With thee it came and goes: but follow me,
> And I will bring thee where no shadow stays
> Thy coming, and thy soft imbraces, hee
> Whose image thou art, him thou shalt enjoy
> Inseparably thine . . . .

$$[4.465–73]$$

An intervening voice comes between Eve and her incipient narcissism and directs her away from her own image, warning her of her mistake while leading her instead to Adam, "hee / Whose image thou art." The voice Eve hears is a Muse of renunciation, whether described narratively as an inner prompting of Eve's imagination or theologically as a form of natural or prevenient grace. The significance of the voice lies in Eve's response:

> what could I do,
> But follow straight, invisibly thus led?
> $$[4.475–76]$$

Eve lives in a world that is more than human. She is subject to modes of discontinuity and denial that shape her experience along lines different from the biases of the natural self. Her state may be contrasted with a remarkable image developed by Jonathan Edwards suggesting the power of the Narcissus myth when held up before the Puritan imagination:

> The water . . . is a type of sin or the corruption of man, and of the state of misery that is the consequence of it. It is like sin in its flattering appearance. How smooth and harmless does the water oftentimes appear, and as if it had paradise and heaven in its bosom. Thus when we stand on the banks of a lake or river, how flattering and pleasing does it oftentimes appear, as though under were pleasant and delightful groves and bowers and even heaven itself in its clearness, enough to tempt one unacquainted with its nature to descend thither. But indeed it is all a cheat: if we descent into it, instead of finding pleasant, delightful groves and a garden of pleasure and heaven in its clearness, we should meet with nothing but death, a land of darkness, or darkness itself . . . .[10]

Eve is distinguished from Edwards's sinner by the presence of that voice which informs her experience and guides her away from the "groves and bowers and even heaven itself" glimpsed in the "clearness" of the water. Edwards, like Milton, perceives the power of the illusory "wat'ry" images; he understands the appeal of a surrogate Paradise centered upon man and freed of the responsibilities of divine order. Each Puritan thinker, however, knows all too profoundly what lies on the other side: "death, a land of darkness, or darkness itself." Unlike Wordsworth, who a little over a century later was to pride himself on having made just that plunge

> Into our Minds, into the Mind of Man—
> My haunt, and the main region of my song,[11]

Edwards and Milton draw back from that "sin . . . we call . . . self-love."[12] Their story is the renunciation that inaugurates all vision and renders possible the mind's discovery of its place in an order extending beyond the self.

Eve's act of renunciation, whether of narcissistic self-image or pastoral plentitudes, is followed by the affirmation of an order in which the individual plays only a subordinate part. Her first sight of Adam leaves her hesitant at his being

> less fair,
> Less winning soft, less amiably mild,
> Than that smooth wat'ry image . . . .
> [4.478–80]

Adam responds as did the earlier voice, by way of invitation:

> Return fair *Eve*,
> Whom fli'st thou? whom thou fli'st, of him thou art,
> His flesh, his bone . . . .
> Part of my Soul I seek thee, and thee claim
> My other half . . . .
> [4.481–83, 487–88]

As she had listened without struggle to the voice at the lake side, she accepts now the lesson offered by Adam:

> with that thy gentle hand
> Seiz'd mine, I yielded, and from that time see
> How beauty is excell'd by manly grace
> And wisdom, which alone is truly fair.
> [4.488–91]

Accepting Adam's vision of human nature as necessarily divided and counterpointed against itself—the "natural" self subordinated to "My other half"—Eve concludes the transition from innocence to a knowledge born of experience. The model of maturation she presents is a paradigm of both the evolution of sublime poetics and of the self's movement outside itself to God through the power and guidance of grace. Her situation parallels in its movement the poet's antithetical progress from pastoral surrender to visionary possibilities.

II

Adam describes postlapsarian Eve as "Defac't, deflow'r'd, and now to Death devote." The Latinate prefix *de* suggests the disjunction which he perceives in Eve: disjoined in appearance ("Defac't") from the inner nature of her thoughts ("Thus *Eve* with Count'nance blithe her story told; / But in her Cheek distemper flushing glow'd"), and denuded of her prelapsarian innocence ("deflow'r'd"). Deflowering also suggests a deeper structural disfiguration that accompanies Eve's fallen relationship to her Edenic world. Often described as a flower who grows in the shade of Adam's sustaining presence, Eve is pictured on her solitary, temptation-defying jaunt through Eden as being

> Herself, though fairest unsupported Flow'r,
> From her best prop so far, and storm so nigh.
> [9.432–33]

To be "deflow'r'd" is to be denied the terms of her relation to Adam, and through him, to the world. Deflowering marks the collapse of a renunciatory poetics. For Eve, it is a form of estrangement; like the term "devote" it suggests a type of "doom": "to give over or consign to the powers of evil or to destruction; to doom."[13] Eve is condemned to a life out of phase with her essential nature; in modern parlance, and in a very modern sense, she is alienated and self-estranged from her true position in the cosmic order.

Milton puns, however, with the Latinate prefix. The alteration in structure of the Edenic world following Eve's disobedience is more than simple disjunction or negation. The term "devote" contains its own inverse meaning, denoting not only condemnation but consecration. Eve is now "to Death devote." It is her task to construct out of the disjunction of her world an order whose starting point is the abyss that separates her from her past. Like Satan, she must make a "Heaven out of Hell," accepting that injunction by which "Death is to mee as Life" (9.954). These words, ironically, are Adam's, for he too shares in the defacement and deflowering entailed in the Fall. His interior monologue, the first discourse divorced from public utterance in *Paradise Lost*, foretells the act of disobedience that will seal the "link of Nature" binding him to Eve.

Adam's monologue also establishes him as a modern poet. If Eve represents, in her prelapsarian origins, a history of poetic beginnings or, more accurately, the emergence of a sublime poetics from pastoral beauty, then Adam traduces his own visionary possibilities by precipitating in his speech a disjunction between inner and outer worlds. What transpires in Adam's monologue is an internalization of space: distances become mental rather than spatial. An incommensurate gap opens between Adam's interior world and the physical space that links him to Eve; their physical proximity belies their spiritual estrangement. Adam's addressed monologue resembles the Romantic lyric of the following two centuries. Like the *Prelude* and so much of Wordsworth's poetry, Adam's monologue is addressed in the second person to a subject whose presence is defined in terms of absence.[14] The form of dialogue manqué suggests the antithetical need for otherness defining the tradition from which Adam and his successors have come, while its residues within an interior monologue betray the deeper surrender of sublime energies to narcissistic demands that the tradition has undergone. Milton's poetry thus raises within itself the possibility of its own inward collapse, a failure of imagination that renders the Fall a study not only in theological but *poetic* miscarriage.

   That the Miltonic sense of fallen man should appear to be so close to the Romantic self-image is no coincidence. The path to Hell is surely paved with the soul of many a good Puritan who in search of God stumbled onto man and never quite regained his way. *Paradise Lost* records within itself that deformation of human purpose involved in the Wordsworthian turn to self-knowledge. Eve sighing at her own image on the "clear Smooth Lake" is Milton's caveat to a future world whose preoccupation with itself will render it careless of other voices of warning, alternative renunciating modes:

>   there I had fixt
>   Mine eyes till now, and pin'd with vain desire,
>   Had not a voice thus warn'd me, What thou seest,
>   What there thou seest fair Creature is thyself . . . .
>   [4.465–68]

Milton's epic poem can hold a mirror to the future only because that future literalizes the poem's own daemonic possibilities. Blake and the Romantic poets were only half-right in their suspicion that Milton "was of the Devil's party." Where they erred was in forgetting that all antithetical verse contains within itself the terms of its own inversion: the temptation to a narcissism corrosive of epic design. To the seventeenth-century Puritan mind, half-author and full-participant in the transformation of post-Renaissance consciousness into a state of increasingly introspective self-consciousness, knowledge of sin came through knowledge of self. Jonathan Edwards was to express it in a sermon of 1738:

> 'Tis Experience *of our selves*, and finding what we are, that God commonly makes Use of as the means of bringing us off from all Dependence *on our selves.*[15]

Introspection proved an insatiable appetite for the saintly Puritan. The inner darkness that often greeted his efforts at self-scrutiny prepared him for the astounding power of grace that elevated him, the "worst of all sinners," into the lap of God. Wordsworth would have found his Protestant progenitors to be strange intellectual bedfellows indeed, yet he shared with them

> such fear and awe
> As fall upon us often when we look
> Into our Minds, into the Mind of Man . . . .[16]

Postlapsarian man was a creature well known to Milton; he was in fact remarkably close to the sort and sensibility that later defined the Romantic self-image. To Milton, as to the Romantics, the individual in a condition of self-knowledge was the starting point for the drama of soul and redemption. Such drama led to God and a visionary poetics for Milton; for the Romantic thinker it turned endlessly upon itself. Eve at the bounds of the lake of self-knowledge, like Narcissus caught in the snares of his own vision, was only a whisper away from the modern world.

III

The impulse toward self-examination occurs in another version of the Eden story, told now Romantically by Thomas Cole, an Anglo-American painter whose three pictures in the window of a New York art dealer in 1825 marked the emergence of an American landscape tradition.[17] *Expulsion from the Garden of Eden* (ca. 1827–28; fig. 27) is a self-portrait of the Romantic mind, created by Cole as a mirror image of his interior world. Adam and Eve (fig. 28), tiny, doomed figures bound hand in hand as they cross the precipice separating Eden from the terrible forces outside the Garden, together image the dilemma of Romantic personhood: she with hand over eyes, stoop-shouldered, gazing groundward as she marches ahead; he with hand over eyes, erect, looking back while marching forward, gazing with shielded vision at the brightness of a past now lost. Their Janus-like posture, earth-bound while heaven gazing, derives from John Martin's illustrations of 1827 to *Paradise Lost* (fig. 29).[18] Cole's figures reverse Martin's roles (Martin's Adam looks down, his Eve gazes back), though like his they represent a humanity torn between future uncertainty and past serenity. Their divided forms confirm the deeper schism that defines the space of Cole's painting. On the right stands Eden, quiet, timeless, filled with the even light of a hazy golden afternoon. On the left, separated from Eden by the massive rock formation that Cole borrows from Martin as the gate to Paradise, rages the world beyond Eden, the home of exiled man, illumined in the chiaroscuro of

27. THOMAS COLE, *Expulsion from the Garden of Eden*, ca. 1827–28. Courtesy, Museum of Fine Arts, Boston, M. and M. Karolik Collection.

28. THOMAS COLE, detail of fig. 27, *Expulsion from the Garden of Eden* (Adam and Eve).

29. JOHN MARTIN, "The Expulsion of Adam and Eve." Illustration in *The Paradise Lost of Milton*, London, Septimus Prowett, 1827, vol. 2, book 12, line 641. Yale Center for British Art, Paul Mellon Collection.

volcanic fire and storm. The individual stands divided and suspended between the two, an eternal voyager in exile from Paradise, condemned not to forget but, as Adam's posture suggests, to remember. Displaced from what he perceives to be his true center, his life is a perpetual transition, just as the waters raging under the precipice he has recently crossed flow continually from one waterfall to the next in perpetual descent.[19]

The displacement that Adam and Eve suffer can be measured by their off-centered relation to the picture's focal point. The geometric center of Cole's canvas is the penumbra of light radiating from the edges of the cavernous archway into Eden. Adam and Eve appear at the far end of the tongue of light that stretches across the bridge emerging from Eden's threshold and spanning the chasm that separates it from time-tossed earth. They are present to the viewer only after searching through the intricately detailed zones of activity surrounding the optical center of the picture. Diminutive in stature, distanced from their true center, they are narrative elements displaced from the visual center of the painting. The story of dispossession that they represent has been formalized into the spatial dislocation that separates the narrative from visual focus and requires that the two be held together across the void that is the true metaphysical center of the picture. They are related to Eden by a web of light and space that spans the chasm separating man from lost innocence; the narrow bridge vaulting the abyss beneath them contains a fracture that runs through its center. Like Edwardsian figures dangling by a narrow thread over the fiery pits below, Adam and Eve walk precipitously over chasms that threaten to overwhelm the bridge-like arch (how massive the rock bridge seems, and yet how perilous when cracked at its center) that supports them over nothingness.

Cole's figures have discovered the experience of loss: they know their own irrevocable alteration as figures displaced into a world of abysses. The fracture running through the rock bridge, the abyss beneath it, the sheer cliffs that seal off Eden and render it inaccessible to the world around it, are all images of their state of mind and being. Cole's figures have entered a world defined by temporal discontinuity. Milton had been careful in *Paradise Lost* to distinguish the effects of time in Eden from those of a postlapsarian world. In the Garden of Eden, "Fruit untoucht" hangs

> incorruptible, till men
> Grow up to thir provision, and more hands
> Help to disburden Nature of her Birth.
> [9.621–24]

Time itself is innocent; it does not contain cycles of decay in its inevitable course; instead prelapsarian time serves only as a backdrop upon which the drama of human growth occurs. So too in Cole's Paradise, where a lush tropical spring experiences endless noon. The uniform diffusion of light through the mist-filled valleys of Eden suggests a stillness in which time records only the absence of change. By eliminating almost entirely all shadowing and chiaroscuro and filling the air with a suffused and nonfocused source of light, Cole creates a world without history, which dwells instead in its own eternal stasis. There is no past distinguishable from the present, no future different from the past, and no memory to recall the differences among the three. When change does occur as a transgression of Paradise's homogeneous space, the garden world responds to it in the only manner it can, expelling change from its midst like a monster from the womb. The Fall thus becomes mankind's first act of history.

On the other side of Cole's Paradise, divided from it by a wild mountain gorge, rages a barren, howling wilderness distinguished chiefly by the destructive presence of temporal processes. Unlike Martin, whose

30. THOMAS COLE, detail of fig. 27, *Expulsion from the Garden of Eden* (struggling animals).

illustration of the Expulsion focuses exclusively on the sublime drama of desolation characterizing the Fall, Cole is concerned as much with the *relation* between prelapsarian and postlapsarian worlds as he is with the separate status of either. The tableau in the lower left-hand corner of the canvas (fig. 30), where a wolf-like creature tears at a fallen stag while a preying vulture circles nearby, introduces the presence of death and the beginnings of narrative within the landscape. The two palm-like trees, bent in the wind as if by the blast of Eden's rage at the painting of its human guests, suggest by analogy Adam and Eve, stoop-shouldered and weighted by the burden of history. So too with the large anthropomorphic tree trunk, a characteristic Cole device that occupies the foreground space of the postlapsarian world and provides the grotesque setting for the drama of wolf and vulture at its feet. Ravaged by time, this tree knows the once-and-for-all character of historic existence. Each moment of its history brings with it an irreversible finality; each experience encountered

31. WINSLOW HOMER, *The Fox Hunt*, 1893. Courtesy of the Pennsylvania Academy of the Fine Arts, Philadelphia.

makes a difference. Winslow Homer, three-quarters of a century later, would fill the long, horizontal canvas of *The Fox Hunt* (1893; fig. 31), with a drama of natural struggle not unlike Cole's. Fox and ravens compete in an environment of raw power—and beauty—for a survival assured to neither creature, though guaranteed perhaps to nature herself in her endless procession of struggle and adaptation. The naturalism of Homer's painting—its unwillingness to accord to human history a position more privileged than that experienced by nature—differs from the more stylized tone of Cole's work. For Cole, nature provides an allegory for human destiny, and man is the privileged center of creation. Unlike Eden, to which one can always go back because one has never gone forward—any real motion means expulsion—the world of the wilderness and its anthropomorphic trees can never regain its mythic innocence nor return to an earlier state. Time is too real to be reversed.

For Adam and Eve, the *reality* of time is the source of its terror. The path before them dissolves into darkness and wilds. The expulsion from the Garden, as a birth into real time, opens onto a future of unknown possibilities. The abyss that spatially lies beneath them stands temporally before them. They enter the Unknown, and their terror lies in the paradox of their dual posture. Looking backward, they must proceed forward, exiles from the security and innocence of the past. Cole's figures inhabit a world defined by change and the imagery of transition: the arch that serves as a threshold between Eden and the wilderness; its inverse presence in the rainbow-shaped clouds that crown the volcanic fire of the background, and again in the bridge spanning the void and gorge over which Adam and Eve have passed. Each image, like the waterfalls that course through the wilderness, suggests the continual flow of time—life as a journey of eternal transition. An older Christian iconography that once conceived of this world as a preparatory stage for eternity has been inverted in *The Expulsion from the Garden of Eden*. The threshold to Cole's Eden seems more to bar entrance than to invite it, and the terror of Adam and Eve is that an existence defined by transition in a world bound by time should have nowhere to go.

Hope, then, is an invention of their own making. Milton had prefigured the process in Adam's remarkable internal soliloquy to Eve:

> How art thou lost, how on a sudden lost,
> Defac't, deflow'r'd, and now to Death devote?
>   [9.900–901]

Like Milton's figures, Cole's too are "amaz'd Night-wanderers" (9.640), "expell'd from hence into a World / Of woe and sorrow" (8.332–33). For both artists knowledge exists as an experience of loss and disjunction. Milton's pun on the word *devote*, suggesting not only condemnation and doom but their inverse, consecration to a new order, hints at a heresy for Milton that will become the basis for a renewed beginning in Cole. Eve's estrangement in Milton, like Adam's proclamation, "Death is to mee as Life" (9.954), occurs within a scheme of redemption that shapes loss into ultimate gain. Though Milton's characters lose sight of that vision, its presence, like the invisible Muse who directs Eve away from her own image in the "liquid Plain," remains the defining force throughout *Paradise Lost*. God is always present to Milton's world if only, as in Hell, as a center against which the boundaries are defined. The new order that Adam and Eve are to know and cultivate as fallen creatures, a world defined by death, remains whatever else a realm with "Providence thir guide" (12.657). Cole's primal Parents, unlike Milton's, have only themselves for guides. They too are to "Death devote"; their hope, however, is not divine. It stems from within and from the earth they inhabit. Eve's downward glance, hiding tears of shame and woe as it fastens upon the ground before her, provides the complementary gesture to Adam's backward look. She represents that side of a divided humanity which looks to the future: not back and up, but forward and down. Condemned to the earth, she must construct from its bowels a new world.

A similar scene occurs a quarter of a century later in American literature in the concluding chapters of *Moby-Dick*. There Ahab, soon to consummate his destiny with the white whale, pursues his rage against ambiguity in a scene in which heaven and earth are related through the image of a quadrant:

> "Cursed be all the things that cast man's eyes aloft to that heaven, whose live vividness but scorches him, as these old eyes are even now scorched with thy light, O sun! Level by nature to this earth's horizon are the glances of man's eyes; not shot from the crown of his head, as if God had meant him to gaze on his firmament. Curse thee, thou quadrant!" dashing it to the deck, "no longer will I guide my earthly way by thee; the level ship's compass, and the level dead-reckoning, by log and by line; *these* shall conduct me, and show me my place on the sea. Aye," lighting from the boat to the deck, "thus I trample on thee, thou paltry thing that feebly pointest on high; thus I split and destroy thee!"[20]

Man assumes in the language of Ahab the dual posture that Cole presents. Torn between the vertical glance aloft to heaven that sears his vision and the horizontal view that, lacking the guidance of heaven, nonetheless confirms man in the "level dead-reckoning" of his fate, Ahab affirms finitude over superhuman (heaven-reckoning) attempts to navigate.[21]

With a vehemence paralleling Cole's in *Expulsion from the Garden of Eden*, Melville pursued through Ahab the earthbound destiny implicit in Eve's stance. Like Milton, he knew the futility behind all gestures of "dead-reckoning." But unlike Milton, whose authorial voice remains above the narrated events of his poem, Melville's delinquent and often absent narrator Ishmael possesses no greater omniscience than his humanity allows him. Unaided by the grace that propels Milton's all-seeing Muse, Ishmael plays the role not of knower but observer, privy to no knowledge deeper than that which passes before the horizon of his experience. Thus Melville's authorial voice, though separate from Ahab, exists at eye-level with him. If it is his task to break the veil that masks the meaning of the novel's events, it is also his fate to have no tools greater than the human eye or ear. Ishmael survives the destruction of the *Pequod* an "orphan": "And I only am escaped alone to tell thee." He, too, like the creatures of Cole's painting, is an exile in eternal pilgrimage. Where Milton could bound man's Fall by the scope of God's design, Melville and Cole remember Paradise only as a lost image, and substitute the finality of dead-reckoning for the promise of redemption. With Stubb they might have cried, "And damn me, Ahab, but thou actest right; live in the game, and die it!"

Ahab's rejection of the sun's power finds its visual parallel in Cole's division of his canvas into two separate but interrelated spaces. For both Melville and Cole the distinction between sky and earth (or Paradise and postlapsarian world) establishes a larger distinction between two different representational modes: an *imagistic* sense of space associated in Cole with the temporal stasis of Eden, and a *narrative* mode of discourse linked with the act of expulsion and the introduction of time (Ahab's horizontal vision). Ahab's rejection of the sun may be read as a denial of what Richard Brodhead has called "epiphanic moments" in the writings of Hawthorne and Melville, moments when the forward-moving momentum of the story is suspended in a sudden shift from "temporal to an atemporal vision."[22] In denying the sun as a legitimate source of human knowledge, Melville is challenging his own tendency to textual interruption, his willingness to suspend the conventions of narrative for an alternative style more centered around symbols than stories and hence less dependent upon *time* for the elaboration of meaning. As Brodhead notes, Hawthorne and Melville

> are fundamentally unwilling to delegate to any one style of vision or organization the exclusive right to represent their world. As a result they generate in their works a conflict of fictions, and the reality of their imagined world, rather than lying in any one of these fictions, comes into existence in their interaction.[23]

In Cole too the lyric qualities of Eden are associated with static and nontemporal modes of epiphany. Narrative exists in the *Expulsion* as the derivative, the residue, of a prior epiphantic mode which gives it birth. Cole's painting not only contrasts the two modes in their entangling and wounding interdependence, but predicates the emergence of narrative forms upon the collapse of past epiphantic possibilities.

The story of the Fall thus presents an account of narrative as a debased and secondary form of cognition. Narrative re-presents or translates Eden's timeless light into tales and myths, forms of accounting that mediate and temporalize the truth they would convey. As Adam and Eve's dual posture suggests, the postlapsarian world suffers from a burden of self-explication that requires of its figures a capacity to unite past and future into a single tale. Adam's backward glance is Cole's way of reminding the viewer that all narrative harbors within itself a lingering memory of its own lyric and epiphantic origins. But as Eve's posture suggests, the story of the Fall may also be understood as a rejection of those antinomian modes of cognition which, like the light of Eden, posit a "pure" truth apparently free from mediation and the demands of narrative form. Cole's affirmation of narrative as the solace of a postlapsarian world is at the same time a denial of all forms of truth-telling that hide or repress their own rhetorical structure through imagery of an all-absorbing sunlight and immediate illumination. The *Expulsion* is not only a tale of the artist's fall into narrative but of the essentially narrativistic qualities of all modes of language in a world where pure truth—light unadulterated by any propagating medium—is itself only a myth, another narrative in an endless progression of *Ur*-myths about the origins of all myths.

Hope, then, as an invention of human making, proceeds from the "level dead-reckoning" that binds man's vision to the horizon. It is the side opposite to Adam's Janus-face, spellbound by the very light that blinds him. In Eden light was a property of the air. Diffuse and anonymous, it dispelled shadows, like time, into ethereal nonexistence. Its source was the sun, an orb barely visible through the haze of Cole's Garden yet present like a lingering afterthought of a divine destiny presiding over all. In the fallen world in which Adam and Eve now find themselves, the remnants of Eden's glow are augmented by a new source of light, earthbound like the vision of Eve. The background volcano, fiery and demonic, represents Cole's visual expression of the furious energy of Ahab. In its seething rage lie both the hope and despair of exiled man. Byron had written fifteen years earlier that poetry "is the lava of the imagination whose eruption prevents an earthquake."[24] His imagery appears to be a more explosive version of Wordsworth's famous formulation of poetry as "the spontaneous overflow of powerful feelings." Both sets of imagery share a common sense of artistic endeavor as a process of mediation whereby internal or affective forces receive linguistic shape and form.

In the *Expulsion from the Garden of Eden*, the artist's transformation of the materials of the wounded self into the stuff of life and dreams is imaged in the erupting background volcano. Here light springs not from divine but from earthly sources. The demonic, which Milton knew to be part of him, clear sign of his need of grace, now becomes the hope and home of postlapsarian nineteenth-century man. Illumination for him comes from within. The fires of his own agony must be transmuted into vision. "So shall ye die perhaps by putting off / Human, to put on Gods" (9.713–14), Satan had warned Eve. His voice becomes the challenge of Cole's age. Adam and Eve must delve into their own volcanic selves in order to hold the candle of their vision to heaven's illumination. No voice guides them, like Milton's Eve, away from the inner images they encounter. Where Jonathan Edwards had once perceived in the myth of Narcissus nothing but "death, a land of darkness, or darkness itself," Cole's wandering pilgrims must "descend" into the self in order to rise again bearing images of light.

They represent a demonization of Milton's antithetical imagination. The forces of otherness—those "intellectual and anti-natural" energies required by Milton—are rewritten by Cole in a nineteenth-century idiom that renames the world as the self. Milton's moral other becomes in Cole's hands an externalization of the ego's own inner voices. The poetics of renunciation are subordinated to a narcissistic sublime in which the other is only a demonized version of the self, a mode of antithetical vision that the Puritan poet would have perceived as false and illusory. For Cole, however, there can be no other mode, for there are no other voices. That is what the Expulsion means: a substitution of inner for outer law, an attention to the wounded language of consciousness, a gift and burden of self-consciousness, a narrative about the origin of narratives. It is all the modern world allows.

IV

The economy of Cole's volcanic imagery is remarkable. It recapitulates within itself the forces within the painting as a whole, while pressing them, condensed and concentrated, to their utmost logic and conclusion. It is, in the first place, an image of the state and condition of Cole's lonely protagonists, isolated, brooding and seething in inner turmoil; it conveys through its own lyric irrationality the gothic character of man's existence and his visions. At the same time it represents a response to their fallen condition: it is an image of the self's capacity to draw upon its inner energies as a means of illuminating the dark. Its light, as opposed to that of Eden, is a product of time and translation, having voyaged the earth's depths in the process of birth. Like the gates of Eden, it too is a threshold image. It marks the boundaries between two spheres of being, external and internal worlds, while suggesting in its own figure neither realm so much as the translation between them. It competes with the light from Eden's arched gate. Situated in the background of the painting, though in the foreground of its meaning, the volcano is present as an alternative to Adam's more nostalgic glance toward Eden, suggesting in its arching trail of smoke and ash a black creation very different from the original. Like the renouncing, repressing "Hence" that begins both *L'Allegro* and *Il Penseroso*, it suggests in its relation to Eden that vision is always an antithetical act, and that epic vision—Cole's New World sublime—commences only when the pastoral pleasures of the Old are left behind.

The juxtaposition of luciferous volcano with the luminosity of Eden is Cole's way of validating his own romantic and imaginative rebellion. The volcano is a signature not only for the mind of Adam and Eve but for the artist himself, and, as such, is profoundly anti-Christian in implication if not intent.[25] The volcano is Cole's artistic answer to God: it represents an inversion of the divine light that illumines Eden and proclaims a new covenant between man and world, replacing an older covenant of hope set before Noah and sealed in the image of the rainbow. The energies unleashed by the volcanic fire are not only profane when compared with the sanctity of Paradise, but derive their authority from laws intrinsic to themselves rather than a morality externally imposed. The mind of man, however demonized in the *Expulsion*, has become the sole arbitrator and legislator of its world. Though Adam and Eve may appear small on the canvas, it is their point of view that defines the painting's perspective. The viewer does not approach the work, as one might expect on first encounter, from the slightly elevated and aloof perspective of an "omniscient" observer, but from a position that places the viewer distinctly to the left of Eden's gates, uncomfortably close to the struggle of predatory creatures in the foreground. Our point of view is that of the postlapsarian world, and we gaze out across the vast abyss that separates us from the promise of Eden. Cole's use of perspective—of the audience's point of view—is both subtle and significant, for it establishes the reality of the postlapsarian world as our point of departure while rendering Paradise accessible only as a visionary project, available to the mind rather than the senses. One can never actually return to Eden or reestablish its protective embrace, but one can create imaginatively a myth of Eden by which to measure and explain one's current state.

Despite the charm and serenity of Cole's Eden, there is a noteworthy ambivalence characterizing the garden world. The fullness of light that stops time and dissolves mystery also renders *history* a mode of *heresy*, for it demands that there be no change to alter Eden's permanence. Paradise lacks those qualities that, according to the postlapsarian viewpoint, render the individual most fully human: the shared bonds of suffering, the passage of time, the possibility of change, and, above all, the capacity to express the self from a vision originating deep within the inner person and authenticated now not by external injunctions but by inner knowledge. Cole's Eden, like Milton's *L'Allegro* groves, is a stultifying place, threatening by the very perfection of its pastoral dalliance to deny the moral and imaginative growth necessary to genuine vision. Cole's Romantic rebellion, then, is, at its most profound level, an act of repudiation, a refusal to abide by the laws of Paradise, and his return in oils to the scene of humanity's original sin is his means of rendering all history, or at least *Ur*-history, an act of rebellion and renunciation. What the myth of the Fall provides Cole is an archetypal account of artistic creation that commences in an act of denial and release. Though experienced initially as an "expulsion" and defeat, it holds forth the possibility of new modes of vision, new sources of illumination, that promise ultimately new forms of redemption. Cole's achievement in the *Expulsion from the Garden of Eden* is to have created a myth of Romantic selfhood that validates the individual's act of assertion by a process of reversal: Cole's *repudiation* of the constraints of Eden is transformed into a tale of expulsion and defeat, masking through its imagery of loss the force of its own refusal.

Milton had always been chary of his powers in *Paradise Lost*. He feared the fine, darkly scrutable line that separated his creation from that of God. His verse soaring beyond the bounds of human vision ("that I may see and tell / Of things invisible to mortal sight," 3.54–55) bore too great a resemblance to Satan's own upward spiraling flights of fancy to allow him easy rest. Milton would most likely have regarded the light of the erupting volcano as an *ignis fatuus*:

> a Flame,
> Which oft, they say, some evil Spirit attends,
> Hovering and blazing with delusive Light . . . .
> [9.637–39]

Such light

> Misleads th' amaz'd Night-wanderer from his way
> To Bogs and Mires, and oft through Pond or Pool,
> There swallow'd up and lost, from succor far.
> [9.640–42]

Could he have replied, it is possible that Cole would have acknowledged the danger of the self-consuming imaginative autonomy that Milton's poetry simultaneously invokes and proscribes. Adam's wistful and rebellious glance Eden-ward suggests the regret (and passion) with which he quitted the Garden. The volcano image opposite Eden, however, is both too seductive and too terrifying to admit return. Milton's proud pastoral renunciation before the otherness of God is no longer possible for a world begotten entirely of itself and sustained solely by its own light.

A final word on Eden. We may understand its significance at two different levels. The first, as discussed above, is the larger and more general import it carries as the scene of the *felix culpa*, the "fortunate fall" that dooms man to the agony of a narcissistic sublime. At a more specific level, however, we might wonder if Cole's Eden doesn't represent a condensation—and potential misreading—of eighteenth-century models of vision, simplified in order the better to be rejected. The Enlightenment's language of clarity and light, its distaste for mystery and ambiguity, its faith in the rationality and intelligibility of its world, and, above all, its failure to comprehend evil and the discontinuities of history, all link it ideologically to the world summarized in Cole's Paradise. One suspects that Cole's rebellion is not simply an abstract struggle against nonhistoric modes of thought or pastoralizing forms of vision, but a profound and revealing encounter between an older and idealizing worldview and a new and radically different one. In *Expulsion from the Garden of Eden*, Cole joins battle with his own (reductive) reading of the eighteenth century, substituting for its continuous, homogeneous, and rational perspective an alternative reality characterized by darkness, loss, and discontinuity. Cole's world knows the ravages of time and the burdens of knowledge and self-consciousness, and it parts company in the *Expulsion* from the classical order and affirmation of an Enlightenment world that birthed it, but that, according to Cole, denied it the darker senses of self—the demands of renunciation and discontinuity—necessary to human growth.

Cole's painting provides an instructive contrast with Charles Willson Peale's *The Artist in His Museum* (1822; fig. 32), painted five years prior to the *Expulsion*. Peale's rationalized space mythologizes Enlightenment values in order to create a coherent and inviting vision of the past that the artist believes is applicable to the present as well.[26] Cole on the other hand creates a myth of the past that serves not only to reject that past by rendering it inaccessible, but to offer an alternative account of the present radically different from the language and aspirations of the older world. Where Peale's interior space with its grid-like perspective creates a present in visual continuity with the past, Cole renders a *breach of continuity* the subject of his work, and requires that break as the source of his freedom. If Cole lacks the faith and studied confidence of Peale's world, he substitutes for them a degree of passion and imagination that Peale's age, with its vision of temperance and moderation, could never have understood. Cole's *Expulsion*, with its womb-like overtones, is at the same time the birth of a new era.

No wonder then the Romantic's nostalgia for a lost and rejected Eden. With Eden fled his innocence, his state of unknowing, which kept him unself-conscious. With knowledge came selfhood, came schism between God and man, came a sublime and demonic narcissism, came time that brings change and death, came self-consciousness and the curse of the self divided and at war within itself. Man seemed to wear two faces when confronting the world, masks that could look simultaneously forward and backward, upward and downward, inward and outward, directions as diverse as the world that now sustained him. This was not necessarily new. The Renaissance had long before understood the individual to be suspended between two spheres of being, a mutable creature whose chameleon-like nature was a source of strength and possibility. But no longer did the halves cohere. The problem was not the self's dual nature.

32. CHARLES WILLSON PEALE, *The Artist in His Museum,* 1822. Courtesy of the Pennsylvania Academy of the Fine Arts, Philadelphia.

Emerson rejoiced in the "bipolar unity"—the play of opposites resolving into unity and then dissolving again into opposition (man and nature, self and other, material and spiritual, freedom and fate)—that constituted the endless dialectic of human existence. It was the incongruity of the two faces that became a source of both agony and possibility for the Romantic thinker. The Platonic myth of male and female as complementary parts of a single being disintegrated in Cole into the division between Eden and the rest of creation. The individual was tethered to a sublime aesthetic predicated on an act of repression while still tied to visions of an irrecoverable world, pastoral and ideal. Where but within the human mind itself was that new threshold which, unlike Eden's granite gates, would permit the self-vanquished wanderer new spaces?

4 Irving, Quidor, and the Catastrophe of Imaginative Vision

> . . .with impious hands
> Rifl'd the bowels of thir mother Earth
> For Treasures better hid.
>
> JOHN MILTON, *Paradise Lost*

> He had begun an investigation, as he imagined, with
> the severe and equal integrity of a judge, desirous
> only of truth . . . . But, as he proceeded, a terrible fas-
> cination, a kind of fierce, though still calm, necessity
> seized the old man within its gripe, and never set him
> free again, until he had done all its bidding. He now
> dug into the poor clergyman's heart, like a miner
> searching for gold; or, rather, like a sexton delving
> into a grave, possibly in quest of a jewel that had been
> buried on the dead man's bosom, but likely to find
> nothing save mortality and corruption. Alas for his
> own soul, if these were what he sought!
>
> NATHANIEL HAWTHORNE, *The Scarlet Letter*

*T*he burden of the psychological self central to both Milton and Cole appears largely absent in the writings of Washington Irving. Where they assume the isolated individual poised, like Eve, upon the shores of self-knowledge, Irving steps outside the "family romance" altogether and substitutes for their narcissistic sublime the rhetoric of folk culture. His artistry is no less self-conscious than theirs: his tales are about their own fictional origins. His quarrel, however, concerns the bourgeois culture they assume. He seeks in his fiction to lend a voice to a world defined not by the individuality or interiority of its figures, but their collective, if unconscious, resistance to the rationalization and commercialization of their world. Irving uses the myth of natural man available in the folk traditions of Dutch New York in order to represent the differences between industrial and preindustrial societies. His figures resemble those "storytellers" described by Walter Benjamin, narrators who arise to assuage the boredom of their own existence, but Irving adds one essential twist to Benjamin's world: he ironizes it.[1]

Storytelling, if Benjamin is to be believed, is an art intrinsically at odds with a culture organized around writing and the dissemination of "information." The storyteller represents an "artisan" form of communication. His stories arise from the rhythms of a preindustrial order: a world with the time to listen, a language that is communal and founded on shared perceptions of reality, a respect for wisdom born of the accrued experience of generations, and a sense of life as still organized around the cycles of nature. With the passing of an artisan order, folk and oral traditions are replaced by the patterns of a written culture. The novel arises to take the place of the tale, and with it the language of the "solitary individual" substitutes for the "wisdom" of the folk. A print culture "teaches us," Benjamin writes, "that the art of storytelling is coming to an end. Less and less frequently do we encounter people with the ability to tell a tale properly. . . . It is as if something that seemed inalienable to us, the securest among our possessions, were taken from us: the ability to exchange experiences."[2]

Benjamin's argument helps explain the resistance we encounter in folk tales to the interiorization of experience so crucial to modern prose fiction. The storyteller resists "psychological analysis" because his tales, like his characters, are not private. They contain within themselves the distilled experience of generations, expressing by the delicately layered frames through which they are told the "communicability" of their worlds. Unlike gothic fiction, which builds upon the separation of public and private voices and presumes the duplicity of its language, the tale-teller requires that the experience of his audience coincide with his own. He believes himself, like the practitioners of what Schiller called "naïve poetry," to be in harmony with nature. His stories are possible because of the "weaving and spinning," the sleeping and boredom, that make listeners—and tellers—of us all.

Irving's stories are different. They arise not from the boredom of his characters but from the interruption of that boredom by forces perceived as intrusive and foreign. The unity his characters experience with nature is not so much "naïve" as a *fiction*, a deliberate denial or repression of the darker encroachment of contemporary culture upon their once pastoral domain. Their boredom and comic repose are only foils by which they simultaneously mask and measure the breakdown of their world. Irving's stories are not born, as Benjamin suggests of true storytelling, from the urge to communicate "something useful" or practical, but instead eschew the effort to give "counsel" in order to record, again and again, their own genesis as tales. They are about fiction-making as a restorative process, for Irving's world, however much it resembles that of Benjamin's tale-teller, postdates Benjamin's artisan culture. It arises from the collapse of the storyteller's world, and proffers in its place a theory of tale-telling in which narrative provides a mode of social discourse counter to the values of the ascending middle class. If his characters seem resolutely comic and undomesticated, perpetual children outside the reaches of a bourgeois work ethic, then they incarnate in their fidelity to natural rhythms the ethos of a prerationalized society unwilling to accommodate itself to the demands of commodity capitalism. Their stories are a means of resisting the encroachments of commercial society: a defeat of Yankee culture by gossip, fiction-making, and the inexhaustible resources of the imagination.

This is Irving's ironization of Benjamin's folk culture. His naïve characters and comic visions are not timeless exemplars of folk forms, but ideologically fraught creations poised as a counter-text to the rhetoric of the liberal tradition. However much his characters may participate in the forms of an oral culture, they possess attributes that distinguish them from traditional folk materials and render them distinctively *modern*: they are almost always marginal figures relative to the culture surrounding them, they are isolated from the recognized channels of productive activity within their societies, they rely on wit and imagination to maintain themselves within their worlds, and they draw attention, through their tales, to the process of fiction-making itself.

They *commodify* themselves in other words, for the irony of Irving's art is that the oral tradition (or the values it represents) survives into the modern world, not solely by a power intrinsic to its stories, but by its ability to render its own precarious history an economic resource within the emerging mores of a written culture. The pot of gold awaiting Irving's characters at the close of so many of his tales, the "golden dreams" that materialize as if by magic, wholly unearned, at the end of his stories, are narrative transcriptions of the new-found value an oral culture possesses when commodified by bourgeois society. The folk traditions of Dutch New York are transformed into a rhetoric of nostalgia, where they enter the cultural mainstream as socially benign and economically profitable artifacts. What began as cultural criticism concludes as a new source of wealth within the complex network of commodity relations governing early capitalism. Or as Irving so marvelously describes the incongruous fate of his comic protagonist Wolfert Webber at the end of *Tales of a Traveller*:

Wolfert Webber was one of those worthy Dutch burghers of the Manhattoes whose fortunes have been made, in a manner, in spite of themselves . . . . His golden dream was accomplished; he did indeed find an
unlooked-for source of wealth; for, when his paternal lands were dis-
tributed into building lots, and rented out to safe tenants, instead of
producing a paltry crop of cabbages, they returned him an abundant
crop of rent . . . a golden produce of the soil . . . . And to commemorate
the origin of his greatness, he had for his crest a full-blown cabbage
painted on the pannels [*sic*] [of his coach], with the pithy motto ALLES
KOPF, that is to say, ALL HEAD: meaning thereby that he had risen by
sheer head-work.³

The unexpected and unaccounted transformation of rural habits into
urban wealth provides in narrative fashion an allegory for Irving's own
art. The world of the tale-teller, when written and reproduced (subject to
the "head-work" of the imagination), provides middle-class culture with a
romanticized myth of its own origins. What has historically been lost or
repressed in the ascendance of Protestant New England society is imaginatively resuscitated in the sentimentalized version of Irving's tales. His
stories internalize within their narrative the irony of their own com-
modification, and they defend themselves against complete assimilation
into the culture surrounding them by the only tools they possess: irony,
laughter, and the child-like glee with which they invert, and thereby
subvert, the demands of the adult work-a-day world.

I

Wolfert Webber led a life somewhat out of the ordinary for cabbage
potentates. The scion of a long line of praiseworthy "Dutch burghers"
whose visages, had they been assembled together, "would have presented
a row of heads marvellously resembling in shape and magnitude the
vegetables over which they reigned,"⁴ presided over a field of cabbages
that were the pride of the "ancient city of Manhattoes" and a source of
family cheer and prosperity for the Webbers. Time, however, marching
to his unheard music and pausing only the length it took him to convert
"rural lanes" into "the bustle and populousness of streets," soon brought
the burgeoning city to the door of the rustic Webbers. Wolfert, the last of
his line, awoke one morning to find himself a "rural potentate in the
midst of a metropolis."

As Geoffrey Crayon relates the story in *Tales of a Traveller*, the
pseudonymously penned volume of Washington Irving, Wolfert's urban
status left the once prosperous burgher strapped for funds; Wolfert was
caught in the vise between rising expenses, a fixed income, and a mar-

riageable daughter. His first remedy, to expel the prospective son-in-law from the family hearth, proved of little value, and the baffled Wolfert cogitated deeply over his troubles. While nursing his cares at a hospitable country inn one afternoon, Wolfert imbibed—along with his brandy—tales of hidden treasures said to dot the Long Island coast, the remnants of buccaneers who once plied the Sound. Wolfert was never the same. Dreams of wealth infected his brain. What were cabbages compared to pots of gold and fabulous sums of money lying just beneath the surface of the earth? Wolfert took to clandestine nightly raids upon his cabbage plot, digging there for the treasure he "knew" to be awaiting him, but with the trials of a severe winter and a neglected harvest, he found instead the pains of want gnawing through his "golden dreams." Friends disappeared with the first scents of poverty in the air, and Wolfert's reveries about pirates' plunder came to be tinged with a fear of the almshouse. One day, stumbling out of his meditations and into the old tavern, Wolfert encountered the mysterious figure of a personage both he and his companions took to be a genuine buccaneer. Wolfert's imagination, never slothful when deliberating an *idée fixe*, kindled into life again.

At the same time, however, the narrator of Wolfert's tale and fictional editor of the book, Geoffrey Crayon, interrupts Wolfert's narrative with a saga told by Wolfert's drinking companion and local historian, Peechy Prauw, about another "Manhattoes" character, the Black Fisherman Sam. This interspersing of separate but interrelated tales affects the reader in a manner similar to its impact on Wolfert himself: it tends to confuse levels of reality, weaving "fact" with fiction in a mixture too delicate to unravel back into its constituent parts. Wolfert subsequently acts upon the tale that Peechy Prauw tells—a comic-grotesque account of Sam's untoward and uninvited discovery of pirates burying their cache—by seeking out Sam so as to retrace the location of the supposed treasure and restore it to the light of day. In so doing, Wolfert completes Sam's otherwise unfinished story by incorporating it into his own; Peechy Prauw's ostensible fiction assumes the authority of real history for Wolfert, proceeds toward a new resolution within the narrative present of Wolfert's story, and comes finally to a close as part of a larger tale told by John Josse Vandermoere to "the late Diedrich Knickerbocker" in the early nineteenth century near Hell Gate, New York, scene of the recent action at all levels of the story.[5] Knickerbocker's papers have passed into the hands of Geoffrey Crayon, who is himself born from the hands of Washington Irving.

That Wolfert should plunge into fiction as if it were history, thereby transforming his own history into the arena of further fictions, brings to the narrative level of Irving's story themes implicit throughout the "Money Diggers" section of *Tales of a Traveller*. Wolfert is besieged by tales of booty buried beneath the paths of unsuspecting wayfarers, and his imagination, crowded with images of supernatural figures and mysterious forces, soon blurs the distinction between fact and fancy that his stolid neighbors and fearful family maintain. This same distinction is blurred for the reader by the ever-retreating presence of the "real" author of the stories of *Tales of a Traveller* behind a series of pseudonymous mantles, each worn as a shield between author and reader like the enveloping red and black cloaks donned by Wolfert and his conspiratorial partner, Dr. Knipperhausen, in their ill-fated pursuit of gold. Like Hawthorne's recollections of his experience at Brook Farm, "essentially a day-dream, and yet a fact," Irving's world inhabits that limbo region of romance between the factual and the "marvelous" where persons and spirits mingle familiarly if not always comfortably. For Hawthorne such territory was the unique province of the artist, whose fiction, though sinning "unpardonably so far as it may swerve aside from the truth of the human heart," was clearly distinguished from the "probable and ordinary course of man's experience."[6] Unlike Hawthorne, however, who was never in danger of confusing his fictions with fact, Irving starts, not with the segregation of poet from world, but with their inevitable conflation. He poses a question like that asked by his English contemporary John Keats at the close of "Ode to a Nightingale." "Was it a vision, or a waking dream?" Keats cries, unable to disentangle the various layers of fiction wrought into the gilded bower of his eternal bird. Wolfert's world at once echoes Keats's question and then proceeds to offer its own unique answer: history is the unending concatenation of tales that man's mind, procreating with a power exceeding his loins, spills forth into the world in endless variety and fashion.

What is most real in Irving's world is the flotsam and jetsam of experience washed up on the shore of daily adventure. "A long pistol of very curious and outlandish fashion, which, from its rusted condition, and its stock being worm-eaten and covered with barnacles, appeared to have lain a long time under water," serves as the vehicle for the "speculation" that leads to the tales of "The Money Diggers." Fished up by one of Diedrich Knickerbocker's picnic-fishing party, it invites attempts at imaginative reconstruction, which are the only forms of accounting that Irving's world knows:

> There is nothing in this world so hard to get at as the truth, and there is nothing in this world but truth that I care for. I sought among all my favorite sources of authentic information, the oldest inhabitants, and

particularly the old Dutch wives of the province; but though I flatter myself that I am better versed than most men in the curious history of my native province, yet for a long time my inquiries were unattended with any substantial result.[7]

Truth comes, as it inevitably must in a world attended by curiosity and the mind's insatiable desire to know, in the "substantial result" of the tale-teller. Among the washed-up pistols and dimly perceived shadows of this world he weaves his tale of accounting, much as an oyster transforms a random grain of sand ingested unawares into a pearl of its own creation. As the oyster coats the intruding presence with secretions, transforming an unwonted fact into a thing of beauty, so the teller of tales spins round the debris of history—its barnacled pistols and unaccounted facts—tales of imagination whose luster and polish are all the mind possesses by way of knowledge.[8] For Keats the true historian is the poet; it is he who humanizes the sublime and terrible beauty of the visionary past into "sylvan" histories and "leaf-fring'd" legends. His stories—true history—preserve through their own sensuality a poetic tradition perceived, like the distant nightingale, as alien and inaccessible in its timeless beauty.[9] The poet's consolation in the face of a tradition too severe to be easily accommodated to everyday desire is the ambivalent tribute that he frames to man's myth-making capacity: "'Beauty is truth, truth beauty,'—that is all / Ye know on earth, and all ye need to know." Beauty is a form wrought from a deeper inability to know. It is an acknowledgment of limits: a refusal of an inhuman and impossible transcendence. Its creation, like the oyster's pearl, is the central fact of its world. It is the poet's single and self-begotten truth; he has no other.

Where Keats humanizes the sublime, as Stuart Ende suggests, through the language of paradox and oxymoron, Irving converts the otherness of history into a fabric of fictions indistinguishable from more "objective" truths. Wolfert's world embraces stories and histories alike. As Geoffrey Crayon writes in the preface to *Tales of a Traveller*:

> I am an old traveller; I have read somewhat, heard and seen more, and dreamt more than all . . . so that when I attempt to draw forth a fact, I cannot determine whether I have read, heard, or dreamt it; and I am always at a loss to know how much to believe of my own stories.[10]

The pseudonymous Mr. Crayon's complicity in the confusion of fact with fiction betrays Irving's attempt, like Keats's in his odes, to redefine the nature of poetic activity. All individuals are fiction-makers in Irving's world, for all individuals are travelers, reading somewhat, hearing and seeing more, and dreaming more than all. Their truths, like their histories, are the products of man's mythy mind in active commerce with the world.

Washington Irving thus is not simply the clever and urbane tale-teller he would seem. His task is more serious than his lighthearted language might suggest. One perceives in a waking dream in Irving's stories because the greatest dream of all, that the world is objectively ordered, no longer exists. No organizing center serves to focus Irving's world. Instead, Irving is content to abide in a carnival of fictionality. Man knows only what he produces, for he is like a Midas of the mind: whatever he touches turns to the stuff of fiction. It is both his curse and his richness.

II

The landlord of Wolfert's rural tavern delivers "a kind of farewell speech" upon the disappearance and presumed death of the mysterious buccaneer:

> "He came," said he, "in a storm, and he went in a storm: he came in the night, and he went in the night; he came nobody knows whence, and he has gone nobody knows where."[11]

By reducing the human condition to an epistemological quagmire, Irving effectively defeats the claims of eighteenth-century philosophy to a world accessible to human intelligence and subject to the authority of the rational mind. Like Charles Brockden Brown before him, he defines in his fiction the limits of the observable and commonsensical world, displaying the vulnerability of empirical thought before the pressures of the imagination and the individual's insatiable desire to know. Brown's novels form an extensive critique of an empirical method unaware of its own limits—a method purporting instead to explain phenomena beyond the range of its own specialized vocabulary. The problem is linguistic: the categories of eighteenth-century empirical science are inadequate to the forces of change they must interpret. For both writers the language of fiction provides an alternative discourse to the failures of an older way of seeing. The emergence of the gothic novel enables Brown through the first-person voice of his narrators to record the machinations of consciousness at a level prior to observable behavior. At the same time Brown establishes a fictional structure that anticipates the later efforts of writers like Hawthorne and James to penetrate the mystery of human behavior through the organizing vision of a character to the periphery of the novel's central action. In a work as early as *Wieland* (1798) Brown frames the tale of his psychopathic protagonist within the epistolary record of his sister Clara, whose baffled recollection of her brother's history subtly transforms the novel from a gothic tale of horror and suspense into a piece of psychological detective work distinguished by the focus it places on the tale-teller herself.

Irving follows in Brown's steps, consolidating the shift from tale to teller by creating a fiction intent upon the process of fiction-making itself. His stories, as John Lynen has suggestively noted, "present fables of fable-making, myths of how myths come into being."[12] They seek to illuminate the world from the point of view of the spectator and dreamer, and direct the attention of the work from the story's center to its circumference, where the reader hears the machinery of consciousness clattering in the wings and substitutes its hum for the buzz of an objectively given world. Irving's greatness was to have discovered that modern man stands at the margins of his own achievements, a baffled and engrossed spectator in a drama he neither controls nor understands. Enlightenment history has been defamiliarized by Irving into a late-night ambush upon the slumbering senses of natural man, a cunning plot devised by eighteenth-cenetury advocates of universal progress to beguile Irving's sleepy protagonists from their ignorance. Unlike Brown, whose quarrel with the Enlightenment turned on its failure to name and thereby know the deeper regions of the inner self, Irving eschews the psychological concerns of the gothic novelist for a critique of eighteenth-century ideology turning on the uses of history. He challenges the notion of historical progress—an idea born of the liberal imagination and the capacity to rationalize experience through the discovery of universal regulatory principles—with a counter-mythology of history as alienating change: inscrutable in nature, tragic in its effects, and disruptive of the bonds between man and nature. "For what is history, in fact," Knickerbocker writes in his *History of New York*, "but a kind of Newgate calendar, a register of the crimes and miseries that man has inflicted on his fellow man?"

> It is a huge libel on human nature, to which we industriously add page after page, volume after volume, as if we were building a monument to the honor, rather than the infamy of our species. If we turn over the pages of these chronicles that man has written of himself, what are the characters dignified by the appellation of great, and held up to the admiration of posterity? Tyrants, robbers, conquerors, renowned only for the magnitude of their misdeeds, and the stupendous wrongs and miseries they have inflicted on mankind . . . . What are the great events that constitute a glorious era? The fall of empires; the desolation of

happy countries; splendid cities tumbled in the dust; the shrieks and groans of whole nations ascending unto heaven![13]

Irving's history is an antihistory: a burlesque parody of an eighteenth-century vision of human self-mastery that transfers to man powers previously reserved for the will of God. He effects in his fiction an end run around a historical center more chimeric than real, accessible to the observer, like the Kantian *Ding an sich*, only as it is assimilated within the precincts of individual perception. Irving's characters willingly render unto Locke the commonsensical world that is Locke's, and abandon in the process a historical consciousness foreign to their epistemologically sealed universe. They substitute in the place of historical achievement their comic thralldom to a world irreducibly textual, where history survives only through the imprint it leaves upon the fecund minds of anonymous narrators, redeemed of its otherness and the "huge libel" it casts upon "human nature" by the capacity of a child's mind to convert facts into fictions, "page after page, volume after volume" of historical catastrophe interspersed with imaginative redress.

The defeat of history, as a swerve around the aspirations of eighteenth-century man, provokes in Irving a profound but deeply disguised sense of guilt. Wolfert exists through most of the story at the edge of society, and his transition from complacent "patroon" to nighttime adventurer chronicles in its pattern the shift from respectability to marginality at the heart of Irving's fiction. Like Rip Van Winkle, Wolfert is divorced from the historical world around him, and he shares with Rip the guilt and castigation that Irving directs toward his naïfs and dreamers. It is their fate to live in the shadow of greatness, estranged versions of a world once larger and more prominent than they. Like the narrator of Hawthorne's "Custom-House" essay, an "idler" borne upon the "topmost bough" of an old "family tree" of "stern and black-browed Puritans," Rip descends from "the Van Winkles who figured so gallantly in the chivalrous days of Peter Stuyvesant . . . . He inherited, however, but little of the martial character of his ancestors."[14] Even the late Diedrich Knickerbocker, "an old gentleman of New York" and chronicler of Irving's most significant tales, represents in his capacity as historian a diversion from the "true" course and interests of society:

> Now that he is dead and gone, it cannot do much harm to his memory to say that his time might have been much better employed in weightier labors . . . . Yet his errors and follies are remembered "more in sorrow than in anger," and it begins to be suspected, that he never intended to injure or offend.[15]

Irving's comic apologia for his characters, like Hawthorne's mock-heroic account of his Salem customs officer, reveals through its quiet posturing traces of a deeper crime. His characters are all speculators and parricides, bound by an oedipal impulse so profound as to seem invisible: each in his own fashion does away with the authority and regulations governing him. The defeat of respectability by magic, superstition, and child's play—the triumph in Irving of natural man over historical man, and in Hawthorne of the idler and visionary over his disapproving Puritan ancestors—represents the author's form of self-accounting, a means of describing narratively the strategy of subversion by which author and audience alike abandon the high ground of history for the surrogate joys of the imagination. The guilt they experience is that of the child who refuses to relinquish his imaginative games for the adult business of making one's way in the world. In a curious twist to a Wordsworthian adage, the child not only spawns the father but spurns him, defeating his castles of stone with figures of air. In Irving's world it is the marginal characters, the children, pirates, and tale-tellers, figures at the peripheries of society, who are exempt from its laws and capable by virtue of their privileged irresponsibility of activities that the mainstream knows nothing of. The fictional onus shifts to them, for they are the true speculators and dreamers, as imaginatively alive as they are financially unstable. The brilliance of Irving's writing lies in its willingness to advance these characters, precisely because of their dreamlike existence, to the center of the stage, trusting to their unerring instincts, their innocence and selfishness, a magical response to the demands of history.

Irving expresses guilt at the parricidal enterprise he has authored by conflating the life of the mind with the habits of the venture capitalist. He exposes each to the hazards and rewards of the speculative life, for "dreaming" and "speculating" in his stories are activities of both the imagination and the pocketbook:

> It was a time for paper credit. The country had been deluged with government bills, the famous Land Bank had been established; there had been a rage for *speculating*; the people had run mad with schemes for new settlements; for building cities in the wilderness; land-jobbers went about with maps of grants, and townships, and Eldorados, lying nobody knew where, but which everybody was ready to purchase. In a word, the great *speculating fever* which breaks out every now and then in the country, had raged to an alarming degree, and everybody was *dreaming* of making *sudden fortunes from nothing*. As usual the *fever* had subsided; the *dream* had gone off, and the *imaginary* fortunes with it; the patients were left in doleful plight, and the whole country resounded with the consequent cry of "hard times."[16]

The defeat of history is founded upon a world of "paper credit," an "imaginary" realm where "fortunes," like "dreams," are made "from nothing," and the "great speculating fever" infects the populace as if a madness or disease. Irving's quiet pun on *speculation* links the habits of the dreamer with the more questionable practices of the "land-jobber" and the real estate broker. Both trade on the willingness of the individual to skirt the boundaries of good business sense, substituting faith and a willingness to believe for the more prudent procedures of the market-place. Irving's language attempts to liberate the individual from the ponderous and respectable machinery of bourgeois life. The speculator builds on "paper," a world entirely textual in its values. He incurs the opprobrium and mistrust of his neighbors by the unconventional nature of his wealth, for where others require bullion for their riches, he builds on "nothing," or at least nothing that their world can recognize as substantial and value-worthy. His imaginative adventures, creations *ex nihilo*, provoke from them a response similar to that of Hawthorne's worldly Puritan ancestors:

> "What is he?" murmurs one gray shadow of my forefathers to the other. "A writer of story-books! What kind of a business in life,—what mode of glorifying God, or being serviceable to mankind in his day and generation,—may that be? Why, the degenerate fellow might as well have been a fiddler!"

And as Hawthorne wryly notes:

> No aim, that I have ever cherished, would they recognize as laudable; no success of mine—if my life, beyond its domestic scope, had ever been brightened by success—would they deem otherwise than worthless, if not positively disgraceful.[17]

The guilt that Hawthorne feels in the face of his literary activities, a guilt premised on the elevation of consciousness to a realm above that of historical achievement, is shared by Irving in his own post-Kantian effort to clear a fictional space at the peripheries of history. Confining his world to the limits of the perceiving mind, Irving unlocks the child within each adult, creating a literary landscape where vision is deflated comically into an act of belief, and facts, like fictions, dissolve into a single dense porridge that is the mind's world. His concerns are those of the dreamer and speculator, who must inevitably in a world of facts fall upon "hard times," but his achievement, and his greatness, is the creation of a fiction of historical estrangement where the myth is less important than its maker and the tales of the fabulist are stories of self-accounting. A generation before Emerson, Thoreau, and the writers of the American Renaissance, Irving fashions a literature pregnant with the shapes of their writing: a concern for the imagination as the bearer of meaning in society (Shelley would later proclaim the poet to be the "unacknowledged legislator of the world"), a desire to account not only for the limitations but the power of imaginative vision, and a recognition that the artist provides society with a counter vision, an alternative voice, to its own standards. These are bold things for an American author to say at the beginning of the nineteenth century, and we must not allow the humor and gentleness of the telling to obscure the radicalness of the vision or the implacable manner with which Irving carries his insights to their logical ends.

III

Irving's Midas touch of the mind was pursued visually—and to rather different ends—by John Quidor (1801–81), a New York painter who often used Irving's stories as the source for his art. Better known to his contemporaries as a creator of signs and fire engine panels,[18] Quidor returned to Irving's tales, especially "The Money Diggers," throughout his life. Though the two men are not known actually to have met,[19] they share a common concern for tale-telling as a primordial human activity. Like Irving, Quidor understood the capacity of the mind to annex the world around it for its own purposes, together with its apparent inability to distinguish what Emerson would soon call the "Me" from the "Not Me." This magical mental transformation of reality into fiction appears as a recurrent concern in Quidor. In the painter's hands, however, fiction-making inevitably concludes in a process of solipsism and self-consciousness. However much his paintings may owe in spirit and composition to the works of Hogarth and Dutch genre painters of the seventeenth century, his focus on the inner self renders his work a burlesque endpoint within a tradition concerned with the demonic possibilities of the imagination dating back to Milton. Unlike Irving, Quidor seems not only skeptical but profoundly alarmed by the prospects of a world shaped entirely to the dimensions of the imagination. He reads his Irving through the filters of a Protestant sensibility obsessed with its inner impulses, and resituates Irving's proto-Borgesian love of fabulation within a context of potential gothic horror. Quidor appears instinctively to have understood the problem of narcissism Milton had posed when he placed Eve on the bank of a lake and left her to her own self-revery. What Quidor lacks is Milton's inner assurance of an antithetical Muse—a voice beyond the pleasures of selfhood and pastoral dalliance—to beckon Eve away from her own "watr'y image." For this nineteenth-century painter and panel-maker, no figure of renunciation exists to guide his characters away from their own narcissistic follies. They are fated instead to that inner plunge—that encounter with an internal daemon—that transpires in Quidor's world as a comic parody of the narcissistic sublime. Beneath the surface humor and bustle of his canvases, we observe in reduced and deflated form the residues of an older visionary tradition.

Quidor painted in 1832 a canvas entitled *The Money Diggers* (fig. 33). Drawing upon the concluding episode of "Wolfert Webber, or Golden Dreams," the picture shows Wolfert and his companion-in-crime Dr. Knipperhausen frozen into postures of fright in response to the "grim visage of the drowned buccaneer" which looms over the ledge facing them. The Black Fisherman Sam hurriedly scrambles from the dark pit he has dug. The night scene is illuminated by the smoky glow of Dr. Knipperhausen's herb-fed fire as it casts a circle of light around the edge of the digging; Wolfert's lantern, dropped in the confusion of the pirate's appearance, together with the light of the white rising moon, augment the smoldering fire that, according to Irving, diffused "a potent odor, savoring marvelously of brimstone and asafoetida." The drama of the composition is enhanced by the sense of claustrophobia and dark mystery which overhangs the painting. Wolfert and his crew are squeezed between the shadowy cliffs behind them and the deep, black, and seemingly bottomless pit before them. The ledge harboring the drowned buccaneer to the painting's right is riddled with dark recesses and gaping cracks, as if it were itself a haunted object of nature, not unlike the sagging house of Usher, which bore on its visage the marks of the mental state of its occupants, until house and inhabitants alike sank forever into a dark tarn. Behind Wolfert and Dr. Knipperhausen spreads a nature as gnarled and grotesque as their worst dreams might provide. Wolfert's startled figure is outlined by the responding contours of a wizened tree whose arm-like limbs seem to grasp his hat and to mirror in their own shape his frightened form. Knipperhausen is visually framed by tree and cliff on either side, and an overhanging dark object, perhaps a fallen tree, enclosing the space above his head. Nowhere is there room to flee (unless of course into further darkness). The cropped effect of the painting, pushing the action to the canvas's margins, heightens the sense of claustrophobia. The leering figure of the buccaneer, like the grasping form of the dead tree behind Wolfert, is as real as any of the three central protagonists of the painting. For the characters in *The Money Diggers*, the world is as real as one believes it to be. No criteria exist within the borders of the painting by which to distinguish fiction from fact. One judges not by the light of reason; no such illumination exists in this nightscape world. Instead there burns only a small smoky fire, fed on herbs and superstition for the purpose, not of expelling the darkness, but of abetting and appeasing its magical powers. In such light man judges.

33. JOHN QUIDOR, *The Money Diggers*, 1832. Brooklyn Museum. Gift of Mr. and Mrs. Alastair Bradley Martin.

In an author's footnote to the story, presumably that of Diedrich Knickerbocker, and in its own way as integral to the tale as its series of narrators, Irving comments on the "divining rod" used by Dr. Knipperhausen to locate the exact spot of the treasure:

> There has been much written against the divining rod by those light minds who are ever ready to scoff at the mysteries of nature; but I fully join with Dr. Knipperhausen *in giving it my faith*.... I make not a doubt that the divining rod is one of those secrets of natural magic, the mystery of which is to be explained by the sympathies existing between physical things operated upon by the planets, and rendered efficacious *by the strong faith of the individual*.[20]

Irving's footnote is peppered with allusions to past explanations of the divining rod's efficacy (including one pseudo-scholarly note in Latin), each in its own way a reminder to the reader of the continual forms of accounting by which man accommodates himself to his world. In the gloss on divining rods, Irving underscores the importance of belief. One need only bring to the rod a faith adequate to its function before results will necessarily follow. The believing is all. Quidor paints Knipperhausen's treasured divining rod standing as if by its own powers at the base of the pit between the knee-locked doctor and the fleeing Sam. Like the other mysterious phenomena of the painting, the instrument is part of the web of belief that knits together Quidor's frightened company. Together they form a tableau inverting the Enlightenment vision of man: creatures of the dark, bound together by their kinship with the irrational mysteries into which they delve, they perceive no further than their imaginations will carry them. Reality is the sum of their beliefs; no "Archimedean point" outside the canvas offers them a vantage from which to view their follies.

Note the black pit framing the emerging figure of Fisherman Sam. The largest single plane of color (or its absence) in *The Money Diggers* is the rounded form of the dark hole that Sam has dug. It dominates the lower foreground of the painting far in excess of the narrative requirements of Irving's story and transforms Quidor's work from a study paralleling Irving's text in the elision of fact with fiction into a more gothic exploration, however burlesque, of subterranean and unknown forces. Like Hemingway's reference to the "abiding earth" as the single triumphant figure of his novels, the black pit in *The Money Diggers*—more than any of the four depicted characters—may be said to be the true subject of the picture.[21] It is the painting's visual statement of its deepest energies. Irving associates the dark hole with black magic and supernatural forces. Quidor pursues this suggestion by placing Dr. Knipperhausen's volume of magical incantations between the incense-burning fire and the pit, as if the book provided a link and direct correlation between the two. As the volume slides into the dark hole, Sam, himself a figure of darkness, emerges. Sam and the book seem inversely balanced; he appears to flee what the book has released at the same time that he himself becomes an image of those darker energies.

Quidor here reverses Irving's comic faith in fiction-making by framing it within a larger context of psychic horror and self-examination. Wolfert seeks in the pit his own dreams, "Golden Dreams" as the story's subtitle reminds us. The dark pit represents, however, not only mystery and unfulfilled visions—a parody of Jacksonian aspirations—but an over-invested image of the mind of man. It embodies the deeper, darker impulses that animate each of the figures in the painting, uniting Quidor's characters with the preternatural forest in which they search. Quidor's money diggers press their irrational world for its deeper secrets, expecting to find riches and gold. What they release instead are the unsanctioned forces of their own minds, imaged in the figure of Sam caught between subterranean depths and surface visibility. Fisherman Sam becomes Quidor's Everyman, as Wolfert was Irving's. Poised between two worlds, one dark, hidden, and unknown, the other, though still dark, at least visible and present for the mind's curious dealings, he images the individual caught and frightened by an act of self-discovery. Linked by his black skin with the pit from which he rises, Sam is both the hidden, irrational self beneath the surface of the conscious man and the everyday self surprised by its inner depths.

He is also the visual counterpart to the drowned buccaneer. We come closer to understanding the claustrophobia of the painting when we define Sam and the mysterious pirate in their spatial relation to the two middleground figures, Wolfert and Dr. Knipperhausen. Quidor's painting, as Christopher Wilson has demonstrated, is related to (whether or not it derives from) Joseph Wright of Derby's *The Earthstopper on the Banks of the Derwent* (1773; fig. 34).[22] *The Money Diggers* inherits from Wright's work not only the terror and possibilities of a nightscape world, but a tripartite compositional arrangement, recurrent in Enlightenment and early Romantic art, that tends to place its protagonists in a middleground landscape sandwiched at either end by naturalized versions of nether and ethereal forces. In compositionally related works as diverse as John Singleton Copley's *Watson and the Shark* (1778; fig. 35) and Charles Willson Peale's *Exhumation of the Mastodon* (1806; fig. 36), a centerground community of individuals is united in a common endeavor that pits their mutual energies against the forces of nature, concentrated in the lower foreground of the painting. In each work a smaller subgroup of the middleground community is present in the foreground. The energy of each canvas, both visually and thematically, moves vertically: the effort of the community is to rescue or redeem forces associated with the foreground space. Watson's deliverance from the sharky sea provides Copley with an allegory of social assimilation. Watson's naked figure shares the foreground plane with the shark: his glazed eyes and open mouth echo the form of the shark and suggest, despite the struggle that divides them, their deeper participation in a realm both creaturely and natural. The shark literalizes Watson's presocial animality. Watson's upward-reaching right arm is suspended equidistantly between the shark to the viewer's right and the inverted triangle of human forms that reaches down to him from the left. Watson is suspended between two realms, natural and social, and his salvation, translated here into an act of acculturation, depends upon the capacity of the larger middleground community to assimilate the isolated individual into its own socially constructed space.

34. JOSEPH WRIGHT OF DERBY, *The Earthstopper on the Banks of the Derwent,* 1773. Collection of the Derby Art Gallery.

The fragility of the enterprise is emphasized by the tension between the heroic and triangulated forms of the centerground figures (they form an isosceles triangle at the center of the painting) and their precarious and off-centered position relative to the boat that supports them; they are threatened not only by the sea, but by their own asymmetric positioning within the craft. Their heroism is constituted through their ability to differentiate themselves from the world of naturalized forces below. Copley's figures represent the power and grandeur of bourgeois civilization-making as an enterprise of both social transformation and instinctual repression (notice the force of the harpoon posed above the shark).

The upper plane of city and sky in Copley's painting provides the foreground action with an abstracted and idealized image of itself. Copley uses the details of Havana harbor to suggest a utopian community:

35. JOHN SINGLETON COPLEY, *Watson and the Shark,* 1778. Courtesy, Museum of Fine Arts, Boston. Gift of George von Lengerke Meyer.

stable, landed, and reaching through its combination of cross-like masts and spires into an etherealized space above. He differs in this regard from Charles Willson Peale, whose skies in the *Exhumation* threaten to erupt with lightning and storm. Peale's figures seek to penetrate the silence of the natural world; their drama lies in their effort to draw knowledge out of a nature not only recalcitrant but at moments ominous and threatening, as the surge of thunder clouds and peal of lightning suggests. Natural history substitutes in the New World for the lack of human history. The power of Peale's painting turns on the ability of his figures to subdue nature through persistence and ingenuity. Though the forces that comprise Peale's world are more benign than those confronting Copley's figures, the threat of the approaching thunderstorm in Peale's canvas (two horses flee in terror in the upper right background)

36. CHARLES WILLSON PEALE, *Exhumation of the Mastodon,* 1806. The Peale Museum, Baltimore.

suggests a retributive power to nature parallel to the savagery of Copley's shark. Peale's figures render nature a commodity of their own world; they fell trees and divert water in order to create an elaborate social machine responsive ultimately to man's own scientific designs. The cycles of nature are subordinated to a crude but efficient process of rationalization defined not only through the division of labor characterizing Peale's efforts but by the social power, based on specialized knowledge, represented by Peale himself. Peale grasps with his left hand a schematized outline of mastodon bones; nature is reducible, as the drawing suggests, to fixed formulas. Peale's outline reminds the viewer, like those two-dimensional maps filling the walls of Vermeer's canvases, of the process of translation—half mystical, half mechanical—by which the artist maps reality into a series of imaginative constructions. Knowledge in Peale's world is power, tantamount, as his *Autobiography* suggests, to a "second creation."

Although the putting these Skeletons together was a long and ardious [*sic*] work, yet the novelty of the subject, the producing the form and, as it would seem a *second creation*, was delightful, and every day's work brought its pleasure.[23]

Quidor's money diggers similarly undergo a "second creation"; unlike Peale's figures, however, they call forth a world that parodies their own powers. Quidor's canvas shares with Copley's and Peale's a tripartite division of space: a foreground plane of dark and recessed forces; a middleground community in intimate commerce with the foreground world; and a background plane above the other two framing and presiding over the action below (note in Quidor the tableau of buccaneer and moon in the upper right corner of the canvas). In *Watson and the Shark* the energy of the painting revolves around the drama of social reclamation in the foreground and middleground planes of the canvas; in *Exhumation of the Mastodon* the central figures—small and mechanical relative to the space they occupy—participate in a larger drama of nature violated (foreground) and vengeful (background). In each canvas the efforts of the centerground community are threatened by events in another plane. In *The Money Diggers* the threat of disaster comes from both planes simultaneously. Knipperhausen fixes his mask-like stare upon the rising figure of Sam at his feet, while Wolfert looks back to the highlighted form of the drowned buccaneer. Wolfert's extended left arm is mirrored in the raised arm of the buccaneer and repeated in the frontally thrust hand of Dr. Knipperhausen. The conjunction of Knipperhausen with Sam and Wolfert with the buccaneer creates a pair of diagonal axes running through opposite corners of the canvas and intersecting at the center of the painting in the startled figure of the frightened doctor.

Like Cole's tragic protagonists in the *Expulsion from the Garden of Eden*, Quidor's centerground figures divide their attention between a world above and behind them and a shadowy realm below and before them. They seem squeezed not only by the margins of the canvas, but by forces internal to it: a foreground plane that allows them no space to stand, and an upper background world that threatens them with retribution. Wolfert and Dr. Knipperhausen are prey not only to the punishing function of the upper plane, but to the subterranean energies of the foreground digging. They encounter in their nightscape foray for riches only doublings and repetitions of themselves (the buccaneer is painted not as a spirit, but as an equal of the solidly modeled money diggers). They are victims, in other words, of the collapse of their own middleground imaginations. In digging for treasure, they are releasing rather than repressing those instinctual forces subversive of the social self. They have uncovered a primitive pleasure principle without sublimating it or deferring it, as

Freud would require, to the mechanisms of the reality principle; and they have precipitated a vengeful and idealized version of themselves (they perceive themselves, after all, as pirates manqué). If, as the tripartite division of Quidor's canvas suggests, the money diggers are also civilization builders, figures whose centerground placement requires their accommodation to, or acculturation of, forces surrounding them, then the culture they create is a narcissistic and subversive one. Their world not only refuses the socialization essential to nineteenth-century liberal ideology, but offers in its stead an alternative vision of the self that is private, gothic, and inherently unsocializable.

This failure of transcendence helps explain the castration imagery rampant throughout the world of *The Money Diggers*. The canvas is defined everywhere by void spaces—pits, caves, hollows—associated with the money diggers' act of discovery. Like the male child who, according to Freud, interprets female sexuality as confirmation of the reality of castration, Quidor's centerground figures recoil in horror at the *locus vacuus* of the pit. Their phallic vulnerability is stressed by their own sexual exposure. A noose dangles from Wolfert's waist, while hanging from the noose—in a marvelous visual metonymy—is a free-swinging fragment of rope. A long chain of keys decorates the crotch region of Dr. Knipperhausen, whose inturned knees, outstretched arms, and gasping mouth suggest beyond his terror the posture of a figure fearful for his more tender parts. The act of discovery—of visionary conjuration—is linked by Quidor, as it is by Poe, to annihilation and loss of power. The catastrophe of vision in Quidor's world concerns the recognition, implicit in *The Money Diggers*, that art both originates and culminates in a loss of ego power, a claustrophobia of the middleground plane that leaves the self with no space to stand. The retributive superego-like function of the drowned buccaneer menaces Wolfert and Knipperhausen as cruelly ("cruel" is Freud's special term for the superego) as the contorted form of Fisherman Sam emerging from the pit below. The release of instinctual forces does not provide Quidor, as it does Copley, with a commerce of psychic realms that defines, when properly assimilated, the heroism of bourgeois existence. On the contrary, Quidor's intercourse of foreground and middleground planes is a dark and magical act, no sooner consummated than responsible for the intervention and punishment of the superego. Quidor's characters, like Freud's personification of the ego, are beset from below and above (reality for them, contrary to Freud's vision of the reality principle, is only an extension of themselves). Nor should the correspondence between Quidor's tripartite canvas and Freud's psychical map of the personality seem surprising, for Freud's division of the territory of the mind into id, ego, and superego may be interpreted as a complex internalization and revision of an older Enlightenment project. "Where id was, there shall ego be. It is a work of culture—not unlike the draining of the Zuider Zee."[24]

In *The Money Diggers* transgression into the midnight region of the mind stands as a *fait accompli*, and the comedy of the painting stems in part from the failure of its characters to understand the implications of their actions. The closest approach to a comprehending vision within the painting appears, if at all, in the figure of the frog who views undaunted from his stage-front seat the drama unfolding before him. Quidor's curious observer figure here resembles Milton's Satan, who, in the guise of a toad, whispers into the ear of the slumbering Eve illusions, "Phantasms and Dreams": "Vain hopes, vain aims, inordinate desires / Blown up with high conceits ingend'ring pride" (4.808–9).[25] Like a burlesque modern Eve, Wolfert is similarly afflicted with "Vain hopes, vain aims," and "inordinate desires." Where Eve can distinguish dream from reality upon awakening (though not without difficulty, for dream is soon to pass into actuality),[26] Wolfert possesses no reference point by which to determine fiction from fact. For him the nocturnal world blurs such distinctions; he is the victim of an unbounded "Fancy," precisely what Milton had feared and Irving affirmed.

Eve tastes the "interdicted" fruit in her dreams, and later narrates the experience to Adam:

> Forthwith up to the Clouds
> With him I flew, and underneath beheld
> The Earth outstretcht immense, a prospect wide
> And various: wond'ring at my flight and change
> To this high exaltation; suddenly
> My Guide was gone, and I, methought, sunk down,
> And fell asleep; but O how glad I wak'd
> To find this but a dream!
>
> [5.86–93]

The dream-like consummation of Eve's temptation is the experience of flight. Eve is lifted above her human condition to see, as from that Archimedean point Kierkegaard would later despair of, the "earth outstretcht immense."[27] The bubble of fancy bursts, however, and Eve returns, having been buoyed by illusion, to the proper boundaries of human vision. She awakes to day. In *The Money Diggers* the story ends differently (as indeed it will for Adam and Eve later). Here the toad triumphs. Perched upon his throne-like rock, he observes the fruition of his labors. Quidor's foreground creature—traditionally associated with witchcraft—seems to embody the brutish and irrational forces of nature that govern man, beasts, and hole. Milton had feared the unbounded Fancy. Quidor shared that fear, now become an actuality, not because it created monsters of its own making, which it did, but because it exceeded the boundaries given to human knowledge. Quidor's figures reverse the demand for transcendent vision by situating themselves within interdicted inner territory. Whereas prelapsarian Eve could soar and then return to earth forewarned, Wolfert must stand the victim of his own unwitting transgression. He has joined forces with the black arts and released from the bowels of the earth terrors best left to night and the frogs. Eve transgressed the bounds of human knowledge by ascending to unwarranted heights, but Quidor's figures, bound in their own fictions, can only plunge. Their sin is to dig and probe where spade and lantern are not welcome. They unearth neither Irving's "golden dreams" nor God's paradise, but, like Milton's Satan, the Hell within.

Aesthetically, then, we are dealing with more than castration anxieties and the formation of the superego. Whatever private significance the psychic components of Quidor's art may hold for him, they represent visually a sense of art as sinning irremediably against its own deepest possibilities. *The Money Diggers* defines artistic vision as a mode of trespass in which the self fails to extend itself beyond its own labyrinthine projections. Unlike Cole's figures, whose inner resources—imaged in the background volcano's explosive illumination—promise to redeem the lost sublime of Eden with their own counter-sublime, Quidor's burlesque heroes remain the victims of their own follies. They precipitate through their quest romance a world whose voided center leaves them with no governing authority—no Muse of renunciation—to untangle their narcissism, and they experience as the price of their vision their comic displacement as characters within their own text. Quidor's art is implicitly conservative: it condemns its characters for the folly of their vision and understands its own energies as violations of a tradition it can no longer sustain. It is a deconstructive mode of art, premised not on the possibility of authentic vision but on its absence. It refuses transcendence as anything but a lingering comic implosion of the inner man. Quidor's void spaces thus become the emblems of an art dialectically defined as the *negation* of prior visionary tradition. Or, in Irving's terms, the treasure the money diggers find is not the treasure they originally sought. The riches of Quidor's subterranean world, as surprising as Wolfert's unexpected wealth at the conclusion of his tale, are instead the products of parody and a revisionary impulse so profound as to draw laughter and renewed vision from an art otherwise consumed by its own energies. Like the death to which Eve is "devote," Quidor's void spaces announce both the end of an old order and the burlesque creation of a new.

37. JOHN QUIDOR, *Antony Van Corlear Brought into the Presence of Peter Stuyvesant*, 1839.
Munson-Williams-Proctor Institute, Utica, New York.

IV

Several years later in *Antony Van Corlear Brought into the Presence of Peter Stuyvesant* (1839; fig. 37), a painting inspired by *Diedrich Knickerbocker's History of New York*, Quidor addresses the social and cultural implications of an art organized around the narcissistic sublime. The failure of the imagination to grow beyond its originating and selfish impulses—to transform self-concern into self-denial—leads to more than a Romantic aggrandizement of inner territory. It opens a Pandora's box of interior energies and unleashes into the commerce of everyday society those forces repressed or denied by the surrounding culture. Quidor's characters pose a threat to the society that produces them. They either disrupt the socially constructed spaces designed to house them or they unravel in their comic quests the conventions and social fictions of their culture.

They are unmaskers, in other words, and they unwittingly expose the artifice and display of those around them. By releasing forces inimical to the public good, energies unassimilable into the larger culture, they reveal behind that culture the deeper strains and wounds that its own rhetoric denies. Their sin therefore is twofold: their very entanglement in their own follies is at the same time an exposure of society's myths and a demythologization of culture. Quidor's characters are not only nature's fools: they are its truth tellers.

Antony Van Corlear Brought into the Presence of Peter Stuyvesant introduces the viewer to one of Irving's more flamboyant characters, "Antony the trumpeter," "matchless champion" of New Amsterdam. Van Corlear has been summoned to the chambers of the peg-legged, irascible Peter Stuyvesant, whose recent assumption of power has put an end to the "unreasonable habit of thinking and speaking for themselves" afflicting his privy council:

> The honest folk of New Amsterdam began to quake now for the fate of their matchless champion, Antony the trumpeter, who had acquired prodigious favor in the eyes of the women by means of his whiskers and his trumpet. Him did Peter the Headstrong cause to be brought into his presence, and eying [*sic*] him for a moment from head to foot, with a countenance that would have appalled anything else than a sounder of brass,—"Pr'ythee, who and what art thou?" said he. "Sire," replied the other, in no wise dismayed, "for my name, it is Antony Van Corlear; for my parentage, I am the son of my mother; for my profession, I am champion and garrison of this great city of New Amsterdam." . . . "How didst thou acquire this paramount honor and dignity?" "Marry, sir," replied the other, "like many a great man before me, simply by sounding my own trumpet." . . . Whereupon the good Antony put his instrument to his lips, and sounded a charge with such a tremendous outset, such a delectable quaver, and such a triumphant cadence, that it was enough to make one's heart leap out of one's mouth only to be within a mile of it.[28]

The martial response of Stuyvesant to Van Corlear's penetrating blast is translated by Quidor into a burlesque sexual comedy. Dangling between Stuyvesant's feet is a phallic saber gilded in precious ornament, a priceless treasure of his manhood. Stuyvesant's wooden leg stands out erect, while his right hand clasps firmly a vertically held cane. In the left-hand corner of the painting a black man wholly extraneous to Irving's text dances wildly to the trumpet blast. This gesticulating character, framed by two of Stuyvesant's three erect members, suggests in his motions libidinal release, while the old man to the right of Stuyvesant seems to recall memories of past exploits stirred up by Van Corlear's blast. His closed eyes, cupped hands, and extended musket echo Stuyvesant's own barely suppressed sexual pleasure. Van Corlear himself is an image of sexual parody. A dark brush stroke marking a crease in his pants suggests a little-boy-like penis, diagonally pointed and almost crushed beneath the weight of Van Corlear's enormous bay window. His belt, resting comfortably above his stomach, does little to contain the expansion of his belly, which literally bursts his breeches. Dangling from the belt, behind his stubby arm, lies the tip of a powder horn, another device of explosive potential. The good Antony's trumpet, however, is his crowning grace. Swathed in ribbons of blue and red received from the women of New Amsterdam, Van Corlear's trumpet, like its counterpart sabers, muskets, and long pipes, is an image of sexual potency. It is civilization's surrogate for the undisciplined energy of the dancing black man, whose status as a figure prior to socialization is emphasized through the image of the baying dog under the window opposite him (a pairing of man and animal reminiscent of Copley's linkage of Watson with the shark). That the dog should respond as the humans to Van Corlear's clarion call links the whole company of *Antony Van Corlear* by comic reduction. Each is a bundle of nervous sexual energies, a stew of life-forces that demands expression whether within or without the constraints of society.

The problem is that the constraints are bursting. Antony's breeches are only the most obvious form of the situation. Quidor's picture abounds with images of constraint and release (fig. 38). Resting against the doorpost of the background entrance with one foot propped up against the opposite sill is a sour-faced personage whose posture and shoulder-propped musket suggest that he is guarding the room. He seems visually to be restraining the background figures of the painting by placing himself as a barrier between them and the foreground action. These figures, who in fact are Dutch burghers, appear pictorially to be dwarf- or gnome-like presences barred from the center-stage action. Their gesticulating hands and limbs, together with the frightening visage floating above the sentry's knee, suggest a deeper potential for chaos and disorder within the picture's background. Framed in the first instance by the doorpost of Stuyvesant's chamber, and again by the restraining image of the stationed guard, the background creatures are themselves contained by the woodwork lattice of the balcony on which they perch. Such visual binding, however, seems to be of no avail. The confusion of strewn objects and diagonal lines that clutters the foreground action, and the inability of the grid-like floor plan to resolve the disarray of bodies and things, confirm the potential chaos of the background figures who are everywhere present in the tone and clamor of Quidor's painting. The world of *Antony Van Corlear*, like its protagonist, is in the process of

38. JOHN QUIDOR, detail of fig. 37, *Antony Van Corlear Brought into the Presence of Peter Stuyvesant* (figures in the doorway).

bursting its breeches in a vast torrent of sexual and social energies about to overwhelm the painting's surface order.

Linked to the explosion of energy informing the picture's foreground is imagery of death, expressed in *Antony Van Corlear* in the painting-within-a-painting (fig. 39). Though blurred and indistinct, two images emerge from the picture on the wall behind Antony. The first is of a crowd surrounding a gallows on a turbulent afternoon, and the other is of

39. JOHN QUIDOR, detail of fig. 37, *Antony Van Corlear Brought into the Presence of Peter Stuyvesant* (painting on the wall).

rowers across a body of water that borders the gallows. Together these images form a *memento mori* within the painting, the gallows providing an emblem of human mortality and the flowing waters a convention for the passage of time. Quidor's quiet allusion to death on the back wall of Peter the Headstrong's chamber transforms the painting in a manner similar to the presence of the black pit in *The Money Diggers*. The framed painting serves as an objective correlative for the energies of the gyrating black man and the surging crowd of threatening figures in the background; implicit in the chaos and libidinal energy they express is the presence of death and destruction. Sexuality and the death instinct, those two great impulses thought by Freud to determine the individual's unconscious life, each spilling over into the self-aware ego only in masked and disguised form, appear in *Antony Van Corlear* as the submerged but essential nature of human existence. Quidor records the fragility of the conscious ego poised above volcanic forces it neither comprehends nor seems capable of containing. Antony Van Corlear's trumpet blast releases energies endemic to each figure in the painting while understood by none. As Irving stresses in his text, Van Corlear is "*sounding my own trumpet.*" He is in burlesque fashion modern (nineteenth-century) man: self-inflated and self-concerned. Van Corlear places the powers of the private person above the restraining conventions of society, and in the process transforms the imagination from an agent of visionary intent into the handmaiden of individual ambition (what is Van Corlear in his balloon-like figure if not a comic reduction of those volcanic forces exploding across Cole's canvases).

The danger Van Corlear runs of bursting his breeches, while metaphorically absurd, is metaphysically significant. As King Oedipus discovered through loss of his sight, one can know too much. One can sound the keyboard of the self only so often before strange resonances and undertones usually heard only in an afterthought begin to make themselves known. The imagination, when narcissistically deployed, opens a Pandora's box, and all the elements of the unprobed self take wing. Note the two flailing whips in the right-hand corner of Stuyvesant's room. Like the muskets and pipes that sublimate and rewrite the individual's darker energies into socially assimilable forms, Stuyvesant's whips are the instruments by which humanity's deeper forces are contained. They are means of repression, reminders of a social discourse predicated upon the suppression of private desire. Their effectiveness can be tested by measuring them against the chaotic energies they oppose, the clamoring crowd at the back door. According to Freud, all repression simply transforms in disguised fashion the manifestation of abiding forces—what is suppressed in one form reemerges in different guise elsewhere. So too with the gnome-like creatures in the background. Though bound literally by the sentry at the door, and figuratively by the whips and images of restraint within the room, they seem destined nonetheless to disrupt the forces of constraint within the painting. The window, after all, is wide open.

There exists what might be termed a second, though less obvious, painting-within-a-painting in *Antony Van Corlear*. The grouping of figures between the doorposts and lintel appears to possess a pictorial unity similar to the picture hanging at its side. This mini-picture announces itself through the figures of the musketed guard and the background imps as a summarization of the tension between containing and contained forces in the painting as a whole. The door serves as a threshold between two contiguous worlds, one blustering, humorous, and conscious, the other darker, more obscure, and potentially frightening. Guarding the threshold as orthodoxly as any Freudianly conceived ego could hope is a censor-like figure whose explicit visual purpose appears to be the policing of the border between inner and outer realms. Referring to the tension between unconscious impulses and their expression in consciousness during sleep, Freud notes that the territory between the conscious and unconscious is policed by a "watchman [that] . . . relaxes its activities during the night," thereby allowing "the suppressed impulses in the unconscious system to find expression." Freud structures his argument through imagery of fortresses and battles, and notes at one point that the "security of the citadel . . . must be guarded." He concludes his discussion of the relation of psychic censor to the conscious and unconscious mind with a description of what occurs in instances of pathology: "the watchman is overpowered, the unconscious excitations overwhelm the preconscious system, and thence obtain control over our speech and actions."[29]

Antony Van Corlear may be described as a world of incipient social pathology, where "the unconscious excitations overwhelm the preconscious system." Unlike *The Money Diggers*, where unsocialized energies liberate the pleasure principle in violation of the individual's mechanisms of deferral, *Antony Van Corlear* focuses more upon the process of sublimation itself (smoking, sword-rattling, trumpet-blowing). What is in question is not the presocial psychic economy of *The Money Diggers*, but the subsequent activities of substitution and self-expression. At a historical level, the painting identifies the sublimating self with the forces of Jacksonian society. It represents a critique of the rhetoric of individualism characteristic of mid-nineteenth-century culture. Van Corlear embodies an ethic of self-aggrandizement that works paradoxically both to define and to undermine the community espousing it. We see in Quidor's canvas a confrontation between two orders organized along oedipal lines: an older world in the figure of Peter Stuyvesant understood as oppressive to the private self and buttressed by the established forces of society (muskets, sabers, guards, and prison-like spaces), and a newer order summarized in Van Corlear, whose Armaggedon-like trumpet blast seems to crumble the walls of Jericho around him.[30] Van Corlear's trumpetry is an act of self-assertion, a caricature of early Romantic individualism. The painting dissolves the distinctions between sexual and social disarray—narcissistic pleasure and economic self-interest—into a single image of wholesale political upheaval. Stuyvesant's desire to protect his power from the masses outside—his fear of the "leveling" tendencies represented by Van Corlear—recapitulates in its tensions the struggle between father and son, traditional values and a rising market economy, that subsequent historians as diverse as Marvin Meyers, Michael Kammen, and Michael Rogin have all noted in their characterizations of the period.[31] In *Antony Van Corlear* we witness older forms of social privilege and family order give way before the new forces of the common man, vaunting his own virtue as his best ticket to success.

Antony Van Corlear is not only a social text, it is a deconstructive one. It legitimates itself by exposing through its theme of repression the tension between text and subtext essential to its own making. The painting focuses in its play between Stuyvesant and Van Corlear on the struggle between self-explication and self-censorship by which texts, like societies, both reveal and conceal their latent energies. It thus thematizes through its story that larger struggle between revelation and repression which governs the operation of all semiotic systems, be they political or artistic. Van Corlear's trumpet leads directly from his lips to the gallows on the wall in the painting-within-a painting, a reminder (1) that texts harbor within themselves alternative texts, (2) that these alternative texts function antithetically to the main text (in Van Corlear's case, through the threat of reprisal the gallows picture presents to the painting's main action), and (3) that such threats are themselves only other stories, alternative instances of a narrative framed and mediated by the tales surrounding it. Quidor's gallows sermon also reminds the viewer of the illicit nature of the libidinal impulses animating the visionary self. Van Corlear's trumpet blast precipitates that moment of self-accounting when any mode of discourse, be it literary or political, must acknowledge the possibility of its own unmaking. From this point of view, Antony Van Corlear functions like the return of Freud's repressed, sounding a note of dissension from within the corridors of consciousness. He articulates through his capacity to disrupt the painting the collusion of text with subtext in the subversion of its own authority. Hence the peculiar uncomfortableness Quidor's characters seem to experience in the face of their own visionary and deconstructive energies. Unlike Irving's comic protagonists, who disappear into the anonymity of their own tales, each figure absorbed into the language of the next, Quidor's heroes (such as they are) carry with them a peculiarly *conservative* resistance to the act of fiction-making that constitutes them. Their presence is an affront to the social and visionary order that gives them birth, and they seem only too ready to validate their own subversive activity through the violation they bring to the world around them.

To understand the complexity of Quidor's vision, we might compare it briefly with William Sidney Mount's early image of artistic self-accounting in *The Painter's Triumph* (1838; fig. 40). Mount's artist in his studio stands next to an admiring, obviously ingenuous spectator whose juxtaposition with a padded chair suggests that he might be the subject of the portrait being viewed. Both figures gaze delightedly upon a canvas that the viewer himself cannot see. In a sweeping diagonal gesture, the artist points down with his right hand to the canvas and back with his left hand (palette and brushes in tow) to the image of a classical figure on the studio wall (the

40. WILLIAM SIDNEY MOUNT, *The Painter's Triumph*, 1838. Courtesy of the Pennsylvania Academy of the Fine Arts, Philadelphia.

only visible painting-within-a-painting). This double gesture suggests that the "triumph" of the artist is to mediate between past and future, drawing on the models of the past to temper the present in order to produce a vision of an idealized future. The artist for Mount becomes a synthesizer and cultural collaborator rather than critic or counter-voice. He accommodates classical conventions (background) to contemporary circumstances (centerground) while forging for his audience a vision of their collective aspirations (foreground). His task is the consolidation of mainstream values through an ideology of cultural self-projection.

In Quidor precisely the opposite occurs. The artist presides over the dismantling of mainstream ideology; his is the voice of cultural conflict and textual transgression. His characters invert the assumptions of the culture that surrounds them by providing a mirror version—a reverse image—of that culture. Quidor was an intellectual heir of Wordsworth's prodigious journey into the mind of man, that voyage which is a strange surrogate in a secularized world for the Christian's pilgrimage through life. Like Cole and many other American Romantics descended from a Miltonic tradition, he feared what the journey would bring. Quidor defines the failure of visionary energies as a trespassing of forbidden inner territory. Hence the *violation* that accompanies all vision. As the gallows imagery reminds us, Quidor's characters plunge themselves and the world around them to an untimely end. Their dalliance arrests the self in its movement to vision and transforms their quest-romance into self-surrender.

For all its serious undertones, however, Quidor's painting concludes not in tragedy but in comedy. Close examination of the picture on the wall reveals that the figure hanging from the gallows is not dangling by the neck but suspended from the waist.[32] The image is an allusion to the reign of William the Testy, Stuyvesant's predecessor who, according to Irving's comic history, punished civic offenders by suspending them from the *waist* upon the gallows. The image and allusion to Irving's tale deflates marvelously the superego-like threat of death and retribution that the painting-within-a-painting raises against the canvas's narcissistic energies. It suggests that the power of art lies in its capacity to transform the transgressions of the private self into the stuff of comic vision. The painting on the wall serves as a paradigm for the canvas as a whole: it images that capacity of the imagination to redeem those gothic tendencies intrinsic to it through parody, comic revision, and cultural demythologization. Comedy for Quidor becomes that privileged mode by which a culture articulates its own countercultural impulses, and in the process confronts the hidden and self-subverting imperatives underwriting all societies. *Antony Van Corlear* teaches us not only the power of art to reflect (and distort) the culture it criticizes, but the importance of art in providing a repository, a home, for alternative ideologies denied or suppressed by the mainstream culture. If for Quidor the artist transgresses a socially defined space in the very act of creation, releasing energies that cultures, like texts, must suppress in order to survive, then the recourse to comedy allows him to redeem his transgression (revise his own history) by simultaneously eliciting and disguising the anxieties of his text.

V

Quidor's characters are not alone. His concern lest man know too much and plunge too deeply, unwittingly releasing forces beyond his comprehension, was shared by Nathaniel Hawthorne. New England Puritanism ran through Hawthorne's veins. A direct descendant of Judge

John Hathorne, who had presided with "stern and resolute countenance" over the Salem witch trials of the late seventeenth century, Hawthorne matured in the shadows of a family history that reads like a tale from Washington Irving: it was rumored that a curse had been hurled upon his family by the husband of a "witch" condemned by "grim Judge Hathorne." As a child Nathaniel Hawthorne had been reared on Spenser, Bunyan, and Milton; his obsessive return as an artist to memories of Puritan New England was an attempt to account not only for his own roots in the Puritan past, but for the shaping influence of the past upon the present. Somewhere buried deep in the Puritan psyche, beneath the stern, grim visages of his ancestors and their sin-ravaged hearts, lay secrets whose meaning—once told—would help unfold the darker riddles of the nineteenth century. What Hawthorne discovered in his Puritan ancestors bore close resemblance to the energies Quidor was unraveling in his fugitive characters.

In 1835, almost contemporaneously with *The Money Diggers* and *Antony Van Corlear*, Hawthorne published the tale of a young man whose inability to disentangle his imagination from reality led him, like Quidor's money diggers, upon a dream-like voyage into the dark night of the soul. We join Young Goodman Brown, together with a mysterious stranger leaning upon a serpentine staff, as they proceed one midnight down an obscure forest path. When the figure of Goody Cloyse appears suddenly in the distance, Goodman Brown seeks to hide himself in the bushes lest the pious old woman recognize him on his ungodly errand:

> Accordingly the young man turned aside, but took care to watch his companion, who advanced softly along the road until he had come within a staff's length of the old dame. She, meanwhile, was making the best of her way, with singular speed for so aged a woman, and mumbling some indistinct words—a prayer, doubtless—as she went.[33]

The particular narrative detail that interests us here is that which describes Goody Cloyse as "mumbling some indistinct words—a prayer, doubtless—as she went." As an instance of indirect discourse—descriptive prose that mirrors the sensibility of the character it describes—Hawthorne's phrase reveals Brown's attempt to render intelligible those "indistinct" and mumbled "words" of Goody Cloyse. By adding the appositive "a prayer, doubtless," Hawthorne interprets a reality that is only dimly perceived, and thereby fashions into predictable form a world otherwise dark and inscrutable. All reality for Brown is a vast tangle of "mumbling and indistinct words"; the labyrinthine and mysterious forest is itself only a figuration of a blurred world that refuses to clarify itself for our anxious young man.

The climax of Hawthorne's imagery of ambiguity and dislocation occurs when Brown hears the sorrowful voice of his wife Faith high on a "black mass of cloud . . . sweeping swiftly northward":

> "Faith!" shouted Goodman Brown, in a voice of agony and desperation; and the echoes of the forest mocked him, crying "Faith! Faith!" as if bewildered wretches were seeking her all through the wilderness.[34]

To lose one's "Faith" in the world of "Young Goodman Brown" is to lose the security and assurance—the principle of order—that guides one in the interpretation of reality. Faith for Goodman Brown is the confidence, born of innocence, that the world is readable and that it conforms to a received standard of truth. The plight of Young Goodman Brown is that neither condition obtains. Reality as a sign system is ambiguous and baffling to the intellect, and what it seems to reveal bears little relation to what one has been taught to expect.

Or does it? Hawthorne's narrative technique includes a conscious disavowal of all responsibility for interpreting the events of the story. By suggesting a series of alternative explanations without confirming any one of them, he forces the reader into the same interpretive stance that confronts Goodman Brown. The text becomes as problematic for its audience as the forest world is for the young Puritan. The form of Hawthorne's fiction thus recapitulates the dilemma that is its central theme: the difficulty of interpretation in a world without adequate guides or signposts. "Young Goodman Brown" becomes a narrative of epistemological quest, and the loss of religious faith marks the failure of an accessible reality.

Were "Young Goodman Brown" to end here, it would remain simply a well-told tale of epistemological doubt. The problem for Hawthorne, however, is that interpretation not only *follows* the perception of ambiguity, it *precedes* it as well. Goodman Brown seems not only to discover, but to inaugurate, the catastrophe of baffled vision. Notice Hawthorne's description of the Salem minister the morning after Brown's midnight vigil:

> The next morning young Goodman Brown came slowly into the street of Salem village, staring around him like a bewildered man. The good old minister was taking a walk along the graveyard to get an appetite for breakfast and meditate his sermon, and bestowed a blessing, as he passed, on Goodman Brown.[35]

What passes between Brown and the old minister is more than a moment's courtesy in the brief "blessing" bestowed by the elderly gentleman upon his young parishioner. With the blessing comes a heritage by which the past imbues the present with the vision and the wisdom that are its legacy. The exchange between the minister and Brown is symbolic of a far deeper transference in which Brown has inherited the sensibility and proclivities of the Puritan heart. And this is a mixed "blessing" indeed. For as Hawthorne's wonderfully understated text reminds us, the "old minister was taking a walk along the graveyard to get an appetite for breakfast." With this simple and wryly comic observation, we are treated to a bold condensation of the Puritan dilemma. Hawthorne's Puritans are obsessed with sin and death. They have dwelt so intensely upon the drama of their own consciousness that they have come to see only themselves and their own worst fears wherever they look.[36] Brown's voyage into the forest is a voyage into himself, and the satanic figure with the serpentine rod is ultimately an embodiment of his own deepest impulses, an alter ego who appears in part as an inverted superego, a figure of authority and knowledge whose purpose is not to confirm man's moral possibilities but to distort them, so that Brown may finally cry, in the words of Milton, "Evil be thou my Good."

Goodman Brown is thus not so different from the old minister "taking a walk along the graveyard to get an appetite for breakfast." They both have an instinct for evil, an "appetite" for sin, born of too long a dalliance, too intense a concern, for the inner promptings of the mind and heart. And this returns us to the epistemological question posed earlier. In a world that requires our interpretation, where objects and events are not complete in themselves but take their meaning from the significance our imagination attaches to them, Goodman Brown's propensity to perceive evil becomes a mild catastrophe, leading him to see sin wherever he looks. What Hawthorne presents in "Young Goodman Brown" is not history but a state of mind in which consciousness comes to swallow reality and mistake the self's darker half for the world. In order to render reality accessible, we transform it into our own self-image, and in so doing *project* the evil we fear to find.

In "Young Goodman Brown" the reality of evil is less important than its perception. Brown's Puritan mind, like a Kantian nightmare, creates a reality it is too weak to disprove and too faithless to construct otherwise. Like one of Quidor's money diggers, he has stumbled into a pit of his own making from which he will never emerge the same: the hole's blackness will constitute the whole of his future vision. Emerson at the same period was pursuing a similar path. What Hawthorne had termed sin Emerson was more prone to call limitation, but for each thinker evil was a state intricately bound to the dilemmas of the perceiving mind. In Emerson, however, the problem of man's radical finitude was continually counterpointed against the possibilities of his visionary power. To understand the role of evil in Emerson's thought, especially in its relation to the act of perception, one turns not to Emerson's explicit descriptions of evil, which are all too rare and which serve too often only as a touchstone for discussions of the doctrine of "compensation," but instead to Emerson's account of the pathos of man's fallen state.

"Man is a god in ruins" Emerson was to write in the year following Hawthorne's publication of "Young Goodman Brown," he is "the dwarf of himself."[37] Possessed of a vision consonant with the gods, he dwells in a self too often "thick-skulled, small-brained, fishy, quadrumanous, quadruped, ill-disguised, hardly escaped into a biped":

> We cannot trifle with this reality, this cropping-out in our planted gardens of the core of the world. No picture of life can have any veracity that does not admit the odious facts. A man's power is hopped in by a necessity which, by many experiments, he touches on every side until he learns its arc.[38]

Like an experienced skater upon the surface of forms, Emerson explored the "arc" of the self's orbit, darting among the visionary expansions and powerless contractions of the soul's life. At moments the "great and cresive self" seemed a quantity of infinite capacity, infinite expansion:

> The life of man is a self-evolving circle, which, from a ring imperceptibly small, rushes on all sides outwards to new and larger circles, and that without end.[39]

Just as frequently, however, the self's expansion outward threatened to overwhelm a center already dislocated by the rapid swim of reality where "dream delivers us to dream, and there is no end to illusion." The law of process characterizing life's flow entailed among its possibilities the dissolution of the self, and Emerson discovered, like Kierkegaard, no greater Archimedean point by which to lift himself above life's train:

> We are incompetent to solve the times. Our geometry cannot span the huge orbits of the prevailing ideas, behold their return and reconcile their opposition. We can only obey our own polarity.[40]

And again:

> This is true, and that other is true. But our geometry cannot span these extreme points and reconcile them.[41]

Kierkegaard countered the Hegelians' claim to systematic knowledge with the charge that existence is a form of radical finitude. One cannot both know and be. The former is reserved for gods, the latter the domain of man. Emerson expressed the dilemma, as did Kierkegaard, in the language of theology as filtered through a post-Kantian consciousness:

It is very unhappy, but too late to be helped, the discovery we have made that we exist. That discovery is called the Fall of Man. Ever afterwards we suspect our instruments. We have learned that we do not see directly, but mediately, and that we have no means of correcting these colored and distorting lenses which we are, or computing the amount of their errors.[42]

Thus Emerson writes in "Montaigne; or, The Skeptic":

Knowledge is the knowing that we can not know.

and he concludes in "Experience":

We live amid surfaces, and the true art of life is to skate well on them.

The alternative is to drown:

I seemed in the height of a tempest to see men overboard struggling in the waves, and driven about here and there. They glanced intelligently at each other, but 'twas little they could do for one another; 'twas much if each could keep afloat alone. Well, they had a right to their eye-beams, and all the rest was Fate.[43]

The same "eye-beams" with which the young Emerson had once "fronted" Nature in a primal embrace:

I become a transparent eyeball; I am nothing; I see all; the currents of the Universal Being circulate through me; I am part or parcel of God,[44]

become for the older man marks of his diminished being. Emerson's "baffled intellect," which once had proclaimed that "the eye is the first circle; the horizon which it forms is the second," and meant by that a deeper unison of self and world beyond the distinctions of "first" and "second"—"eye" and "horizon"—no longer could maintain its earlier holism:

I know better than to claim any completeness for my picture. I am a fragment, and this is a fragment of me.[45]

The sad and inevitable conclusion followed shortly:

As I am, so I see.[46]

Radical finitude for Kierkegaard meant the absolute incapacity of the self to know a world beyond itself. "Truth as subjectivity," Kierkegaard's response to this dilemma, substituted interior modes of being, the dynamic of decision and commitment, for more systematic and objectively conceived notions of truth. In Emerson "subjectivity" had other connotations. It suggested the capacity of a fragmented self, creating all in its own image, to play what had become only a game of unity:

Once we lived in what we saw; now, the rapaciousness of this new power, which threatens to absorb all things, engages us. Nature, art, persons, letters, religions, objects, successively tumble in, and God is but one of its ideas.[47]

Kierkegaard in his lonely vigil of faith could mark with the Trinity—that paradox of incarnation—a limit to the subjectivity of human vision. Here and here alone stood one absolute fact that brooked no dispute nor could be swallowed into the imaginative abysses of the human mind. Against this one Fact the self must conform itself and accept its destiny. Emerson had once hoped to find in nature such an absolute. Though its name occasionally varied—now nature, now Idealism, now even the soul—its reality for Emerson provided the single abiding anchor to a world otherwise engulfed in motion. But vision turned upon itself, and the prism of the eye soon became the prison of reality, not refracting but creating its world. "It is the eye which makes the horizon," cried Emerson, and in the process transgressed the one boundary that had kept Kierkegaard sane. Where Kierkegaard had seen Paradox, hurled himself against its massive impenetrability, and called it God, Emerson found only the ripple that continues across the water until ultimately the whole of the lake is confined within its perimeter. This is Emerson's evil, counterpointed against that good it so often resembles. Evil consists not in the deeds that render us lesser men, for which an act of compensation may restore the universe to its original harmony, but instead in the deeper deed, the single fact of finitude, that reveals us to be radically limited in our existence, at the same time as it threatens paradoxically to consume the cosmos. There is something sublime in the failure of this solipsistic evil to distinguish itself from that original unity whose loss it is an expression of.

With the publication of "The Minister's Black Veil" in 1836, Hawthorne had come to experience that Emersonian sense of an evil defined by the very nature of man's finite existence rather than any older theological context. For Hawthorne's gentle protagonist, Parson Hooper, the black veil he wears signifies, beyond the "ambiguity of sin or sorrow," that deeper mortality which links men together in a community of the dead and dying. He resembles one of Emerson's drowning individuals, linked by shared "eye-beams" to other drowning souls while yet alone with his own fate:

"Have patience with me, Elizabeth!" cried he passionately. "Do not desert me, though this veil must be between us here on earth . . . . Oh! you know not how lonely I am, and how frightened, to be alone behind my black veil. Do not leave me in this miserable obscurity for ever!"[48]

Despite the isolation it describes, Hawthorne's tale of Parson Hooper differs from that of young Goodman Brown in being more than an account of epistemological failure. "The Minister's Black Veil" is a study in the social implications of overabundant vision. Goodman Brown enters the wilderness of the mind—in the words of Henry James, Sr., "an unsubdued forest where the wolf howls and the obscene bird of night chatters"—never to emerge again from the darkened labyrinth of his perceptions. Hooper metaphorically has traversed the same path but, unlike Brown, what he sees is not only self-projection, but the dark inner logic of human existence. The paradigm of the Fall, which informs the progress of Goodman Brown through the midnight forest, rendering the journey into self-consciousness an exercise in solipsism, becomes in "The Minister's Black Veil" the shock of recognition that occurs when the individual breaks through the platitudinous fictions of society to discover beneath them the brutal fact of his mortality. What Hooper perceives, and the community of Milford by an apparent act of repression fails to perceive, is the finitude that constitutes their common humanity.

The result is socially disruptive. The opening paragraph of the story describes in stereotyped and domesticated terms a society of apparent health and vigor prior to the appearance of the veil. Hawthorne's language resembles the popular fiction of his day; it represents his effort to compete with those "damn'd female scribblers" dominating the magazine market:

> The sexton stood up in the porch of Milford meetinghouse pulling lustily at the bell rope. The old people of the village came stooping along the street. Children with bright faces, tript merrily beside their parents.... Spruce bachelors looked sidelong at the pretty maidens, and fancied that the Sabbath sunshine made them prettier than on week-days.[49]

The Milford community, wearing its childish innocence like Sunday finery, suggests a community as close to Eden as Hawthorne's Puritans were likely to achieve. They resemble in this respect the parishioners of Salem at the close of "Young Goodman Brown." What distinguishes the two is the process of disintegration that the Milford community undergoes. With the appearance of Mr. Hooper, both the buoyant tone of the opening paragraph and the conventions of popular fiction disappear. The minister, like the author, intrudes his own darker vision upon the world of middle-class frivolity. The rhetoric of social coherence characterizing the women scribblers dissolves as Hooper's black veil, like Hawthorne's dark prose, makes its effects felt:

Some gathered in little circles, huddled closely together, with their mouths all whispering in the centre; some went homeward alone, wrapt in silent meditation; some talked loudly, and profaned the Sabbath day with ostentatious laughter. A few shook their sagacious heads, intimating that they could penetrate the mystery; while one or two affirmed that there was no mystery at all, but only that Mr. Hooper's eyes were so weakened by the midnight lamp, as to require a shade.[50]

The veil's power lies in the act of recognition it elicits from its beholders. They perceive in it their mortality—that sum of sin and death that most constitutes their humanity—and seek, as is only human, to escape the burden of recognition entailed. Hooper represents what might be called in twentieth-century terminology an instance of "ontological shock" when the self is thrown out of the protective embrace of daily habit and forced, in a moment of great anxiety, to confront its own mortality. Then, in the language of Martin Heidegger, one discovers death to be "one's own most possibility."[51] The Heideggerian individual flees such recognition, seeking refuge in the anonymity of "das Man," that driven urban creature whose bourgeois life is a series of masks that protect him from the scent of death and finitude. So too with the community of Milford. They "longed for a breath of wind to blow aside the veil." Unwilling or unable to acknowledge the implications of the two folds of black crepe, they construct a veil around the significance it portends. *They*, and not the Reverend Mr. Hooper, interpose a screen between themselves and reality by attempting to transform the veil into a series of accountable explanations (whether of Hooper's secret sin or simply his over-fatigued eyes). The Milford community staves off the moment of recognition by reducing the veil to a manageable quantity, holding its mystery and portent at arm's length.

Yet perhaps the greater sin is Parson Hooper's. The vision that he brings his parishioners—human mortality, the darker sins of the heart and soul, the ultimate isolation of the individual in the face of death—are facts whose revelation must invariably rend the social fabric of the community. Hooper sees where vision is not welcome, bringing to light truths whose articulation destroys the bonds and social masks necessary to the congenial operation of society. Hawthorne's achievement in "The Minister's Black Veil" is a complete demythologization of what Emerson would call the "optative mood." The myth of primal innocence, whether of individuals or societies, is rejected by Hawthorne, dismantled into a fiction whose poignancy lies in its social necessity. The call of the young Emerson for an "original relation with the Universe" is transformed by Hawthorne into the self's discovery of the alienating fact of death. Where

Emerson, in his more affirmative moods, would strip away the mask from divinity to discover there the human mind, Hawthorne follows suit, carrying through the Emersonian program. Holding his humanity to the mirror, he sees not the gods, but the grim reaper staring blankly back. Hawthorne understood both aspects of Emerson's evil: he described the finitude it entails and the solipsism it suggests. Unlike Emerson, whose evil was only a moment of counterpoint in an endless dance between life and death, Hawthorne, like the good Reverend Hooper he writes about, perceived not the dance, but the long black shadows that fell from its figures.

If "The Minister's Black Veil" represents at a social level Hawthorne's awareness of the plight and consequences of overabundant vision, then the story at an aesthetic level represents a self-conscious investigation into the nature and power of Romantic symbolism. Hooper's parishioners, after all, are frightened not only by the vision of mortality that Hooper offers them, but by the very fact of the veil itself. This "simple piece of crape," as Hawthorne somewhat disingenuously refers to his symbol,[52] generates out of its very blankness a repository of meanings that betrays the apparent simplicity and innocence of its material components. The veil is Hawthorne's brilliant and perverse image for a Lockean world gone awry. Its blackness provides a counter-image to Locke's *tabula rasa*. Both are receptacles for foreign impressions, but whereas Locke's blank slate records the data of an external world commonsensically assumed, Hawthorne's mysterious symbol receives the projections of the inner self in all its dark and sequestered significance. The veil represents a rupture within the public world of the Puritan community. Its ambiguity marks an elision of public meanings, a slippage of significances in a culture predicated on communally established and univocal modes of authority. What separates the veil from the traditional typology of the Puritan community is its failure to conform to the sanctioned codes of Puritan society. Its lack of determinate meaning creates a linguistic void or hiatus—a gap in the public discourse—that is filled by those *private* meanings otherwise excluded from social intercourse. These latter meanings are determined by the shape of the Protestant imagination when freed from the constraints that bind it socially and theologically.

The veil then is not a modern symbol—a Borgesian artifact—creating meaning *sui generis*. It lacks the playfulness and metaphysical irresponsibility that characterize not only Coleridge in his confrontation with the collapse of traditional systems of intelligibility,[53] but the ebullient figures of Irving in their willingness to substitute the fecundity of narrative form for the lost (and irrecoverable) specificity of historically determined meaning. Hawthorne's symbol instead derives its significance from a division between public and private selves attendant upon the breakdown of an older typology. The Romantic symbol introduces into the old order a moment of silence to which the private and demonic subject attaches itself. It becomes the focus for meanings latent in the culture but repressed (or denied) by its rhetoric. Hence the curious affinity between symbolic activity in Hawthorne and Freudian states of neurosis or dream behavior. The symbol literalizes or expresses those latent meanings denied by the communal language or assimilable only in alternative forms. It intrudes into the public discourse meanings or impulses foreign to it, evading the process of socialization governing the formation of all public language and disrupting the existing psychic or social economies of repression. Hawthorne's veil thus resembles in its symbolic structure the dynamics of representation present in Freud. The veil exists as an overdetermined symbol, translating into the realm of public discourse (what Freud would call consciousness) meanings otherwise understood as private (what Freud would call the unconscious or preconscious). The veil provides a conduit or mode of access between these two realms, and in the process disrupts the operations of the former by the introduction of elements subversive of its stability. This conflict between tenor and vehicle, between the language of the private heart and an imagery of public meanings, allows the unsocialized self to evade the mediations and repressions of the established order, bypassing the socially sanctioned categories of Puritan typology with a rhetoric inherently nonsocial and individual. The result is a pitched battle within the house of language. The Romantic symbol—the visionary act—stands at odds with the culture that produces it, and harbors within itself a tension between latent and overt meanings that threatens to erupt (note the volcanic imagery again) with explosive fury in the interstices and silences of the artist's oeuvre.

Hawthorne's resemblance to Quidor is great. Each figure, unlike Irving, perceives a limit—both psychic and social—to the proper advance of the imagination in its own self-recognition. Fiction-making becomes as much a defense against the dilemma of overabundant vision as it is a means of unmasking truths the artist fears to pursue. In a work like *Antony Van Corlear Brought into the Presence of Peter Stuyvesant*, Quidor sounds a note of caution against that impulse to self-knowledge and self-transparency—that invasion of the body politic by the private self—which would soon launch Emerson upon his visionary career. The Emersonian enterprise of the "transparent eyeball"—the call to a selfhood transparent to itself and in contact with its deepest animating forces—seemed for Quidor, as for Hawthorne, to transgress the boundaries by which the self is protected from its own deeper instincts. Emersonian man, when truly liberated, must remove the walls that shelter him from the darker currents of the cosmic ether. He must raise the windows, pull down the balcony guard rails, dismiss the sentries, and welcome as his brothers and equals—ultimately as himself—the demon-like forces that people Quidor's world. It is a bold plunge to make, and Quidor, like Hawthorne, seems frightened of its issue. Death in the image of the hangman, and forces dark and terrible in the figures of the dancing black man and balcony imps, suggest Quidor's response to an age of Emersonian men for whom self-reliance begins with self-knowledge. No individual can survive a world without walls, an ego without repressions, a society without sentries. The self requires mediation. It requires the fictions that hide the deeper alonenesses among men, the secret sins of their inner beings, and the fact of death, which ultimately isolates them from one another. Better the evasions of history and comedy, and the illusion of community, than to open Pandora's chest of truth.

VI

Hawthorne includes in *The Blithedale Romance* a remarkable passage that parodies at the same time as it repeats the experience of loss and yearning that informs the Romantic sensibility. The passage appears as part of a tale told by Zenobia to the Blithedale inhabitants; the story, like its counterpart in a Shakespearian play-within-a-play, unravels through analogy and allusion truths hidden or unstated within the larger story. Zenobia tells of a certain "gentleman" by the name of Theodore whose skeptical disposition and hardy common sense lead him one night to the chambers of the mysterious Veiled Lady (a shadowy heroine-image drifting throughout Hawthorne's novel) in an attempt to discover her identity. The veiled presence proves more elusive than Theodore had expected, and he finds himself confronted with two alternatives if he is to learn her true identity. Unwilling first to pledge eternal troth by a simple kiss to the figure behind the veil, he prefers alternatively to remove her mask before proceeding to more amorous matters. The trembling figure forewarns him that when unmasked before kissed, she is "doomed" to become his "evil fate":

> Grasping at the veil, he flung it upward, and caught a glimpse of a pale, lovely face beneath; just one momentary glimpse, and then the apparition vanished, and the silvery veil fluttered slowly down and lay upon the floor. Theodore was alone. Our legend leaves him there. His retribution was, to pine forever and ever for another sight of that dim,

mournful face—which might have been his lifelong household fireside joy,—to desire, and waste life in a feverish quest, and never meet it more.⁵⁴

Theodore's fate recapitulates in its own deflated manner the destiny of Cole's Adam and Eve. To each is vouchsafed a solitary, parting glance at some paradisal state lost to all but memory. In *Blithedale*, Zenobia's tale is ironically told. Theodore's fate is to be repeated by Miles Coverdale, who does not, like Theodore, pine romantically away for a lost vision, but who instead achieves in piecemeal fashion a vision made possible only by the distance that separates him from the protagonists he observes. Hawthorne's novel of social disintegration subverts Zenobia's tale of conventional romantic emotion by dissolving the myths of romantic love and social vision into the failed and often selfish schemes of individuals baffled by the reality they would reform. Only one illusion does Hawthorne let stand: the capacity of an observer to draw an imaginative order out of the chaos before him.

> It is his office to give applause when due, and sometimes an inevitable tear, to detect the final fitness of incident to character, and distil in his long-brooding thought the whole morality of the performance.... And, after all was finished, I would come, as if to gather up the white ashes of those who had perished at the stake, and to tell the world—the wrong being now atoned for—how much had perished there which it had never yet known how to praise.⁵⁵

At the same moment that Hawthorne is transfiguring the romantic experience of Theodore—"to pine forever and ever...in a feverish quest"—into the more tragic vision of Coverdale, he is affirming the fictionality of even Coverdale's vision. Like Irving before him, the author of *The Blithedale Romance* perceives all attempts at meaning as proceeding from an intellectual Midas-touch that turns all in its path to fiction. Where Irving could revel with childlike ecstasy in the world of fantasy created, Hawthorne developed Coverdale as a detective-like figure to distinguish order from chaos (paralleling Poe's creation of more ironically defined sleuth-like heroes in many of his short stories). That order should prove the product of Coverdale's imaginative capacities is a source of deep ambivalence for Hawthorne, who distrusted the mind of man as deeply as Emerson once rested his hopes in it. The real loss of *Blithedale* is not the innocence and domesticity that Theodore laments in Zenobia's tale, but the bifurcation that separates vision from action. Hawthorne's artist figure exists at the peripheries of his own world; he retains his perogative of vision only by relinquishing large portions of his humanity. In John Quidor's monumental canvas of the period, *The Return of Rip Van*

41. JOHN QUIDOR, *The Return of Rip Van Winkle,* ca. 1850s. National Gallery of Art, Washington, D.C., Andrew W. Mellon Collection.

Winkle (ca. 1850s; fig. 41), Quidor similarly pursues with the full power of his artistic vision the role of the Romantic imagination in its estrangement from the world around it.

The imagery of containment and eruption woven into the composition of *Antony Van Corlear Brought into the Presence of Peter Stuyvesant* appears in altered form in the later *Return of Rip Van Winkle*. At the center of the picture stands the bearded, bewildered Rip, larger than life in body and gesture though clothed in tattered and crumbling garments. Surrounding him in the shape of a "U," like a horseshoe round a post, are the townsfolk of Rip's tiny Hudson River Village. At one end of the "U" stands Irving's "self-important old gentleman, in a sharp cocked hat . . . with one arm akimbo, the other resting on his cane," while capping the other end stands an equally singular, though less belligerent, personage with a ruddy face, an exotic pipe, and a gesture of curiosity and astonishment. The motley crew of townsfolk who complete the "U" bear a striking resemblance to the round-faced, vacant-eyed figures peopling the public spaces in the art of Honoré Daumier in the second quarter of the nineteenth century in France.[56] Again, like the stricken humanity in Goya's later work, Quidor's staring faces, sometimes leering and grotesque, sometimes plaintive and suffering, belong to a human comedy too deep for laughter. They subsume in their common and contorted humanity the passions, bestiality, and concerns of man's quotidian existence. Rip's position within the encircling crowd is highlighted by the pattern of light and shadow that defines the foreground space. He stands in the center of the "U" in a pool of light blocked out by alternating sequences of light and dark that correspond roughly with the position of the townspeople. The effect is to place Rip in the center spotlight, bordered on either side by darkness and humanity, and to create in the lower half of the canvas a shallow stage space in which the action of the painting occurs.

The result of this arrangement is not unlike the neoclassical composition of Benjamin West in a painting like *Agrippina Landing at Brundisium with the Ashes of Germanicus* (1768; fig. 42). Quidor shares with West the sense of human gesture as exaggerated and theatrical that lends both paintings their Baroque quality. Again like West, though in less explicit fashion, he presents his *dramatis personae* as upon a stage by containing the painting's action within a shallow medium-ground depth. Each painter frames and limits the background recession into space by the presence of architectural models that highlight the stage space before them, pushing it forward into the viewer's perception, while commenting thematically on the action of the figures. For West the historically accurate reconstruction of Roman excavations reinforces the crisis of values that his foreground stage action suggests. The background architecture frames the "stoicism and dignity" of Agrippina, cradling the ashes of her martyred and equally heroic husband, against a heritage of classical virtue. That heritage is repeated in the eighteenth-century present through its effort at a scientific reconstruction of the past.[57] The background "arcaded façade" thus telescopes past history and eighteenth-century scholarship into a single image of enduring human vision. The picture speaks to the present in the language of the past. It establishes the classical heritage as a model for West's own audience over half a century before Mount's efforts in *The Painter's Triumph*, at the same time as it "friezes" all history into a timeless image of human aspiration. Though time passes, West suggests no essential *change* that would obviate the capacity of the eighteenth century to carry on in the footsteps of the second. Individuals of both

42. BENJAMIN WEST, *Agrippina Landing at Brundisium with the Ashes of Germanicus*, 1768. Yale University Art Gallery. Gift of Louis M. Rabinowitz.

eras, as of all times, are linked by West through their common moral makeup and rational faculties, not unlike the reasonable and judicious humanity whom Thomas Jefferson eight years later assumes as his universal audience in the Declaration of Independence.

Quidor's composition employs a similar use of architectural imagery to frame and contain his foreground action. Like West, he includes, in one corner of the canvas, an opening onto an unbounded background vista of distant mountains. For Quidor, however, the period of time spanned between past and present involves decades rather than centuries. History is distinguished not by its continuity but by the disjunction that in the course of two decades can render a man a stranger in his own land. The disaffection in West's painting, the treachery that has marked the death of Germanicus, is an aberration from a higher, timeless ideal of human behavior. West's concatenation of past with present, though it suggests a linear quality to history by which one age assumes the mantle and tasks of another, ultimately subsumes all such progress into a present outside the bounds of time and impervious to the demands of change. The static, frieze-like character of his composition and muted colors of its figures emphasize its ultimate disregard of time. Quidor's modified Baroque composition with its stage-like arrangement underscores his concern, like West's, for the drama of human history. Quidor's figures, however reduced and grotesque, are the proper progeny of West's center-stage characters. Rip's framing on either side by a chorus-like humanity is an exact counterpart to West's proscenium stage action. Unlike West's heroes, however, Rip is the victim rather than the redeemer of time. His world is defined by temporal discontinuity where West's figures know time only as a form of immortality. There is a "historicity" at work in Quidor, a sense of the *difference* that time makes, that West knows nothing of.

Quidor's time is both social and personal. The public character of West's painting, where private grief is transformed into a ritual of public import, bespeaks a world whose sense of identity is very different from that of Quidor. West's figures, especially Agrippina and her party, possess simplified, idealized faces, more like masks than individuated personalities. Grouped as actors upon a stage, their identity seems constituted entirely by the public role they enact. The individual virtues of stoicism and courage that they represent are qualities to be found not on the periphery of society nor engendered in private opposition to social convention, but within the body politic itself. Agrippina *is* her social role and not a private person forced to public tasks. She is most herself when most the exemplar of classical virtues. Quidor's Rip Van Winkle, though present like Agrippina within a public space, is baffled by the social world that surrounds him and bars him, prison-like, from the one familiar image within the picture space, his son Rip, whom he mistakes for his own younger self. Agrippina, like Rip, is pictured returning to her homeland; her arrival is assimilated into a pattern of values and responses that both she and her audience assume in advance. Rip's return is a chronicle of *nonassimilation*. The world he enters bears no relation to the one he left, and, unlike Agrippina, he has no reasonable account of the intervening time.

Irving situates his narrative in the decades preceding and following the American Revolution. The pathos of Irving's protagonist stems in part from the genuine social revolution that confronts the unwary Rip, and that Quidor, like Irving, uses to suggest how profound a dislocation has occurred in Rip's life. Signs of the American Revolution suggested by Irving's text dot Quidor's canvas. A portrait of General Washington smiles where once the visage of George III stared (fig. 43); hanging from the flagpost (once a "great tree that used to shelter the quiet little Dutch

43. JOHN QUIDOR, detail of fig. 41, *The Return of Rip Van Winkle* (portrait of George Washington).

inn" of Nicholas Vedder) are the stars and stripes of a nation wholly un-known to Rip, and above the lintel of the new hotel a sign proclaims "The Union Hotel by Jonathan Doolittle"; in the foreground of the canvas, at the feet of the pipe-smoking observer, lies a pamphlet on which is writ-ten "ELECTION/RIGHTS OF CITIZENS/LIBERTY/BUNKER'S HILL" (fig. 44), phrases directly from Irving's text, while the pocket of the pipe-smoking gentle-man carries a wad of papers on which appear the words "seventy-six," the year of the Declaration of Independence. Rip's relation to this world is summed up in the image of the youth in the right-hand corner of the crowd, who has a crossbow poised upon his shoulder: like the dated weapon, Rip Van Winkle is a social anachronism. He lives in a world where change occurs without mediating rites of passage. Like Wolfert Webber, Rip's life can be divided into "before" and "after" with no tan-gible moment of transition to account for the difference.

His story thus literalizes the theme of social dislocation that surfaces frequently in Irving's fiction. Quidor's Rip Van Winkle shares with

44. JOHN QUIDOR, detail of fig. 41, *The Return of Rip Van Winkle* (handbill)

Irving's that sense of baffled incomprehension of a character in search of a reality. There is an anger in Quidor's painting commensurate with the pathos in Irving's tale. The agrarian displacement that underlies the temporal discontinuity in Irving is echoed in Quidor, though only vaguely, by the city/country division of his background. Behind Rip and the villagers stands the closed space of the town buildings,. while to the painting's left, under the tree against which the young Rip leans, the landscape continues back into the hazy blue Catskills, the scene, presumably, of Rip's recent adventure. The contrast between father and son, urban and rural backgrounds, suggests the social revolution that has accompanied America's political one, especially as the young Rip embodies through his rustic attire and his father's misconceptions a past lost and irretrievable to the older man. Rip initially mistakes his son for his past self:

> Rip looked, and beheld a precise counterpart of himself, as he went up the mountain; apparently as lazy, and certainly as ragged. The poor fellow was now completely confounded. He doubted his own identity,

and whether he was himself or another man. In the midst of his bewilderment, the man in the cocked hat demanded who he was, and what was his name.

"God knows," exclaimed he, at his wit's end; "I'm not myself—I'm somebody else—that's me yonder—no—that's somebody else got into my shoes—I was myself last night, but . . . everything's changed, and I'm changed, and I can't tell what's my name, or who I am!"[58]

The relation of Rip to his son is as problematic as that of the individual to society. Like the Veiled Lady before Theodore, or Eden before Cole's peregrine parents, the younger Rip hovers before his father as an image of a past no longer available. The irony of *The Return of Rip Van Winkle* is that there is *no* return; there is instead only a past one did not leave, but that one no longer possesses, and a present one did not enter, but from which there is no escape.

Linked to that past are the virility and life that an old man fears lost. In the crowd, at the painting's right, an elderly woman with capped head bends over to stare at Rip (fig. 45). Dangling from her belt are a pair of scissors and a pincushion. The cushion is red and heart-shaped, while the scissors, like the pins piercing the cushion, are sharp and pointed. In her hand is a small stick, a little too short to be an adequate cane, but slender and pointed enough to be a formidable club. Together with the anachronistic crossbow that appears next to the sewing tools, these artifacts suggest not only a linkage between love and aggression, but in their sharp, pointed, and weapon-like character, a peculiarly threatening and destructive mode of sexuality. Rip's vulnerability is suggested by the noose—an image of mortality—that Quidor has draped around his neck. Like the rope that encircles Wolfert Webber's waist in *The Money Diggers*, hanging before his crotch like an attenuated phallus, Rip's noose extends down his chest to the old, outdated flintlock, which he grips tightly at groin level. The rope proceeds to Rip's powder bag which it supports at waist level (fig. 46). Sexuality and death, linked comically in *Antony Van Corlear,* reappear in *The Return of Rip Van Winkle* through the juxtaposition of phallic rifle with noose-like rope. Their combination suggests the struggle and bewilderment within Rip between a past perceived as vital and a present distinguished by unaccountable loss. Rip reaches after his son as after a missing part of himself, his line of vision and clasped rifle meeting as by triangulation in the outstretched arm that directs the movement of the painting toward the phantom figure under the leafy tree. To lose the past is to lose one's roots and, as a consequence, to forfeit one's virility.

Quidor builds upon Irving's prose. Rip cries in the short story, "I fell

45. JOHN QUIDOR. detail of fig. 41,
The Return of Rip Van Winkle
(woman with cap and boy with
 crossbow).

asleep on the mountain, and they've changed my gun, and everything's changed, and I'm changed . . . ." Uprooted by a social revolution that orphans Rip in a present unfamiliar with his past, betrayed by processes of time that taunt age with memories more real than their aftermath, Rip experiences in this painting of "return" the irreversibility of time in a world of change. Unlike Cole's Adam and Eve, whose consolation as exiles is the adventure of pilgrims, Rip has no known pilgrimage to re-

46. JOHN QUIDOR, detail of fig. 41, *The Return of Rip Van Winkle* (Rip Van Winkle and leering man).

cord; the past evaporated as he slept, the present transpired un-announced. What is left is the moment of recognition when self-image and reality enter into painful colloquy. Not that time, the mother of all discontinuities, is ever understood. She remains for Rip a mystery. But her offspring—age, death, and a failure of powers—demand recognition.

Rip's gesture of recognition transforms the painting. It is an act of creation as much as an acknowledgment of kinship. Rip's heroic and larger-than-life stature, his flowing white beard and patriarchal pate, together with his extended arm, arched hand, and crooked index finger, all suggest a moment charged not only with the recognition implicit in the encounter of father and son, but surcharged with the powers and energies of creation. Rip's potent hand reaches out toward the young Rip in a manner parallel to that of God the Father in Michelangelo's Sistine Chapel fresco. The younger Rip in turn, as John Wilderming has noted, resembles Michelangelo's *Bound Slave*, and the figures of father and son, creator and created, are bound together in Quidor's painting by the curious congruence of their right hands.[59] As the young Rip leans dreamily against a supporting tree (his figure is as elusive and unreal as it is present and perplexing), his right arm extends downward the length of his side until it too forms a shaped and pointing gesture that mirrors almost exactly Rip's own baffled and accusing pose. Whether or not Quidor was aware of Michelangelo's work, the power and creative potential of Rip's gesture is unmistakable. It transforms the painting from a study in social orphanhood—the crisis of Rip's estrangement and social dispossession—into a deeper account of creation and the dilemmas of artistic paternity. What Rip's gesture tells us is that he is not only displaced by a world present and inscrutable, but that he is himself its author and father.

Notice the gnome-like and gnarled children who leer and gesticulate between Rip and the pigtailed old man to his right. In the engraved source for Quidor's painting, an illustration by Richard Westall of *The Return of Rip Van Winkle* in an 1824 London edition of Irving's *The Sketchbook*, three grinning, well-groomed children stand in the picture's left foreground (fig. 47).[60] In Westall's illustration, the three youths are demonstrably real: they stand on solid ground and inhabit a space measurable in its relation to the bewildered Rip. In Quidor's painting, however, the children have lost their quality of reality and seem to emerge from an undefined shadow space directly behind Rip, like so many demons from a nether region. Neither old nor young, they are simply small in build, pudgy and gnome-like in feature, and amorphously clustered in a group whose number cannot be accurately counted. Like their more visibly menacing counterparts in the doorway vista of *Antony Van Corlear*, they populate a background space framed on one side by the extended figure of Rip and on the other by the glaring old man whose wooden walking stick resembles the musket of the watchman guarding Stuyvesant's chambers in the earlier work. Though contained by the visual rectangle of Rip and the pigtailed man, the gnome-like children, like the creatures on the balcony in *Antony Van Corlear*, threaten to erupt into the shallow center space of the painting. They are related to the mannered figure of the young Rip not only in their common roles as children and progeny, but through their deeper figuration of forces on the peripheries of consciousness, energies attendant upon the act of creation itself. One figure

47. RICHARD WESTALL, illustration of "The Return of Rip Van Winkle" from Washington Irving's *The Sketchbook,* published by Hurst, Robinson and Co., London, 1824. Collection of American Literature, Beinecke Rare Book and Manuscript Library, Yale University.

in particular, standing with hat upon head immediately behind Rip's elbow, points directly up at Rip, as if returning Rip's own accusatory gesture. The creator stands confronted by powers he himself has created, who now come to haunt and accuse him. What we witness in the larger confrontation between father and son—and in an intervening background space of uncertain depth, filled with creatures of uncertain origin—is a crisis of paternity, Rip's encounter with forces of his own making, released like so many fugitives from Pandora's box at the very moment of recognition that defines the painting's center. Ghost-like forms in a fluid space, these impish children emerge from shadows like Fisherman Sam from *The Money Diggers*'s pit, figments of Quidor's own imagination. They confront their creator—as they seem to confront Rip—as a host of misshapen progeny who embody within themselves the artist's deepest fears for his own creation and powers of figuration.

These fears are twofold. They center first in the image of the taunting children, whose peculiar placement and hallucinatory qualities suggest the presence of nonsocial and unsanctioned energies. The catastrophe of artistic creation—as Milton had foreseen when paralleling Satan's flights of pride with the artist's own imaginative excursions, and as Hawthorne had probed in the power of the black veil to disrupt and destroy even as it refused to swerve from the truth it proclaimed—this capacity of creative catastrophe lies in the power of art to probe with scalpel-like surety beneath the tissues of social fiction, and beyond the limits of natural vision, to depths too deep for social man to accommodate without disruption or disaster. If we learn from "The Minister's Black Veil" the power of mystery, and, in those two pieces of black crepe, the power of symbolic discourse to unleash forces whose very truth requires their continued repression and denial, then we see in *The Return of Rip Van Winkle* that moment of recognition when the ability to create as gods returns full force upon the creator, making his necessary usurpation of divine prerogatives an act of terror and isolation.

Contrast for a moment Rip's balding and exposed head, in its prophetic power, with the hatted visages of virtually every prominent figure surrounding Rip. Not only are the hats themselves exaggerated and comic in their various shapes and distensions, but they seem to announce their own function as covers—as articles of clothing like pants or shoes designed to hide human nakedness within a social context—when seen in their collective contrast with Rip's own exposed and more vulnerable figure. This contrast between images of exposure and closedness (or coveredness) runs as a secondary undertone throughout the painting; it is present in the contrast between Rip's physical isolation and the collective security of the crowd, and in the very tattered and disintegrating state of his own coat and breeches as compared to the proper and occasionally colorful dress of the citizenry. The point that most draws our attention to the brigade of hats dotting the picture is the visual interlude that occurs between Rip's extended index finger and the black tricorner of the pigtailed gentleman. Though the shape of Rip's Michelangelo-like hand directs the viewer from Rip's lateral gaze to the figure of his nearby son, the action is momentarily deflected, if not actually disrupted, by the presence of the tricornered hat that hovers just beyond the tip of Rip's downward-bent finger like a trough awaiting water from a spout above it. This curious comic interruption of the more serious visual flow from Rip to son serves an important function. It seems to deflect the intensity of the father-son sequence with a comic intrusion that defuses in part the passion of the former even as it furthers it along its visual route. Comedy thus functions here as a mode of deflection—a means of clothing in acceptable social dress energies otherwise unassimilable by the community. Rip's naked head, balding and prophetically fashioned, contrasts with the hatted visages of those around him as recognition contrasts with social disguise. The moment of truth is an unmasking, and its energy can be contained only as deflected through comic discourse, which both disguises and reveals that which it communicates. In the marvelous interlude of Rip's arched hand and the tricornered hat, we have a larger *apologia* for Quidor's work as a whole. Comedy for Quidor appears to be the self's defense against its own deepest vision; it is an extended visual trope that transfigures the artist's rage and vulnerability by deflecting what it would repress but cannot, revealing what it must know and would not.

Beyond the concern for energies unleashed by the act of creation, a second fear implicit in Rip's crisis of paternity centers upon the figure of young Rip and the larger relation of the father to the community surrounding him. Rip has been betrayed not only by time, which caught him napping two decades, but by the very world that he as father has unwittingly authored. What one sees in the baffled accusation accompanying Rip's authorial gesture is a belated recognition that Romantic creation is a self-alienating process. Rip is displaced by his own vision. Lounging against a supporting tree, young Rip Van Winkle becomes in the painting more than an image of a past no longer accessible to the present world—a past whose absence is tantamount to a loss of identity and creative power. Both logically and chronologically, he represents the present and future as well. He is the progeny of old Rip Van Winkle, and the community that surrounds him (almost as if shielding him from the angry old man) dwells in a historical present that it shares with the son to the exclusion of the father. We might term this situation a state of reversed belatedness, understanding "belatedness" to mean a condition in which the poet or artist believes himself doomed for reasons of birth or temporal sequence to a role of secondary activity relative to an imaginative precursor. For Harold Bloom, from whom the term is taken, poetic activity is a continual struggle for priority, an oedipal-like encounter between a poet and his precursor, in which the poet fights to create an imaginative space for himself in a world perceived as closed and over-burdened with the language of the poetic past.[61] The sense of belatedness afflicting the young poet (and dooming the weak one) lies in his fear that the precursor poet has already cleared the ground to which he aspires, and erected there a poetic edifice that the younger, and belated, poet can experience only as exclusionary.

What is intriguing about *The Return of Rip Van Winkle* is the manner in which Quidor's work seems to extend and then reverse the pattern Bloom describes. Rip's bafflement and outrage may be explained initially as a latecomer's confusion upon entering a world created prior to his arrival. By sleeping through the American Revolution, Rip has doomed himself to perpetual belatedness. The picture, however, hinges upon an irony that reverses its ostensible meaning. Rip is not only the latecomer in a world defined by a prior revolution, he is at the same time its author: he is both father of the young Rip Van Winkle and an artist-creator who calls into being his progeny and the mysterious world accompanying it. The confrontation between Rip and son is thus more than the encounter of past with present: it is the confrontation of the artist with his creation, the symbol-maker with his symbols, and the recognition at the heart of that encounter that the creator is displaced most by that which is most his—his own flesh and blood, his own vision. It is not the precursor who demands priority and seems thereby to exclude the artist from the vision he seeks, it is the vision itself, the poised and completed work of art, that con-summates its birth by denying its paternity, relegating its author to old age and to the irony of a belatedness brought about by his own success. The precursor is none other than the creator himself, the visionary dis-placed by his own vision.

The issue, phrased alternatively, is one of representation: the artist violates by the very act of figuration the object he would portray. He consigns himself instead to a world of doubles and misrepresentations, figures whose realization is never one with their conception. The con-fused relation of Rip Van Winkle to his son introduces into Quidor's painting the problem of doubling and repetition first explored in *The*

Money Diggers. Rip is caught in a narcissistic web that limits his vision of the world to variant possibilities of himself. As in *The Money Diggers* and "Young Goodman Brown," he can render the world intelligible only by rendering it a form of self-reflection. The demand for recognition emanating from the crowd surrounding him functions, like Milton's antithetical Muse, as a voice of renunciation drawing him away from his own "watr'y Image" to a reality different from the one he knows. For the older Rip, however, such a lesson is anathema. He is baffled by the crowd and by their difference from him, and he points angrily at his son as a misrepresentation of himself, a betrayal of his own possibilities. His wish to be his younger self is at bottom a desire for presence and identity, a bewildered and nostalgic wish for a world where the object is one with its representation. But representation, by definition, is a revisionary act in *Rip Van Winkle* (that is why there is no *return*). It alters what it touches and constitutes itself through the re-presentation (misrepresentation) of past forms. To be belated is thus to be caught in the tangles of language, to discover the gap that places all tropes at a distance from their object and binds the self in a world of endless doubles. To seek identity over difference (and that is Rip's fate) is to remain a diminished version of oneself: to be nothing more than a reduced and impotent version of one's deepest possibilities.

   The Return of Rip Van Winkle is Quidor's statement of self-accounting, and it is filled with anger and retribution. Unlike the earlier *Money Diggers*, in which punishment was confined to the upper right corner of the canvas, Quidor's late masterpiece suffuses its anger throughout the canvas: the background imps gesture accusatorily at the pointing Rip, Rip reaches in anger and confusion to his son and self, the crowd menaces the blustering old man. However diverse the circuit of retribution may appear, it coalesces both formally and thematically in the single gesture of recognition linking Rip to his son. The collapse of the imagination into a single narcissistic circle dooms the artist-creator to his own displacement. His work remains perpetually secondary relative to a visionary tradition it can emulate only by way of parody and self-accusation. Quidor's painting records within itself both the history of its own evolution and the agony of its vision. Its curse is to be a witness to its own secondariness.

VII

Quidor's concern for an art that dispossesses its creator is shared by other mid-nineteenth-century figures. In *The Scarlet Letter*, Hawthorne expresses a similar fear through the character of Pearl, Hester Prynne's elusive and uncontrollable fairy child. In "The Custom House" essay prefatory to *The Scarlet Letter*, Hawthorne appears to pun on the word "custom" to suggest a world freed from the burdens of history. He notes what seems to be his family "destiny to make Salem my home":

> My doom was on me. It was not the first time, nor the second, that I had gone away,—as it seemed, permanently,—but yet returned, like the bad half-penny; or as if Salem were for me the inevitable centre of the universe.[62]

The narrator interprets this sense of historical inevitability between himself and Salem—a family destiny dogging his heels—as a sign of ill mental health:

> This very sentiment is an evidence that the connection, which has become an unhealthy one, should at last be severed. Human nature will not flourish, any more than a potato, if it be planted and replanted, for too long a series of generations, in the same worn-out soil. My children have had other birthplaces, and, so far as their fortunes may be within my control, shall strike their roots into *unaccustomed* earth.[63]

The silent pun on the root word "custom" is repeated several pages later when the narrator notes that

> There was always a prophetic instinct, a low whisper in my ear, that, within no long period, and whenever a new change in *custom* should be essential to my good, a change would come.[64]

As the narrator's apparent gamesmanship with the term "custom" seems to suggest, "The Custom House" essay is a study ultimately in a particular state of mind, a habit of historical consciousness not unlike original sin: it is assumed at birth and relinquished only at death. The encounter of the narrator first with the present occupants of the Salem "Custom House," and ultimately with the moth-eaten "A" that the Custom House retains from its secret and unknown past, is a figuration of those deeper energies by which the novelist in his prose first constructs an imaginative repository for the past, a custom house, and then seeks to enter and inhabit it. His purpose is in part antiquarian, the effort of the present to account for itself by first accounting for its origins. But there is a counterhistorical impulse at work also. Hawthorne's narrator seeks to know and possess the past in order ultimately to acquit himself of its burden. That is the significance of his desire for "unaccustomed earth." The narrator of "The Custom House" essay must provide the past with a voice that it could not provide for itself, and in lending it narrative form, he brings to completion its hinted but unstated significances. In so doing, he not only invests the past with the power of its own possibilities, but he also frees the present from its responsibility to a beautiful, frightening, and almost forgotten world. Fiction-making becomes a means of discharging one's historical obligations, just as "grace" had once been the Puritans' language for the resolution of original sin. But for Hawthorne as for the Puritans, grace is a gift not shared by all. The promise of "The Custom House" essay is a possibility of freedom directed to a future generation; not the author but his progeny may hope to enjoy the fruits of "unaccustomed" existence. "My children have had other birthplaces, and, so far as their fortunes may be within my control, shall strike their roots into unaccustomed earth."

Only one character in *The Scarlet Letter* actually achieves the freedom that Hawthorne describes in "The Custom House." Pearl is born with the "freedom of a broken law," and she comes to actualize for Hawthorne that movement outside the constraints of history that Hester alone could never accomplish. Hester dwells on the periphery between society and wilderness, and her freedom is achieved through acts of social mediation that link her destiny as an individual to her past as a transgressor of an established social code. Pearl, by contrast, is a creature untouched by social convention. Her natural wildness—she is associated with birds, motion, and unrestrained energy—is an expression of her deeper freedom from historical ties. Hawthorne presents Pearl as fatherless. When asked by Mr. Wilson who had made her, she "announced that she had not been made at all, but had been plucked by her mother off the bush of wild roses that grew by the prison door." She responds to Hester's admonition that her "Heavenly Father" had sent her by crying, "He did not send me . . . . I have no Heavenly Father." Pearl's metaphoric orphanhood—her unfathered state—is the image by which Hawthorne describes her independence from the bonds of the past, and as such, she represents for Hawthorne an imaginative approximation to a state of unaccustomed existence. To be unfathered is to be freed of history's demands, to exist as a creature wholly natural and unaccountable to social convention.

Hawthorne's attitude to Pearl, however, is not what one might expect from the author of "The Custom House" essay. Hawthorne, like Hester, finds Pearl to be "beautiful and brilliant," but he also perceives in her wild energy a.being "all in disorder." In her perverse strangeness and innocence, her energy without perceptible organization, Pearl comes to assume for Hawthorne an almost Frankenstein-like quality:

> The mother felt like one who has evoked a spirit, but, by some irregularity in the process of conjuration, has failed to win the master-word that should control this new and incomprehensible intelligence.[65]

In her very innocence and freedom from law, Pearl is more monster than child; she is too natural and hence too alien to be comprehended by historical man. She represents for Hawthorne, as the encounter of Rip Van Winkle with his son does for Quidor, the terror and estrangement of a world unbounded by the canons of the past, a future and self-centered world created by an act of social or artistic transgression and imaged through the metaphor of parents and progeny. Pearl may be interpreted as the product of Hawthorne's imaginative striving to be done with history; she is a creature freshly plucked from the resolutely nonhistorical world of Emerson (a trope for Emerson's "transparent eyeball") and deposited, with great tribulation, into the heart of Hawthorne's morally constituted universe. What she reveals, beyond the initial exhilaration of unaccustomed existence, is Hawthorne's terror in the face of his own creation. She is an energy let loose upon the earth by an act of moral trespass (whether the trespass be that of Hester socially, Hawthorne imaginatively, or Emerson metaphysically), and she haunts her creator by her refusal to conform to recognized patterns of behavior. Related to her maker by ties of both love and fear, she is Hawthorne's caveat to those who would be rid of the past.

For Quidor, the issue is not the presence or price of history, but its disappearance altogether. All time for Rip Van Winkle occurs in the aftermath of history, and all creation is a mode of metaphoric orphanhood in which the created denies and betrays its parental origins. Where Quidor and Hawthorne meet is in their mutual fear of their own artistic powers. For Hawthorne the privilege of vision entails simultaneously the curse of social transgression; artistic performance threatens to overwhelm the carefully wrought distinctions by which a society protects itself from truths unaccommodated to the social fabric. The very task Hawthorne assumes of freeing the individual from the bonds of the past turns into a monstrous endeavor in which a visionary future returns to haunt the present with the reproach of its own alien being. For Quidor visionary activity is not only disruptive of social and psychic stability (as expressed in *The Money Diggers* and *Antony Van Corlear*), but threatens the artist with his own imaginative displacement. What we have termed the dilemma of reversed belatedness in *The Return of Rip Van Winkle* is ultimately an expression of the artist's fears not simply for the change occurring around him, but for the transformations inaugurated by the catastrophe of his own vision. To experience the alienness of one's own work is to know the foreignness and strangeness that attaches to all vision when the imagination, in its prophetic and creative power, violates boundaries perceived as socially, textually, or theologically established. Quidor records in *The Return of Rip Van Winkle* the power of the Romantic symbol (and of prophetic vision in general) to bring the future proleptically into the present, and in the process to render what was once present into a socially anachronistic and belated past. This crisis of reversed belatedness, of the artist's displacement by his own vision and his ensuing sense of impotence and anger, is more than an ancillary aspect of Quidor's painting. It signals the development of an awareness within the artist of the dilemma of his overabundant and textually subversive vision, and, through the narrative of Rip Van Winkle, an attempt to lend that awareness a pictorial voice.

At last we can return to the one figure as yet undescribed in *Antony Van Corlear Brought into the Presence of Peter Stuyvesant*. Against the threshold of the background door, perched upon the post opposite the leaning guard, stands the lounging form of a highly feminized and youthful-looking figure. The curly locks and soft features suggest a woman in what is otherwise a man's world. The androgynous nature of this person reflects her ambiguous position within the painting's composition. Situated behind the raised leg of the sentry, while not yet a part of the background balcony figures, she belongs neither to the foreground world of Stuyvesant's males nor the background of demonic creatures. Her closest visual correlate is the sentry with whom she shares the midground space, but from whom she differs by the expression of reflective comprehension on her face (the sentry appears to gaze into Stuyvesant's room with mute incomprehension). Where the watchman's aggressive figure dominates the threshold space and extends his presence beyond the doorposts into the room itself, Quidor's quizzical female seems wholly confined by the space of the threshold into which she seems to melt, for she is less than half the size of the brown-jacketed guard. Her passivity is reinforced by the loose white and gold brushwork with which she is painted; her body is modeled by soft painterly brushstrokes rather than the more linear, muscular forms of the sentry opposite her. She seems an observer figure, the only person in *Antony Van Corlear* capable of comprehending, as from a distance, the action and significance of the whole. Her presence completes the picture-within-a-picture formed by the doorway, sentry, and background figures. Like an artist surveying his work, this unidentified personage seems an image of Quidor's own presence within the painting.[66]

She is the true progeny of Rip Van Winkle's awakening into vision. Like Freud's censor and Stuyvesant's watchman, she straddles a narrow corridor between consciousness and the unknown; unlike either of these two figures, however, her presence is defined through its contrast with their power. She is a creature fitted for visionary activity only, possessing neither the musket nor the muscles requisite for their tasks. It is she who appears to observe the carnival of life before her, to trace the circus of forms that fill the air, and to note, beneath the surface riot, the drama of containment that it both masks and expresses. Yet if she alone is possessed of a vision that comprehends the whole, she alone is dispossessed of a participating role within the pageant before her. She represents the artist manqué, a voyeur figure whose fated gift is to behold what he or she cannot affect. Miles Coverdale in *The Blithedale Romance* describes his role within the novel as that of

> the Chorus in a classic play, which seems to be set aloof from the possibility of personal concernment, and bestows the whole measure of its hope or fear, its exultation or sorrow, on the fortunes of others, between whom and itself this sympathy is the only bond.[67]

Hawthorne's greatness in *The Blithedale Romance* is his achievement of a novelistic structure predicated upon the schism of visionary activity from worldly enterprise. Coverdale represents the disembodied presence of the artist whose very exclusion from the precincts of ordinary human intercourse renders him capable of an imaginative power not granted to those in the midst of life's fray.[68] In *Antony Van Corlear*, Quidor's feminized threshold figure is his visual equivalent to Hawthorne's diminished narrator. The voyeuristic powers of Quidor's enigmatic female are a figuration of the artist's self-conceived isolation. Simply to see is to remove oneself from the train of action, to suffer, like Rip Van Winkle, the fate of the creator displaced by the power and presence of his own creation. Quidor's figure comes to represent within herself that bifurcation of vision and action which is the hallmark of Hawthorne's "Minor Poet," thereby providing an image for the artist who not only sees where others are blind, but whose vision itself condemns him to self-parody and powerlessness.

That is the final meaning not only of *The Return of Rip Van Winkle* but of *Antony Van Corlear Brought into the Presence of Peter Stuyvesant*. Quidor's artist-figure stands next to a Freudian-like watchman, and with him must share the responsibility for what passes through the doorway of consciousness. Like Freud's censor, she appears to mask the painting's meanings—perhaps even from herself—with tropes and visual disguises; where society can avail itself of guns, horns, and whips to dissemble and defuse what it cannot otherwise assimilate, the artist resorts to metaphor—to the mystery of two folds of black crepe or the language of the comic imagination. The sin of the artist, however—a form of original sin, for it is one that he brings with him into the world—is the very fact of his visionary power. His compulsion to vision is no more containable than are Antony's bursting breeches, and yet like Antony in the narrow corridors of consciousness, he risks with each new sound of the trumpet an upheavel he is powerless to control. This is the catastrophe of imaginative vision, the fate of the artist for whom all creation is a mode of psychic or social disruption that returns Frankenstein-like to haunt its creator. Intrinsic to the very process of vision is the engendering of worlds that seem alien to the creator and appear to him to exist by laws foreign to his own self-definition and inimical to the canons of order by which he exists.

Part Three

Romanticism and the
Unconscious:
Thomas Cole

5

Thomas Cole and the Creation of a Romantic Sublime

Dedicated to the memory of
Thomas Weiskel

The youth of a science is its prime of life; before this age it is old, its age the age of the preconceptions by which it lives, as a child . . . [lives] the preconceptions and hence the age of its parents. . . .

Freud had to cope with the following situation: to be himself his own father, to construct with his own craftsman's hands the theoretical space in which to situate his discovery, to weave with thread borrowed intuitively left and right the great net with which to catch in the depths of blind experience the teeming fish of the unconscious, which men call dumb because it speaks even while they sleep.

LOUIS ALTHUSSER, *Lenin and Philosophy*

To reach back into the power animating Cole's early major canvases, the sublime landscapes of 1826–28, we must unravel a thread that hides like Arachne's web a silent story within its beautiful patterns.[1] Cole's paintings of the period, together with his writings, disguise as do so many Romantic texts the inner machinations and sources of energy behind his imagery. The soaring peaks and dramatic chiaroscuro of the sublime generate within themselves a vocabulary of conflict and resolution. Behind the terror and exhilaration of Cole's paintings the viewer encounters a moment of psychological reversal when an oppressive burden is lifted and the soul receives an influx of power, which it experiences in an ecstasy of liberation and release.[2] For Cole the drama of oppression and release is expressed through a massing of mountain peaks in a formulaic pattern common to most of his early works. A foreground hillock or promontory is juxtaposed against a larger and often threatening middleground peak. In between the two lies an abysmal valley, usually saturated with rising mists, while in the distant background the clearing skies open onto a prospect of green meadows and expanding space. Though the pattern varies from canvas to canvas, its persistence throughout Cole's oeuvre, dominating in the early years and recurring in the later works, suggests more than the play of convention and reality. Cole's sublime landscapes, in fact, are pointedly nonrealistic. They draw their energy from the drama of the psyche in the struggle of self-definition, and they reach into the uniqueness of an *American* topography only as that topography reinforces their own aesthetic or psychological needs.

What occurs in Cole is more than a layering of private experience upon a two-dimensional canvas. Cole is Allston's successor as the person of greatest influence in American painting in the second quarter of the nineteenth century. For Allston, the loss of referential meaning and the accompanying sense of the mind's self-entrapment culminated in an aesthetics of parody, an art form that makes a virtue of its limitations. The parodic imagination provided Allston with a mode of self-referential discourse that freed him from the constraints of traditional, semantically oriented systems of meaning and pointed him in the direction of early modernism. In Cole this process is both advanced and reversed. The sublime replaces the parodic as the primary language of the imagination: its task is to defeat the claustrophobic and imploding centers of meaning surrounding it by substituting for past forms of art the narrative of its own peculiar genesis. The sublime painting tells but a single tale. It repeats on each canvas the history of its struggle with older systems of meaning, which it perceives as exclusionary and prohibitive. Like the struggle of David with Goliath, the sublime turns upon the capacity of the humble to defeat the mighty by an act of wit and imagination. The triumph of the sublime depends ultimately on its ability to appropriate the energy of antecedent art forms for its own ends. The liberation effected by this defeat and reversal of the past not only validates the original effort, but substitutes for the loss of narrative structure (paintings *about* something and not simply records of their own composition) a landscape suffused with autobiographic meanings. Through the Romantic sublime, Cole invents his own story, filling the silence of nonnarrative vistas with the clamor of self-discovery. The emotive quality so often attributed to Romantic painting thus develops as a secondary rather than a primary characteristic; it is present not because the artist wishes primarily to generate emotion and engage the feelings of his viewers, but because he has come to substitute the drama of his intellectual maturation for more traditional modes of narrative.

When successful, the sublime painting not only reproduces its struggles for the viewer, but engages in its own narrative reinterpretation. It recasts its story into a tale of self-origination, claiming to have possessed all along powers that it only recently obtained. In Cole, this rewriting of the sublime is called the beautiful. The primal battle between father and son, antecedent art and modern revision, is recast from the vantage point of the victor to appear as an inevitable and foregone conclusion. The scars of battle are smoothed into the harmonies of an integrated landscape, and the terror of the sublime passes over into the refuge and comfort of the beautiful. The beautiful then is a fiction, a carefully composed rearrangement of an earlier score. It recasts sublime history into an edited artifice, manipulating in the best tradition of managed news only those facts that are fit to print. Or as Emerson phrased it, recasting the Wordsworthian enterprise with characteristic insouciance, "history is an impertinence and an injury if it be anything more than a cheerful apologue or parable of my being and becoming."[3]

Cole sought to rewrite history into a "cheerful apologue" of himself. His sublime paintings form an "allegorical narrative" that both masks and reveals the inner turmoils of his assumption to artistic power. He forms in this respect an interesting contrast to Washington Irving, with whom he shares a common sense of guilt for having dispatched history before the seductive blandishments of fiction. For Irving, as we have noted, fiction-making defends the self against the wounds of historical time. What cannot be comprehended rationally is simply repressed and rewritten until a substitute set of tales—consciously fictional in their origins—can placate the urge to know and reintegrate the baffled self, as if by magic, into a restored present. The reader is left with a sense of "before" and "after," an awareness of how the world once was and to what it has returned, but he lacks any true insight into the character of change itself. Irving calls our attention to the effects rather than the causes of history, leaving to the dream-work of his characters their ability to survive. In Cole precisely the opposite happens. The sublime becomes the record of that struggle which Irving's narratives avoid, a detailed account of the disequilibrium and recovery that marks the artist for greatness in his encounter with history. The gaping hole at the center of Irving's fiction, the historical void that his characters seek again and again to fill, is rendered by Cole into the subject of his art. The sublime is Cole's battle against the forces that shackle and baffle him. Only in the beautiful does he attempt to recast the terrors of that struggle into a fictionalized and reintegrating myth.

Cole in other words supplies a term missing in Irving. He provides us with a front-row view of an event that Irving, having slept through it, can only report secondhand from the gossip and speculation of his characters. Not that Cole's private experiences or artistic strategies in any way duplicate those of Irving. They don't. But they help us to demystify the complex and perplexing relations of imaginative experience to the realms of history and convention. In Cole we find what Irving hides: a privileged moment in which the artist reveals the mediating and fictionalizing tendencies by which he constructs his Romantic identity. In Irving the father has already been slain, and all we can do is feast on his remains, tantalizingly prepared. In Cole we witness the combat itself, and may judge of victor and vanquished from our own observations.

I

In 1825 Thomas Cole made his first trip up the Hudson River, a refugee from his studio in the narrow garret of his father's New York house. Cole painted during this period in a small and confining quarter on Greenwich Street, his "room so narrow as to afford him barely space enough, in his process of painting, to retreat the requisite distance from the canvass":

> To increase its inconvenience, it [Cole's studio] had only the half of a small window. Could the young artists of these better days look in upon that poorly lighted closet, they might possibly wonder how anything good could have been done in a situation so pinched and blinded. There it *was* done, nevertheless. There, perpetually fighting with a kind of twilight, and that too almost in fetters, elbowed and pushed by mean partitions, worked the young man of serious mind, and strong heart . . . .[4]

Cole's situation is no doubt mythologized in the passage; his nineteenth-century biographer, Louis Legrand Noble, appears to cast Cole as a spiritual Benjamin Franklin, working his way from rags to artistic riches in an exemplary fashion. Though the drama of the "strong heart" overcoming adversity is an appealing one, and perhaps even an accurate one, the deeper truth of the passage lies elsewhere, in the language and imagery with which Noble constructs Cole's state of mind. The sense of the passage is of a state of constriction: a "narrow" garret of claustrophobic dimensions that leaves the artist in a plight so "pinched and blinded" that he is "almost in fetters, elbowed and pushed by mean partitions." The physical condition of Cole's "poorly lighted closet" bespeaks a psychological state of severe claustrophobia. Noble himself grasps the implication of his description, commenting at a later point that it was the painter's mental state that distinguished his relation to the garret in his father's house:

> Unlike the impatient person in an old play, he was one that could sing with truth, as well as with a grace, "My mind to me a kingdom is:" and

so, in the narrowness of his father's garret, he had a wide patience, and a lofty spirit, and a luminous chamber in his soul.[5]

Noble counterpoints the "luminous chamber" of Cole's "soul" with the meaner "narrowness of his father's garret," setting spiritual response against physical environment in a triumph of mind over body. The complexity of the passage may be extended a step further, however, by reconceiving and redeploying the terms Noble gives us: father, claustrophobia, liberation. If, as Noble suggests, Cole triumphs over adverse conditions by the force of his imagination, then those conditions must themselves represent in metaphoric fashion deeper states of consciousness. It is not only poverty Cole struggles against, but the burden of a world associated with his father and conceived as dark and fettering. The liberation Cole seeks is an imaginative overthrow of his own claustrophobia, and he turns for release to a world unhampered by "partitions" or the narrowing conditions of "half of a small window."

Noble recounts two incidents from the fall of 1823, when Cole was still uncertain about his vocation as a painter, that highlight the underlying tension between Cole and his father over the issue of a career:

> With the return of autumn, ripened the resolution, expressed the year before in that parting conversation with his friend in Zanesville, to seek a more favourable field of action. In this *he was discouraged by his father*, who urged some substantial calling. His mother, though, who had taken the truer measure of her son's genius, entered, as she did at the outset, warmly into all his wishes, and incited him forward in the path of his choice. *From her sympathy and encouragement did he gather heart to face the disapproval of his father*, and strengthen himself in his determination.
>
> A mere trifle, often, lights up a person's circumstances and character, and instantly decides a question that affects his whole life. A singular illustration of this is the following incident. Cole was taking a solitary walk, *unusually agitated by a recent conversation with his father*: "Well," said he to himself aloud, at the same moment picking up a couple of good-sized pebbles, "I will put one of these upon the top of a stick; if I can throw, and knock if off with the other, I will be a painter; if I miss it, I will give up the thought forever." Stepping back some ten or twelve paces, he threw, and knocked it off. He turned, and went home immediately, and made known his unalterable resolution.[6]

In both situations, Cole's vocational conflict merges imperceptibly into an oedipally defined encounter between father and son. Cole's mother supports her son's desire to become an artist, and allies herself, according to Noble, with Cole in his opposition to the father. The anecdote of the two "good-sized pebbles," however mythic in nature (it probably represents what Freud would call a "screen memory," expressing in displaced fashion childhood emotions unperceived by the conscious mind), demonstrates a linkage in Cole's mind between an act of disruption (toppling a stone) and the "unalterable resolution" to become an artist against his father's will. To dislodge one stone with another is to act out in veiled terms that larger struggle between father and son at the heart of Cole's sublime. As we will later note, Cole reintroduces the memory of the mother in the maternal imagery of the beautiful, that state which issues from the sublime after the son's defeat of the father.

Cole ventured in 1825 under the sponsorship of an early patron, George Bruen, beyond the Palisades and the "Highlands" to the heart of the Catskills. There he sketched scenes of lakes, rivers, and cataracts that he translated upon returning to his New York studio into a series of oil paintings that brought him to the attention of the New York art world and launched him upon his career.[7] His early canvases demonstrate his desire to encompass broad masses of land within a single visual sweep. He returns repeatedly to spaces organized around a vertical axis, and painted a series of views of Kaaterskill Falls that attempt, with varying degrees of success, to capture the vertiginous quality experienced by the viewer at the prospect of descending rock ledges and falling waters. Even in his predominantly horizontal canvases (*Lake with Dead Trees, Catskill*, 1825 [fig. 48], and *The Woodchopper, Lake Featherstonhaugh*, 1826 [fig. 49]), Cole experiments with chiaroscuro and receding passages of water to create a sense of depth and perspective. The foreground inevitably includes a lanky vertical tree or stand of trunks that transforms an unbounded horizon into a framed visual unity, limited by the perspective implicit in the viewer's stance. Such framing brings the horizon under the artist's visual control, a first step toward the imaginative appropriation and reworking of a natural space.

When populating his scenes with pioneers or woodsmen, Cole frequently introduces the figure of a lone axman engaged in the felling of a tree. The motif, which will recur to the end of Cole's career, though often only as an abandoned ax wedged in the corner of a stump or log, translates Cole's own mastery over the landscape, altering and shaping it to the demands of the imagination, into substitute narrative terms. Both Barbara Novak and Nicholas Cikovsky, Jr., have noted the ambivalence attached to ax and stump imagery in nineteenth-century American painting.[8] The woodsman is an image of power, his mastery and view contingent upon an act of despoliation. As a surrogate for the artist, he expresses at what is presumably a preconscious level the painter's sense of struggle with nature for mastery. Though the woodsman's tools are physical rather than imaginative, they share with the artist's brush the

48. THOMAS COLE, *Lake with Dead Trees, Catskill,* 1825. Allen Memorial Art Museum, Oberlin College. Gift of Charles F. Olney (04.1183).

capacity to reverse the power of nature by the ingenuity of their handling. They are the first in a progression of visual motifs that will play an increasingly significant role in Cole's works as instruments of release and liberation. Whether the woodsman's ax, the Indian's staff, Daniel Boone's rifle, Saint John's cross, or the artist's brush, they constitute a series of implements—all linear in shape, wooden in nature, and small in relation to their world—designed to conquer the forces around them. In varying degrees, their power is associated with both vision (or conquest) and destruction, and to each is attached the irony that the derivatives of nature, the sticks and branches that turn into brushes and crosses, can subdue the mighty forests from which they originate.

Cole's efforts to break the monotony of the horizon line—to free himself from flat bands of land and sky mounted horizontally in a two-dimensional space—lead him in works like *Snow Squall, Winter Landscape*

49. THOMAS COLE, *The Woodchopper, Lake Featherstonhaugh,* 1826. University Galleries, University of Southern California, Los Angeles. The Elizabeth Holmes Fisher Collection.

in the Catskills (ca. 1825–26; fig. 50) toward a massing of ascending forms along a vertically defined axis. The desire for spatial depth, for a canvas that recedes at the same time as it rises, combines with an impulse toward vertiginous prospects to produce a structure that exhibits, despite the weakness of its handling, the major elements of the Colean sublime. A foreground promontory or cliff thrusts itself forward at a diagonal to the picture plane. Its stark and dramatic placement, following the canons of the Burkean sublime, exposes the spectator to the terrors of the scene before him while protecting him in its dark and sheltered spots from the dangers he views.[9] A valley of undefined depth separates the promontory from a larger peak at the center of the canvas. The vertical rock slabs of the latter continue and extend the line of ascent suggested by the foreground outcropping. In the upper right-hand quarter of the canvas a mass of black clouds blots out the view of heaven, while below them a white snow squall rages through the valley. Only in the distant background, on the other side of the center peak, can the viewer discern a serene stretch of calm and populated space.

The atmosphere of the painting is pervaded by a sense of loneliness and desolation, deriving in part from the contrast between the pastoral world in the distant left corner and the savage isolation of the foreground. The scene depends for its effect upon an unstated, but implicit, play of contraries: the nakedness and brutality of nature in the foreground contrasts with its apparent passivity in the left background; the foreground promontory is poised in dialectical tension with the jutting peak behind it, the former's rocky massiveness belied by the height and power of the latter; and the sense of ascent in both outcropping and mountain peak contrasts vividly with a vertiginal feeling of depth created by the abrupt drop of the valley and the dislocating walls of snow that defy the viewer's desire to measure and thereby define the space.

50. THOMAS COLE, *Snow Squall, Winter Landscape in the Catskills,* ca. 1825–26. Courtesy of the R. W. Norton Art Gallery, Shreveport, Louisiana.

The affective structure of the painting centers upon Cole's use of verticality. By drawing on the capacity of vertical spaces to create magnitudes at once ascending and descending, Cole can conflate the experience of elevation with the sensation of abyss, combining the two opposite states into a single highly charged and profoundly ambivalent moment of vertigo. The void of the valley is thus only an inversion of the heights by which it is defined. The experience of vertigo is summarized in the aggressive ascent of the outcropping, where the apparent solidity of the rock is counterpointed by its liability to collapse. The sense of vulnerability is emphasized by the shadows and chiaroscuro that permeate the promontory, and by the exposed and disfigured creature and trees upon it.

The viewer relates both physically and empathetically to the foreground plane, while finding in the valley a barrier of almost metaphysical proportions separating him from the centerground peak. The wolf and trees that accommodate him, however uncomfortably, to the promontory world, individuating it and rendering it on human scale, either disappear in the middleground space or reappear in the case of the background forests in such proportions that their scale seems threatening and annihilating. The central mountain remains, for all its power, an unhospitable and uninhabitable space; it cannot be humanized by individually known objects as in the foreground. By traversing the valley and encountering the change of scale it implies, the viewer undergoes a process of "defamiliarization." The veil of familiarity is lifted from the face of nature and an alien strangeness left in its stead. Just as dreams often translate temporal sequences into spatial relations, depicting for example a period of four years as a building of four stories, Cole renders in his sublime space a temporal process of estrangement through the spatial relations of two planes.[10] The time elapsed in the temporal movement from normalcy to estrangement, from the moment when the everyday erupts into the uncanny, is figured spatially in the presence of the valley, whose signification is that of an *interval* between two states in immediate relation. To move *visually* from one to another is to undergo *experientially* the moment of angst and unmasking when the individual finds himself alone and confronted with a world that is an estranged version of himself.

The significance of the dichotomy between foreground and middleground planes thus becomes clearer. The composition enacts visually an experience of estrangement as the isolated self slips from a state of normalcy to one of terror and self-regard. Cole has seized intuitively upon the conventions of the sublime (isolation, terror, and the safety of observation) and the attributes of verticality (elevation and abyss) to ratify an experience of discontinuity that arises from the breakdown of those systems undergirding the individual's everyday relation to the world. The dualism of the work, its division into parallel and problematically related planes, represents more than Allston's imaginative defense against the monism of the mind. It provides the viewer with a visual correlate to an affective state, an expression of an ambivalently charged experience in which the nakedness of the self (like the exposure of the outcropping) is an occasion both of assertion and negation. The Colean sublime commences with a program of defamiliarization. It begins with the collapse of the everyday ego in a moment of self-alienation,[11] and it proceeds to the goal of recovery, as we shall soon note, by reappropriating through an act of identification those forces that challenge it.

One model for this procedure, as Thomas Weiskel has pointed out, is the Oedipus complex, in which the autonomy of the psyche is tied to forces outside itself; these forces (usually the image of the parents) are subject not so much to defeat as introjection and identification.[12] The parental figure exists for the child as both an external reality and a parent-imago, an imagined figure neither wholly real nor yet wholly incorporated into the child's own mental operations as the beginnings of the superego. The child must resolve the conflict with this ambiguous authority by transforming the parental figure from an object-attachment, the end point of a libidinal desire, into an internalized source of authority. This process ushers in the latency period and diverts the intense erotic desires of the child away from the parent by a combination of sublimation and what Freud calls "desexualization." With the dissolution of the Oedipus complex, the libidinal and aggressive components of the object-attachment are freed for other purposes, among which is the growth of the superego.[13]

Freud's categories provide us with a language helpful in articulating the logic of Cole's painting. We need not accept Freud's terms literally in order to tap their suggestiveness as metaphors. In *Snow Squall, Winter Landscape in the Catskills*, Cole deploys the sublime in a manner that parallels the patterns of an oedipal encounter. *Snow Squall*'s dichotomous structure revolves around the juxtaposition of the foreground promontory with the visually superior middleground peak. The two are related—as the dynamics of an oedipal situation would suggest—by counterpoint and identification. The squat and almost step-like ascent of the outcropping culminates visually in the crown of the central peak, while the pointed tip of a foreground tree penetrates the sloping left bank of the centerground mountain. The mountain thus appears as a paternal continuation and fulfillment of the vertical aspirations of the foreground promontory. The painting differs, however, from a Freudian text in its inability to transform its object attachment into an act of identification. Cole's topography, unlike Freud's, commences from the estrangement that distinguishes foreground from middleground. The larger mountain offers at once a visual extension of the foreground plane and, through its transformation of size and scale, a distortion and alienation of the foreground space. The central mountain provides a model for authority external to the self; yet when joined to the self in a Hogarthian 'S-curve' of beauty—the pattern behind the spiral of promontory and mountain—it produces an image of autonomy alien to the foreground viewer.

The central peak, then, operates like an over-invested symbol; it exists as the repository for a series of contradictory operations. In its positive modes, it is aspired to as an extension of the foreground self, an image of both rivalry and attempted identification. In its negative valuations, it transforms the indefinite threat of the valley into the concrete symbol of a crushing height, an embodiment of that ambivalent power attached psychologically to the parent figure and visually to all verticality. It mocks the self with a counter-image at once distant and familiar, and defies the identification its mysterious presence seems to offer.

The question of visual sources in relation to the oedipal understructure of Cole's sublime works is a perplexing one. The general range of images available to Cole in the years leading up to his sublime period is known. What is less certain are the specific sources Cole might have seen in developing the characteristically Freudian structure of his landscapes. The work of John Martin, which Cole knew from reproductions, was not readily available in the United States until 1826 at the earliest, and more likely 1827. Martin's painting *Joshua Commanding the Sun to Stand Still* (1816) was engraved and published on 9 May 1827 (fig. 51). Were it not for the problem of chronology, the reproduction could well have provided Cole the model he sought. Joshua stands on a small foreground elevation and gestures toward the sun, hidden in the right background by a large centerground promontory. The tension between foreground figures and centerground peak parallels almost exactly Cole's own sublime formula, but the date of the Martin engraving suggests that Cole saw it only after his own sublime topography was largely developed. There is little doubt, however, that the Martin reproduction served as the source for Cole's *Moses on the Mount* (fig. 52), one of the least typical and most clearly derivative of Cole's early sublime landscapes. In Martin's engravings for Milton's *Paradise Lost,* we again find landscapes suggestive in their composition of Cole's own methods. Especially the illustrations for book 1, line 314, and book 11, line 226, remind one through their counterpointing of figures and precipices of Cole's similar arrangement of space. But again, Martin's illustrations were not available until 1827, and

51. JOHN MARTIN, *Joshua Commanding the Sun to Stand Still*, 1827 (mezzotint). Yale Center for British Art, Paul Mellon Collection.

could have done no more than confirm Cole in a landscape vocabulary already his own.

Cole is known to have seen reproductions of the work of Salvator Rosa as early as 1820, when he studied an English book on the art of painting in the possession of an itinerant painter named Stein. He again encountered Salvator's works while a student at the Pennsylvania Academy of Fine Arts in the early 1820s. As Esther Seaver has suggested, Cole learned from Salvator how to transform his paintings into "turbulent and storm riven landscapes."[14] Whether he also found in Salvator the terms for an oedipally conceived nature is less certain. In his various landscapes of *banditti* and the *Landscape with a Lake, Mountains and Five Soldiers in the Foreground* (fig. 53), Salvator places his foreground figures at ground level relative to a centerground mountain or abutting peak. Though the relation between foreground and middleground planes lacks the compelling and intense drama of Cole's canvases, the terms are at least present in certain of Salvator's works for a landscape shaped to the contours of oedipal struggle. Without further and more exact knowledge of Cole's sources (and for that matter the precise dates of his early paintings), we can only speculate where Cole's sources end and his genius begins. My

52. THOMAS COLE, *Moses on the Mount,* 1828. Courtesy, Shelburne Museum, Shelburne, Vermont.

own guess is that he moves instinctively toward a massing of forms along oedipal lines, borrowing and rearranging from images linked loosely together in his mind by their sublime possibilities.

By establishing the sublime along the contours of an oedipal struggle, Cole has created a visual arena in which to work out the project of artistic selfhood.[15] Cole's crisis of vocation and self-definition in his early adult years appears to reinvoke the patterns of a similar but earlier struggle for identity dating back to infancy. The energy of that past conflict, together with the terms of its resolution, attaches itself to the present struggle, acting not only as the suppressed but animating force behind the conflict, but as the hidden agenda that the current crisis must resolve. The painting, however, is not simply *about* the oedipal conflict, nor is it a disguised but direct translation of childhood emotions onto the artist's canvas. Instead, the strategies adopted by the child in the process of ego formation reappear in transformed but still recognizable versions in the efforts of

53. SALVATOR ROSA, *Landscape with a Lake, Mountains and Five Soldiers in the Foreground.* John and Mable Ringling Museum of Art, Sarasota, Florida.

the adult to establish his own vocational identity. Cole appropriates the language of the sublime according to the terms of an older and more infantile history of conflict and resolution, and proceeds through the course of his painting to rewrite that history in a modern natural idiom.

To trace the oedipal underpinnings of Cole's sublime canvases, therefore, is to pursue psychoanalysis as a system of tropes leading to larger cultural generalizations. Our concern lies not so much within the province of Cole's private life as with those larger patterns and mental operations that together constitute a recognizable moment in the history of the sublime—a moment known to us today as Romantic. Psychoanalysis enables us to map an American version of the Romantic sublime, taking as our starting point the strategies of Cole's text (rather than his person), and unraveling from the dense tissue of intention and disguise that one finds there the history of artistic consciousness in its efforts at realization.

In dallying with psychoanalysis and the process of ego formation, we need not reduce the sublime to an adventure in ego psychology, whether the latter is defined along Freudian lines as "the analysis of resistances and the strengthening of the subject's ego," or understood simply as a successive series of life crises. We are warned against the perils of ego psychology by the French psychoanalyst Jacques Lacan.[16] Lacan revises the traditional Freudian typology of childhood evolution through his introduction of the "mirror state," an encounter of the child with his mirror image that results in a fictional—and alienating—self-projection that forms the basis for all future identifications. According to Lacan, the infant exists in a world radically different from that of the adult: its experiences have not yet been organized into a consciousness centered around the self and differentiated from the world surrounding it. Instead the child of six to eighteen months passes through a phase of "transitivism" in which the body parts of other human beings (or creatures) are perceived as if they were his own. It is from within this precentered and preindividuated state that the individual first encounters his image in a mirror, and projects upon the bodily wholeness perceived there a completion and autonomy the child lacks in his own life. The specular image endows the child with a sense of motor control and bodily permanence that on the one hand establishes the groundwork for all future acts of identification while at the same time alienating the child from the deeper flux and ambiguity of his affective life:

> The *mirror-phase* is a drama whose internal impulse rushes from insufficiency to anticipation and which manufactures for the subject, captive to the lure of spatial identification, the succession of phantasies from a fragmented body-image to a form of its totality which we shall call orthopaedic—and to the assumption, finally, of the armour of alienating identity, which will stamp with the rigidity of its structure the whole of the subject's mental development.[17]

Though Lacan considers the mirror phase as an act of "identification, in the full sense which analysis gives to the term: namely, the transformation which takes place in the subject when he assumes an image," it is not to be understood as the first of many identifications that mark the history of the subject's ego. Rather, the mirror phase establishes that *Ur*-identification which consolidates the self into an agency capable of all future acts of identification. The child recognizes through the mirror phase "a form of himself projected in space, and in that form discovers himself."[18] The essence of the mirror phase is the creation of an *imago* that idealizes the "still very deep motor incoordination" into an "ideal unity," precipitating the "I" or ego in "primordial form."

> But the important point is that this form situates the instance of the *ego*, before its social determination, in a fictional direction, which will always remain irreducible for the individual alone, or rather, which will only rejoin the development of the subject asymptotically, whatever the success of the dialectical synthesis by which he must resolve as *I* his discordance with his own reality.[19]

The ego is born of the drive toward permanence and stasis, an idealizing and alienating imago precipitated in the gap of motor insufficiency and destined to bridge a distance it is always insufficient to fill. Hence in Lacan the tragic and unavoidable motion of the subject in an effort of self-repair. Prior even to the crisis of the oedipal years and what Lacan, following Heidegger, will call the "insertion of the subject into History," the individual stands estranged from himself in a rupture of inner being from self-image.

Lacan's language is peculiarly adapted to the purposes of art history. The locus of experience in the period of the mirror phase is the "Imaginary," a term denoting the influence of the imago in the construction of reality. Lacan's "Imaginary Order" is not to be confused with more traditional conventions for speaking of the imagination. The "Imaginary" for Lacan is a specifically delimited term contrasting with the Symbolic, the realm of language operations, and is defined through its uniquely "spatial and visual connotations" as "a kind of pre-verbal register whose logic is essentially visual."[20] Inaugurated by the mirror stage and the visual transitivism it entails, the Imaginary is characterized above all by the absence of any mediation—or the perception of any mediation—between self and other. The perceptual field is experienced and appropriated as indifferently one with the self, though the appearance of feelings of ambivalence in the early months of infancy releases into this preegoistic world a surcharge of aggressiveness that will figure prominently in the oedipal years.

The category of the Imaginary provides a tantalizing clue for understanding the operations of the sublime. We may return to Cole's *Snow Squall* to find in it not only the energy of an earlier oedipal crisis, but the very origins of identity formation in a process of self-alienation that resembles Lacan's account of the mirror phase. The elements are all there: a foreground image that we may read as a representation and visualization of an affective-psychological state; a sense of self characterized by a jumble of part-objects (trees, wolf, rocks) to which is attached the subject's narcissistic love; a drive toward an idealized image (the centerground peak) distinguished by its permanence and solidity and understood as a spatialization of the self into an autonomous structure; and a gap, a *béance*, built structurally into the very terms of the relationship between actual self and desired imago and expressed visually through a dialectic of alienation and self-estrangement.

II

We can best understand the significance of mirror-phase elements in

Snow Squall by placing it within a series of early sublime paintings that together provide a perspective on the changing mental topography of Cole's work. In *Snow Squall* the predominating visual energy is assertive. The forward-thrusting promontory advances aggressively to meet the idealized projection of the central peak, while the negative and threatening forces of the painting—the raging walls of snow and vertical drop of the valley—coexist with the central mountain without being directly identified with it. In later canvases the explosive potential of the *valley* is attached directly to the dominating *mountain*, whose features become increasingly generalized into large and undifferentiated masses of dark space. Accompanying this demonization of the central peak is a reversal of the earlier values associated with it. Its position as a projected imago is subverted by the growing threat it poses to the safety of the foreground world, its capacity to crush now overshadowing the vertical uplift it offers. In its most stylized and condensed form, the center-ground peak ceases altogether to function as an aspired-to object and is transfigured instead into a *blocking agent* that intervenes between the foreground promontory and distant pastoral landscape, preventing the issuance of the former into the latter. Psychologically we may describe this transformation in Cole's sublime canvases as a move from works organized around narcissistic energies (images of the child's love for itself) to canvases more object-oriented (attachment to objects understood as other than the self). This latter pattern revolves around the Oedipus complex and a shift of erotic energy away from the figure of the father to that of the mother. Despite the maternal promises of the distant meadowlands, the deepest affective moments within Cole's sublime works remain centered around the male-male conflict of the central space.

Two canvases illustrate the point. Painted within a period of two years subsequent to *Snow Squall*, *Winter Landscape in the Catskills*, they demonstrate a maturity of style and facility in handling lacking in the earlier work. Though there is no historical evidence to link the two as either pendant pieces or even repeated versions of the same scene, they possess a striking visual relation that suggests their common psychological (and aesthetic) underpinnings. The viewer may grasp their significance by measuring the extent of their differences. In the earlier of the two works, *Sunrise in the Catskills* (1826), Cole achieves as naturalistic an expression of the sublime as his own skills or the genre will permit him. As Barbara Novak has noted, Cole's career was torn between the "polarity of the real and the ideal":

> Cole, the dreamer, the arch-romantic who preferred to paint Arcadian compositions—waiting for "time to draw a veil over the common details, the unessential parts, which shall leave the great features,

whether the beautiful or the sublime, dominant in the mind"—found himself an idealist in a world that demanded a more discreet blend of the real with the ideal.[21]

The impulse in Cole toward the "real" is genuine and not simply or even largely the result of cultural pressures external to his own predilections. It expresses an imperative to naturalize the processes of revelation and authority previously reserved for either the Church or society. Like Emerson, with whom he shares an attitude of profound ambivalence toward received modes of authority, Cole sought in nature a metaphor for the self unburdened of history. History was the province of the Old World, of human nature shackled to social definitions, and the battle to free the self from the debts of history was waged on the fields and vistas of unstoried nature. As Cole wrote of the American landscape:

> All nature is new to art, no Tivolis, Ternis, Mont Blancs, Plinlimmons, hackneyed and worn by the daily pencils of hundreds; but primeval forests, virgin lakes and waterfalls.[22]

The attempt to create a self prior to all socialization was, at its profoundest, an effort to relocate the sources of authority from outside the self to within. It was, as Weiskel points out, "a massive transposition of transcendence into a naturalistic key," wresting from the gods the power they so jealously guarded and transferring it instead to a new mode of discourse revolving around the individual and expressed somewhat disingenuously through a dialectic of self and other. The "other" as a rule meant "nature," a metaphorical substitution for the self's own powers, a presence whose occasional distance or difference from the self expressed the failure of that self to recognize or appropriate its own possibilities.

The impulse to naturalization thus represented the defeat of an older mode of historical discourse. Naturalization heralded the triumph of a Romantic counter-Enlightenment against the more social modes of secularization associated with the eighteenth century. It substituted on a linguistic level a grammar of the self for a grammar of society. In the hands of first-generation Romantics like Wordsworth or Coleridge in England, Friedrich and Schleiermacher in Germany, and Emerson and Cole in America, the process of naturalization pursued two routes simultaneously. On the one hand it advanced and validated a world "involuntarily secular" where the limits of knowledge were confined to the sensory apparatus of a sentient observer, while on the other hand it preserved for that world the possibility of transcendence by harboring within itself a promise of theophany. If man were confined by the limits of the natural, bound by an empirical philosophy that it was his fate both to inherit and revise, then his historical destiny seemed to lie in rupturing and then rewriting the boundaries of the real, admitting the transcendent, in effect, through the back door. Romantic naturalism turned on a concerted effort to wed God to the world of appearances:

> If the only route to the intellect lies through the senses, belief in a supernatural Being finds itself insecure. God had to be saved, even if He had to marry the world of appearances. And so, in the natural sublime, He did. The first development, in the seventeenth century, was the identification of the Deity's traditional attributes,—infinity, immensity, coexistence—with the vastness of space newly discovered by an emergent astronomy. The emotions traditionally religious were displaced from the Deity and became associated first with the immensity of space and secondarily with the natural phenomena (oceans, mountains) which seemed to approach that immensity. Soon a sense of the numinous was diffused through all the grander aspects of nature. The mental result was enormously to enhance the prestige of the sensible imagination as the faculty which mediated the divine presence felt to be immanent in nature, or at least likely to be evoked by nature's grander aspect. Indeed, the imagination became the surest guide and recourse for the moral sense.[23]

In Schleiermacher, as in all idealisms sprung like Athena from the troubled brow of Kantian thought, the numinous was imported into the natural in a moment of precognitive ecstasy. The individual experienced a moment of *ek-stasis* or standing outside himself during which a transcendent oneness erupted through the sequence of normal cognitive operations. This breach of epistemological etiquette was later repaired by the Understanding, which resumed its epistemic functions by sorting reality into the categories of subject and object. For Cole the creation of a naturalism fraught with the energies of the transcendent was mediated less by Kant and the tradition of German idealism than by the history of British empiricism and its recent love for Longinus and the *Peri Hypsous*:

> Longinus had made Nature the demiurge responsible not only for man's physical being but also for that which "transcends the human"—thought, imagination, speech (*logos*). This emphasis was congenial to the English mind, for it seemed to authorize an alternative to the more reductive and empirical conception of the natural which was gaining ground. It was a way of having it both ways, a transcendence without any controversial theology, a natural religion.[24]

The sublime developed within the empirical tradition as a special case of Romantic naturalism. It authorized an account of the natural that spared the secular mind the embarrassments of an overt supernaturalism while still allowing for the power and mystery that conventional empiricisms lacked. The sublime defended naturalism from its own limit and endpoint in the literal. It thrived along those fault lines and fissures of eighteenth-century thought where new modes of affective and intellectual experience challenged the reductive tendencies of classical empiricism with the threat of collapse. The sublime tended to exaggerate the terms of empirical discourse to such an extent that their very distortion forced a rupture in the older system and provided, through its breakdown, new forms of expression empowered by the dissolution of the old. Like the gothic novel, whose emergence and history in the eighteenth century it closely parallels, the sublime remains a vocabulary with one leg rooted firmly in the past. It represents an attempt to resolve and replace an older idiom by transforming its discontinuities into an explosive and surcharged version of itself, a naturalism subversive of its own limits.

"We cannot," remarks Weiskel, "conceive of a literal sublime," and we perceive in Cole a naturalism equipped with its own metaphoric brake, a counter-empiricism wary of the real while committed to the great program of secularization. The tension in the sublime between the real and the ideal can be understood as the attempt by the Romantic imagination to rescue reality from the burden of normalcy and the fate of the "literal." Like Schleiermacher's nontemporal theophany or Emerson's "transparent Eyeball," the irruption of the numinous into the sphere of the natural is the formula by which a generation of post-Enlightenment thinkers and artists made their peace with the Understanding and the constraints upon knowledge that it entailed. The commitment in Cole to the real, and in particular to the natural landscape, represents more than an effort at recovering for the isolated self the pristine energies of a presocial world. It is an attempt to disengage that self from the yoke of all authorities that challenge the autonomy of the individual. The task of the sublime, like that of the oedipal encounter, is to reconceive the self from the vantage of autonomy, and the language of nature, when shaped to the stylized dimensions of the sublime, provides the means by which Cole achieves what Emerson would soon describe as an "original relationship with the universe."

We have been using the term "naturalization" to this point at a generalized level to suggest that particular form of secularization associated with the return to nature and the end of historical and social modes of discourse. The advent of "Romantic naturalism" in the closing decades of the eighteenth century adds a unique twist to this process of naturalization: it remystifies the natural world by restoring to it the "thunders of the deep,"[25] a demonization of reality that guarantees the transcendent a place within the secular. The process is not unlike the efforts of Claude Lorrain in the opening decades of the seventeenth century to preserve a role for the numinous within the desacralized world of Renaissance history. Claude's quiescent and time-wearied canvases suggest in their incantatory moments of stasis a world beyond the reach of secular history, a world defined as an imaginative hiatus from the business of everyday life. Claude creates worlds presided over by the artist, whose visual magic must serve as a surrogate for powers once reserved for a priesthood. Claude stands as a prototype of the modern artist who fashions for himself priestly functions in a secular world, reversing by an effort of imagination the stampede of history toward its own naturalization. In Cole this defense against naturalization proceeds a step further. Romantic naturalism operates as a reaction formation to the forces of secularization of which it is a part; it resists the secular on its march toward the literal. It also characterizes that sequence of movements at the heart of the sublime which results in an influx of energy.

III

Let us return to *Sunrise in the Catskills* (fig. 54) in its relation to a work of the following year, *Sunny Morning on the Hudson* (1827). Both paintings present a prospect view of a centerground mountain.[26] *Sunrise in the Catskills* positions the viewer on a flattened ledge flanked by a large trapezoidal outcropping that blocks the viewer's visual access to the left and directs the eye instead to the open vistas of the center and right. The angled remains of a smallish foreground tree, withered and uprooted, span the space between ledge and valley and point the viewer toward the vapor trails that arc around the right foot of the mountain and disappear in the brown and tan mists of the background. In the center of the foreground ledge, surrounded by vegetable forms, fallen trees, and massive rocks, sits a boulder-like fragment relatively small in size, blockish in stature, and crowned by a protuberance of vegetation and a solitary stone. Situated between the trapezoidal outcropping and the withered tree, this boulder defines the geometric midpoint of the canvas along its horizontal axis. Visually its position is more problematic. On the one hand it seems to sit at the bottom of a series of vertical slopes: at the top, directly above it, stands the summit of the central peak, while in the middle a smaller hillock repeats the curve of the peak and reinforces the rhythm of undulating surfaces rising above the central boulder. The outline of a distant peak to the left of the central mountain extends the movement into the distant space. The result is the creation of a wave pattern of alternating rhythms, now ascending, now descending, that binds the foreground boulder to the forms above it and allows the observer either to ascend with the rising forms or feel inundated by their concentrically massed

54. THOMAS COLE, *Sunrise in the Catskills*, 1826. Private collection, New York.

weight. This tension along an essentially vertical axis is balanced on the other hand by the diagonal line of mist and vapor that extends the zone of high-intensity light from the foreground boulder and tree to the right-hand corner of the canvas before angling once more to the upper right center of the painting and into the background.

The foreground boulder thus launches the viewer along two different directions, the first a vertical movement of circular forms confined to the lower center and left of the canvas and the second a more narrow movement of light along a diagonal to the right, which eventually links the viewer with the mist-filled space above the centerground mountain. The same pattern may be observed in the organization of *Sunny Morning on the Hudson* (fig. 55). Though Cole has dispensed with the rocky outcropping on the left, he has retained the sense of visual inhibition that it creates by dramatically extending the centerground mountain into a wall of black space filling the upper three-quarters of the left border. The more naturalistic vegetation of *Sunrise in the Catskills* has been stylized into the frozen and distended forms on the left, while the smaller boulder defining the viewpoint of *Sunrise* has been transformed into a prominent altar-like

55. THOMAS COLE, *Sunny Morning on the Hudson,* 1827. Courtesy, Museum of Fine Arts, Boston, M. and M. Karolik Collection.

shape dominating the foreground space and juxtaposed in bold chiaroscuro against the dark centerground peak. *Sunny Morning* gives evidence of being a radically condensed and compacted version of the forces that went into the making of *Sunrise.* It dispenses altogether with the latter's progression of valley, hillock, and mountain in a realistically intelligible space, and instead collapses foreground and centerground into two flattened and juxtaposed planes whose relation is stylized and visual rather than natural or serial. Though bordered by an adjoining hill on its right-hand slope, the centerground mountain defines the middle third of the canvas as a single mass of black and undifferentiated pigment, crested at the top by a tuft of white cloud. The valley at its feet baffles the viewer's expectations for an intelligible space, retaining its trails of vapor and mist only as visual signs to indicate depth and direction. The mimetic impulse of *Sunrise in the Catskills* has been superceded by a deeper urge toward allegory and the marshaling of space in a stylized manner.

What remains constant between the two paintings is their underlining organization. The same spatial armature holds each work together. The starkly outlined altar-shaped form of *Sunny Morning,* like the less obtrusive boulder of *Sunrise,* defines a foreground point of observation situated at the fulcrum of two opposing and asymmetrically balanced directions. The play of altar and mountain pulls the eye up and to the left, while the path of mist draws the viewer through the valley to the right and on to the pale blue peace of the river world beyond. The two pictures, like *Snow Squall* before them, develop through the tripartite movement of the viewer from foreground to centerground planes and thence to a background occupying the upper portions of the canvas. The differences among the paintings—modulations in style, proportion, and visual or tonal emphasis—are all variations upon a common visual structure and form in sequence a paradigmatic narrative of the Colean sublime.[27]

The story reads thus: the enjambment upon which *Snow Squall* is predicated—the extension of a single line of thought into two separate planes such that the completion of the painter's identity requires the movement of the eye over the gap separating foreground from centerground—this visual enjambment locates the originating energies of *Snow Squall* at a preoedipal moment when the mirror stage crosses over into the oedipal crisis. The painting is largely narcissistic in its attempts to achieve an idealized imago for itself, though its efforts at self-definition contain implicitly the terms out of which oedipal struggle will transpire. In subsequent works like *Sunrise in the Catskills,* the narcissistic assertion of the foreground promontory in its extension into the middleground peak is muted into a more clearly oedipal rivalry between foreground and middleground planes. The central mountain no longer exists as an enjambed extension of the self, unifying and alienating at the same time, but appears in its separation and contrast from the foreground ledge as a distinctly different body, distinguished tonally and coloristically from the mottled gray and white of the foreground boulder. The narcissism of the earlier painting has been replaced by an erotic object attachment, an attempt at both identification and rivalry along oedipal lines.

What distinguishes *Sunrise in the Catskills* as a later painting is the more ambivalent state of early oedipal desires that it represents. The assertive aggression of *Snow Squall* has disappeared, and in its place a *small* boulder situated at a lower point on the canvas suggests an emerging sense of impotence and inferiority, a visual parallel to the helplessness of the child in face of the incalculable superiority of the parent. Note everywhere the signs of secondariness cluttering the painting as an obsessive and recurrent motif: the central boulder that appears small and diminished in comparison to the larger outcropping to the left; the relation of both these rock formations and the ledge upon which they sit to the dominating mountain beyond them; the framing of the central mountain with a smaller hillock at its feet; the tufts of greenery that crown the tops of the gnarled trees to the left, instances of secondary growth upon the death-like trunks that support them; the strands of vegetation that grow as if by miracle along the crevices and tops of the larger rocks upholding them; and the placement of a small rock, isolated and exposed, upon the foreground boulder, a compact summary of the sense of secondariness underlying the painting and a motif that Cole will repeat frequently in the future, most famously in *The Course of Empire* series. Each of these instances expresses a fear of failure and hopelessness, a sense of the fated defeat to which the oedipal aspirant is doomed in his inability to measure up to the stature and power of the parent figure.

The conflict is exaggerated and further emphasized by a revision of the ratio of centerground to foreground space. The foreground promontory is reduced in size and centered at a lower point on the canvas relative to the earlier *Snow Squall*, while the area occupied by the central mountain is expanded laterally, darkened in tone and contrasted more prominently with the lighter boulder. Hogarth's 'S-curve' of beauty, which previously linked promontory and peak in a single visual sweep, narcissistic and alluring in *Snow Squall*, has been replaced in *Sunrise* by an open expanse of dark and threatening space defined more by its difference from the foreground ledge than its identity with it.[28] Not only is the central mountain defined now as the Other rather than a mirror-phase extension of the self, but its relation to the foreground ledge is only one of two possible modes of movement within the painting. These alternative visual itineraries coexist simultaneously. They each originate from the foreground boulder. The second route, however, carries the viewer around the foot of the mountain to the inchoate forms of the upper background. The relation of boulder to mountain has in effect been challenged by an alternative relation of boulder to background, and though the nature of the latter remains undefined in the painting, its presence suggests a deep structural transformation in the painting's energies and their deployment.

Only with *Sunny Morning on the Hudson* do we find the issues finally clarified. In a remarkably intense economy of expression, Cole simplifies and reduces his drama to its barest terms. The relation of foreground to centerground and background planes is consolidated into a single though complex visual narrative that begins with the foreground altarpiece, concludes with the prospect of the distant valley, and confronts the center mountain as a blocking agent en route to the background vista. The energies of the earlier works have been reversed. Where *Snow Squall* directed the observer to the peak immediately behind it, and *Sunrise* divided its attention between the central mountain and an alternative swerve into the unknown space to the right, *Sunny Morning on the Hudson* places the viewer in direct visual relation with the background landscape. Cole moves the central peak to the left, expands the open space of the background, and reconceives the central mountain as an interfering presence mediating between foreground and background planes. The painting attempts to navigate from the natural stone altarpiece to the background meadows as quickly and effortlessly as possible, and encounters the dark and ominous visage of the central peak as a diversion and barrier to its appointed end.

The significance of this realignment of visual energies lies in the corresponding shift in oedipal object choices it implies. The male-male bonding that characterizes the struggle of foreground and middleground planes in both *Snow Squall* and *Sunrise*—the former narcissistic and potentially autoerotic, the latter the homosexual love of the child for the father[29]—this liason of like forces undergoes a profound transformation in *Sunny Morning* and reaches for the first time beyond the figure of the father toward more maternally defined imagery. The background of the painting consists of a serene and reposeful space characterized by a lack of aggression and conflict. When expressed in the context of the oedipal energies underlying it, the imagery suggests that the child's love for the father has been overcome and reversed by his greater desire for the mother. The central mountain's interference with the visual sweep backward reveals that the father has been transformed from an object of attraction to one of rivalry and reproof, an impediment to the child's deepest heterosexual fantasies.

The problem with this account is that it is partial and potentially misleading, for it fails to understand the nature of the turn to the mother. Freud assumed that all human beings are bisexual by nature, developing in the genital and postgenital years in the direction of the opposite or same sex according to the relative intensity of their differing sexual and cultural circumstances. The choice of object depends primarily on the history of the subject's psychic development.[30] Freud identified what he considered to be active and passive components in the child's relation to both his father and his mother during the oedipal years. He assumed that women, like men, develop from earliest infancy an attachment with the mother that the male in the normal course of development learns by a complex series of psychological operations to transfer to other women as the basis for his later heterosexual love. For women the transition to a heterosexual love object is more complicated, for it involves a complex realignment or withdrawal of the daughter's affection from the mother and a corresponding redirecting of her love toward the father.[31] What distinguishes the psychic energy undergirding Cole's sublime landscapes is its parallel to the oedipal processes of a woman rather than a man. It begins with a homosexual bond that undergoes in the course of its development an apparent reversal that seems to lie at the heart of its successful resolution. Even in *Sunny Morning on the Hudson*, in which we appear to have a more classical statement of oedipal rivalries in the child's competition with the father for the love of the mother, the primary energy of the painting, like that in *Snow Squall* and *Sunrise*, remains centered in the foreground relation of altar to mountain. The painting tells us more in its stark chiaroscuro about the affective engagement of father and son than it does about the desire for maternal love, a concern relegated literally to the background.[32]

IV

We have noticed from the beginning a sense of alienation attached to the mirror-phase identification in *Snow Squall*.[33] The oedipal conflict, we may theorize, inherits from the earlier mirror phase the terms of all future acts of identification, acts that are destined to repeat the sense of ambivalence and self-estrangement associated with that primal narcissistic identification. The oedipal conflict also inherits from that earlier stage a tendency to fictionalize in the face of its own frustrations. The illusion to which the subject falls prey in the mirror phase may be described negatively as an unavoidable act of self-deception, but in its positive effects, it represents a capacity for fiction-making as a means of resolving psychic trauma that (1) lays the groundwork for all future acts of sublimation and displacement, and (2) fixes the subject upon linguistic modes of substitution—symbolic exchanges—as a response to the resistances it encounters. Our interest here, to rephrase the point, lies not only in the self-alienation that is an inherent part of Lacan's world, but in the predisposition to *fictionalize* that underlies the activities of the mirror phase and makes possible its enjambed identifications. It is this predisposition that the mirror state actualizes and builds into the fabric of all future operations.[34]

We witness in Cole's paintings not only a program of identity formation, but a bias to resolve the dilemmas of identity formation through a series of operations that are *fictional* in nature and *linguistic* in their tendencies. In *Sunrise in the Catskills* the narcissistic anxiety of *Snow Storm* has been transformed into a fear of the Other expressed rather dramatically in a dread of annihilation and more poignantly through the theme of secondariness. The alternative visual pathway that the painting allows us around the foot of the mountain provides the key to the dilemma of secondariness and an answer to the forbidden love masked in the fear of annihilation. (Freud notes that all fears express repressed desires.) Whether the love object be narcissistic and autoerotic as suggested by *Snow Squall* or more specifically homosexual as one would expect from the negative Oedipus complex, the hidden agenda of the painting lies in forging an alternative psychic economy that allows an outlet for the repressed love while disguising its actions so as to ward off the threat of reprisal. *The vapor trail of the valley is Cole's answer*. It is a remarkable and exact transcription of a psychic need into spatial terms. Commencing visually from the foreground boulder and the world of secondariness that it represents, the trail of vapor skirts the base of the threatening power—literally circumventing it—and leads by a process of indirection, again literalized in its circuitous route, to a world of mist and light in the background. We are not to understand the background haze as an actual alternative to the forces of the foreground, as if the forbidden love object had suddenly been renounced, but rather as a *sublimation* and disguise of the earlier object. For that is the significance of the mist that forges a trial along the valley floor before leading us to the upper background. It is a pun, a verbal and visual emblem of the transformation and sublimation of matter from one state to another. Cole's mist reminds us that we are dealing with a process of conversion in which all acts of substitution are metaphoric exchanges of objects into their analogues and surrogates.

The painting turns on a pun. It is a study in *sublim*ation in the rudimentary sense that links the sublime to an influx of power achieved through the liberation and appropriation of forbidden and illicit forces. The devious trail of mist enroute to a world of light and energy marks the creation of an imaginative pathway around that which is taboo. It achieves by indirection what is unavailable by direct frontal assault. Cole's mist represents the capacity of symbolic operations (displacement and substitution) to convert the forbidden object into disguised but acceptable—and accessible—form. The mist is an emblem of that conversion. It inscribes into the painting a reminder of the secret that is the key to the painting's success. Like a dream image, its minor and apparently peripheral role within the painting, together with our ability to account for it naturalistically, are all foils and disguises by which it masks its central importance as the summation of a series of symbolic operations that are the true heart of the painting's meaning.

These symbolic procedures are important not only for the specific answer they provide to Cole's oedipal concerns, but for the underlying reliance on language patterns that they reveal. Dating back to the mirror stage and the precipitation of the ego in an act of fiction-making, the faculty of language provides the subject with a complicated set of linguistic rules which operate in a manner resembling Kant's *a priori* forms: they determine the very pathways along which mental energy can travel prior to any specific act of language. Beyond the threat of punishment or fear of castration in *Sunrise in the Catskills*, we sense the extraordinary excitement and exhilaration that accompanies Cole's own discovery of the power and significance of creation, the latter defined as the capacity of the mind to generate a grammar. *Sunrise in the Catskills* records Cole's first encounter with language as the power of the subject to subvert and conquer the real: the capacity to appropriate not only a particular discourse available within a culture at a given point (as the language of the sublime was for Cole), but the deeper mastery and invention of the very rules of rhetoric itself. The painting records the power of metaphor to convert forbidden fruit into noontime fare. Creation marks for Cole the individual's assumption into language, portrayed psychologically in terms of fear and trembling and structurally as a covert bid for autonomy against the power and rules of the Other.

We can understand now the appropriateness of those earlier images of the woodsman inscribing with his ax his presence into the landscape, or in the language of the sublime, the persistence of valley routes at the foot of mountain-obstructions. The imagery of the former (woodsmen) shares with the latter (valley routes) a sense of incision and the creation of pathways from recalcitrant matter, whether by the hands of man or the powers of nature. Together these trains of imagery present the rules of symbolic operation, the pathways of language, as they are carved into the fabric and body of the real. Cole's axmen and trailblazers, cutting in nature a history of their own movements, literalize through their actions the efforts of the artist to generate a grammar through the tangles of reality. By what we may term an "inscriptive necessity," each incises into the wilderness traces of his own existence, and claims in the process to possess the world that now bears his name.

What distinguishes Cole's language system and points it firmly in the direction of the *modern* is its grounding, as with almost all modern literary texts, in a strategy of indirection. Except for chronology, it would be tempting to say that Cole takes his cue from Melville rather than Emerson, or, to internationalize the analogy, that he assumes in his work what his contemporary, Søren Kierkegaard, was pioneering in his writing. Both Melville and Kierkegaard sought an order of symbolic discourse that, unlike Emerson's, did not measure its fragmentation and deviation against a nostalgically recollected wholeness, but took instead as its standard its right to indirection and disguise. The economic principles of Cole's language system are based, as are those of Freud, on Occam's razor and the expending of minimum amounts of energy to achieve any given end, but the linguistic principles, on the contrary, require subterfuge and delay. To gain in Emersonian fashion a direct alignment of things and thoughts, objects and eyes, so as to produce an exact analogy between language, nature, and the divine mind, would defeat Cole at the very game he must play in order to reverse a deck stacked ontologically against him. The world of the ego, and of the liberal tradition that has historically espoused it, might deploy its forces in metaphors of rectitude, straightness, and an analogical world view grounded in symmetry and congruence, but the linguistic realm of the modern—the region in which Cole plays—has staked its boundaries around the margins and peripheries of consciousness. The reasons for this transformation are complex and may be explained in part by a sense of "belatedness" owing to the dominance of a humanistic discourse that can be revised, appropriated, or repudiated by the only weapons left to secondariness: subterfuge, subversion, and disguise.[35] In Cole, as we shall see, the promise of language is its ability to reverse and defeat a larger opponent by seizing his power metaphorically, a mode of conversion by which matter is subtilized into energy and a superior force brought to heel before a wittier one. The path of wit in *Sunrise in the Catskills* is the trail of vapor that traduces the mountain to its left and gains by means of sublimation what it cannot achieve through direct assault. Cole follows the route of displacement in mapping out his linguistic strategies, and offers us in his quest for power not bouquets of symmetry but the fleeting sideward glance of indirection.

V

The first step in this process of indirection is *naturalization*, a word that operates at two different levels in Cole. At its first and more general level, naturalization partakes of that larger cultural effort discussed earlier to divest the self of its social and historical determinants. The naturalized self is a being assimilable to the language of nature, a creature shorn of all social definition and reduced to the barest terms of his humanity. This ratter-tatter collection of flesh, bones, and blood, represented in Cole by the natural landscape itself or occasionally by figures of pioneers, woodsmen, and Indians (man in his more original and primitive state), resolves all human aspiration to a drama of natural forces and renders nature, like death, the great equalizer of individual rank and station. Naturalization in its political dimensions is related to the great bourgeois revolution of the seventeenth and eighteenth centuries, where it was not nature but divine grace that cut a revolutionary swath through established social institutions and replaced traditional historical alliances with a new aristocracy of the elect, a community that grew with time and the doctrine of free will into a democracy of the saved. Cole's democracy is a fleshly one, bearing greater affinities to Thoreau's cunningly reductive experiment at Walden Pond to seize life by the marrow and know it in all its meanest and ugliest beauty, than to John Winthrop's and John Cotton's revolution of the saints two centuries earlier. It begins with a radical realignment of power in which an older system of authority is undercut through a new confluence of forces. For members of Cole's generation, nature was the magic word that toppled old dynasties and meanings and erected in their place the geography and standards of the natural world.

Naturalization represents more, however, than a faith in the unfettered possibilities of the physical and moral landscape. It becomes in Cole's hands a deliberate means of mystifying the threatening and illicit forces confronting the subject. At this second and psychologically more complicated level, naturalization represents a strategy for defying the power and priority of the past by denying it the terms of its authority. By means of a bold program of reduction, naturalization wrests the past into a colossal anonymity, disguising the forces it opposes by massing them into a single and overwhelming presence bristling with energy but shorn of name and authority. In Cole the process of naturalization, implicit in the very act of landscape painting as a revolutionary gesture, is highlighted through the topography of the centerground mountain. The tendency toward anonymity is present as early as *Snow Squall*, where the lack or diminution of individual object-parts on the central peak forms the basis for the alienation underlying the painting's narcissistic identification. This drive toward anonymity is further elaborated in *Sunrise in the Catskills* and *Sunny Morning on the Hudson*. In each work the central peak becomes progressively darker and broader, a process of generalization that blurs its individuating features and emphasizes instead its presence as a threatening force. In *Sunny Morning* the stylization has become so extreme that the link between realism and visual allegory is severed, and the central peak looms as an anonymous black mass in a frankly mannered psychomachia. This demonization and mystification of the central mountain enables Cole to confront directly the forces he must challenge (or that challenge him), and yet to mask the directness of that encounter through the disguise and "derealization" of the central peak.

The project of naturalization places Cole in a position of great jeopardy. Though it denudes the Other of a specific identity, blurring the details by which it might be recognized or named, it situates the artist directly before the threatening agent, locked in a confrontation with no assurances beforehand as to the outcome. Naturalization is a Promethean act in which the artist hazards his identity for the sake of his goal (which is also his identity). It is accompanied in Cole by imagery of sacrifice and secondariness. The heroism of naturalization lies in its refusal to ignore the power of the Other. The Other is present in the full force of its fury, denied the name by which to wield its authority over the subject but massed with all its potential energy intact. Without that energy it would mean nothing to the artist, for the sublime draws its power from its ability ultimately to defeat (and ingest)[36] the constraining force, reversing the threat of annihilation into a promise of liberation.

The reversal comes in the second moment of the sublime encounter through an act of *signification*. Signification follows immediately upon the heels of naturalization and redeems secondariness by absorbing the power of the Other into a new sign system. In naturalization the Other is denied its symbolic authority and reduced to the level of an image, a visual or material presence prior to any symbolic investment, hovering on the brink of meaning while not yet integrated into a particular discourse. Signification follows upon this process by reinvesting the image with alternative authority. Its new meaning is determined by the terms of the signifying moment rather than any former, and now defeated, grammar. The naturalized image—massed for confrontation, generalized into an anonymity that masks its identity, pregnant in its potential power—ceases to threaten the foreground self, which feels during the process of naturalization its relative smallness and powerlessness before the larger presence, and instead comes to function as a signifying term within the new discourse of the sublime subject.[37] The act of signification redeems secondariness and frees the subject from his repressed attachments by sublimating desire, rerouting it along an alternative pathway in a new psychic economy.

Signification then is an act of renaming. It is the triumph of the child over the parent, David over Goliath, through an activity as simple and profound as language, the arcing of a small stone along an invisible route until it reaches its target virtually unseen, bringing to fruition a desire otherwise impossible to achieve. Language is the subject's weapon against the massive authority of the Other, capable of defeating the resistances and threats of the natural world by operations so agile and swift that they leave in their wake only mists and vapor trails, fleeting traces of their hidden presence. The signifying act is represented on the canvas, appropriately enough, not by images of mass and substance, but by hollows, voids, and incised spaces that record pathways carved out of matter. Grammar is generated along a sequence of visual pathways, and its rules, like the valley trails, operate according to the larger swerves of desire around the resistance of mass. Naturalization thus provides the signifying subject with the necessary space and freedom to operate. It blurs that which cannot be confronted directly by eradicating the authority of its name. Naturalization enables the subject, facing heroically an anonymous and threatening presence, to reverse the direction of the threat through a subsequent act of signification in which the power of the Other is appropriated linguistically in moments of displacement and sublimation.

VI

The appearance in *Sunny Morning on the Hudson* of a detailed background vista completes the process of sublimation begun in *Sunrise in the Catskills* by giving it a "local habitation and a name." Cole has lifted the background haze to reveal behind its gauzy mists the meandering serenity of a river valley extending to the horizon (fig. 56). The prospect is situated like an inverted isosceles triangle along the descending slopes of the center-ground mountains. Its relation to the foreground is visionary: it is presented to the eye as a *view* framed by the nearer peaks. Its attraction lies in the distance that allows the observer to comprehend it in a glance as a unity, inviting the mind to contemplation rather than actual contact or travel. To attain the view, however, we must crane our necks over the intruding lower ridge of the mountain, which partially obstructs our view by its careful placement at an angle high enough to interfere with the vista but not so high as to block it altogether.

Where *Sunny Morning* differs from *Sunrise* compositionally is in the closer alliance of the observer's point of view with that of the foreground observation point. In *Sunrise* the foreground block of stone is clearly subordinated to and dominated by the central mountain. The larger overview available to the observer is not directly accessible from the foreground ledge, and the background world must be attained instead by the valley route that skirts the mountain's base. In *Sunny Morning* the background vista and larger overview are shared by viewer and altarpiece alike. The role of the vapor trail diminishes as the visual accessibility of the meadow region increases. The work of sublimation has now been completed. Libidinal energies have been converted into visual ones and the struggle of the sublime redirected and disguised into the quest for the beautiful. The central mountain, though still a focus for foreground energies, has been reconceived as an impediment on the way to the background, while the distant river valley presents itself as a reversal of the forces of the center and foreground. It is defined horizontally where they are constituted vertically; it occupies a void in space where they exist

56. THOMAS COLE, detail of fig. 55, *Sunny Morning on the Hudson* (background valley).

positively (its contours are shaped through their absences, literally inverting their forms); and it is passive and serene where they are aggressive and threatening. Like all reaction-formations, however, the background world embodies within its disguised imagery the very forces it is designed to suppress directly and therefore fulfill indirectly. Whether the eye moves from the tip of mist at the apex of the triangle to the distant horizon line, or along the winding waterway from left to right, it traces a progress through time that recapitulates in its motion the dialectic of foreground and centerground. The central river repeats the mist-filled gap between promontory and peak, smoothing the jagged discontinuity of the foreground world into a more continuous-seeming space. It retains nonetheless the record of a separation between two realms of land. That both shores of the river should appear equally paired and matched, neither side exhibiting a clear superiority of size or proportion to the other, only confirms the role of the background world in rewriting the struggles of the center space as a tale of harmony. The clear priority of power and prestige that the central mountain maintains over the foreground altar-form is here recast into a myth of equality in a landscape that is now conceived as continuous and uninterrupted. Only the innocuous-seeming bend of the river, with its juxtaposition of slightly asymmetric rises of land at either fork, remains as an almost direct—*but now detraumatized*—reminder of the far more frightening clash of power in the sublime world of the foreground.

The beautiful thus arises in Cole as a reaction to the forces of the sublime. It represents a sublimation of those forces along a visual pathway that fictionalizes its own origins and history by resituating them in a detraumatized narrative founded on a myth of continuity and equality. This fictionalization of the sublime into the terms of the beautiful—a sublimation of a terrible beauty into a pastoral one—occurs through an act of renaming in which the old and threatening language of the past is replaced by a new one in a moment of reversal. In Cole this means that the power of the Other is liberated for the purposes of the subject by the capacity of the latter, as in Irving, to spin a web of language around the former, recasting the sublime as a stage on the way to the beautiful. According to this revised narrative, the sublime is present first as a hindrance to the desired object and then as a disguised force recognizable within the contours of the object itself. Those contours are noteworthy, not only for the way in which they both mask and reveal the subject's true ends, but for the manner in which they fulfill the original terms of the subject's desires. As a fictionalization of the sublime, the beautiful allows a consummation of the subject's forbidden desires that is both passive and visionary. Whether, as the evidence of the mirror stage would suggest, the object of the self's love is narcissistic and autoerotic, or whether it is, in its more oedipal constructions, homosexual and parent-oriented, the effect of the beautiful is to fulfill the terms of the earlier love.

As a visionary state the beautiful grows out of the scoptophiliac tendencies of the child, his desire to see, and allows us to specify the exact route that sublimation once took. That which could not be possessed directly was appropriated visually. What he could not *have* he could at least *see*, and so the desired object was achieved by means of the eye rather than the hand, a mode of displacement and a privileging of vision that were to play significant roles in the later choice of the beautiful as a *visionary* state answering to the forbidding energy of the sublime.[38] The inability of the child to consummate his desire directly, or his dread of the consequences of such an act, expresses itself in turn in the need for distance implicit in Cole's framing of the beautiful. The gap experienced by the child between his intentions and their fruitions reappears in the large vistas of open space, and especially in the forbidding presence of the center-ground mountain, which separate the foreground promontory from the river valley world. Distance and framing become Cole's means of alerting the viewer to the sublimating operations occurring at his feet (just as scoptophilia is his means of bypassing the authority of the hand with the powers of the eye).

The passivity of the beautiful functions similarly to fulfill earlier needs implicit in the autoerotic or homosexual tendencies of mirror and oedipal states. In its narcissistic tendencies, passivity allows the erotic energy of the subject to remain within the circumference of the self and simulates the desire of the child for the passive arousal associated with acts of stroking, whether autoerotic or initiated from outside. In a more clearly oedipal context, the desire for passivity reflects the child's desire to make love with the father either through fantasies of masturbation or by assuming the role of the mother.[39] Cole's construction of the beautiful renders it a pointedly passive state. The space it fills is horizontal and supine, and its accessibility is dependent on its being viewed rather than actively engaged. It recreates through culturally sanctioned imagery the conditions of childhood sexuality and the terms of their fulfillment. The beautiful thus provides Cole with a means of redirecting the energies of a male/male homosexual love into an object attachment that remains passive in its constitution and is conceived in apparently feminine imagery.[40] In addition to the qualities of passivity and supineness already noted, the beautiful is fashioned from those compositionally void spaces that exist in the intervals between positive and usually masculine images. Given the strong fear of castration expressed in the painting through the language of secondariness, the association of the beautiful with void spaces expresses not only a sense of the feminine as a vessel, but a fear of punishment tied to the fulfillment of one's forbidden desires. To be passive and feminine is a means not only for the fulfillment of the child's libidinal fantasies, but represents the form of punishment that those pleasures inevitably incur: castration. As Freud notes, the male child during the oedipal phase associates the girl's lack of a penis with the punishment all children receive for enacting their forbidden desires. The beautiful *qua* feminine is Cole's means of representing both the solution to his desires and the retribution that that solution entails.

The beautiful then is Cole's act of signification, a renaming of a love inherently autoerotic and homosexual. It is the magic that redeems secondariness by allowing access in disguised and visionary terms to a realm otherwise forbidden. It is born of the energy of scoptophilia, and constituted in imagery that is both passive and feminine. Though it appears to confirm a classical oedipal preference of the male child for the opposite sex, it functions in Cole not as a moment of genuine reversal of affection from the father to the mother, but as a disguised transformation of the original homosexual love into alternative terms that preserve the pattern, if not the object, of the earlier attachment.

The beautiful substitutes coherence for power; that is its essential move. It provides a continuous narrative about a discontinuous state, creating a fiction of timeless repose in a world marching inexorably to death and ravishment. As a post-sublime experience, it presents a nature divested of its original awe-fulness, substituting a myth of integration and domesticity for the repressed and demonic energies of the sublime. It domesticates the sublime by reconceiving its struggles in pastoral terms, providing us—unlike the sublime—with a world we can live in.

The beautiful is related to the sublime as a palimpsest to the original text. It rewrites its earlier history from the vantage point of victory, disguising its phallic goal and the profound anxiety of its struggle by substituting its own visionary consummation for the desire for identification with the central mountain. By claiming priority for itself, the beautiful defeats the authority of the mountain. It redirects the foreground energy away from the central peak and focuses it on the background vista. This process of sublimation is the means by which the sublime creates a revision of itself, accomplishing its original ends through an act of renaming.

The turning point in the history of the sublime, then, is its transformation into the beautiful, an alternative text that functions as its fulfillment and resolution. As the scoptophiliac child learns to redeem the failure of the hand through the world of the eye, so the sublime painting comes to defeat history by its own textuality. It substitutes a continual rewriting of the same text for a genuine alteration of history, preferring to retain in disguised form its autoerotic love for the father to any actual desire for the mother. The tendency to fictionalize, precipitated in the mirror phase, bears strange fruit in the capacity of the text, of language, marshaled in the service of vision and the eye, to defeat the strictures of the hand. The beautiful represents the consummation of mirror-state fictions. From the distance separating the beholder from his beloved object—the visual hiatus essential to all scoptophilia—is born the endless circuit of desire in quest of its unattainable object. The beautiful is as fulfilling as all sublimations can be, and as alienating as all displacements must be.

VII

Louis Noble records in his biography of Cole three journal entries dating from the years 1826–27 in which Cole describes, or purports to describe, his adventures while hiking through the Catskill Mountains. The adventures they narrate are so wild and fantastical that even Noble, usually an unflappable advocate of Cole, must qualify his presentation of the third account with a mild disclaimer:

> The following singular story, very likely in part a fiction, is, nevertheless, a lively and exciting sketch of the poetic artist in the midst of the fatigues and dangers not unfrequently incident to his walks for the picturesque.[41]

Noble's concern for the reader's credulity reflects his awareness that Cole's accounts offer more than a simple narration of a wilderness outing. Their stylized nature and singular subject-matter point them well in the direction of fiction, and Noble asks the reader to accept them, not for their literal truth, but for the powers of imagination in the "poetic artist" that they exhibit. We might do well to heed Noble's advice, noting the freedom Cole seems to feel in these pieces to allow his imagination to roam at will over the material of private experience. Like the paintings we have just been treating, these quasi-autobiographical sketches subordinate the literal transcription of an observed landscape to the different purposes of psychic self-expression. Their relevance to the modern reader lies precisely in their fictionalization, the process by which the natural landscape receives its shape and affective coloring from the mental topography it reproduces. Cole's narratives, like his paintings, operate according to the laws of a specific textuality. They function as publicly accessible and culturally mediated dream-texts, dependent for their language on the conventions of contemporary travel and wilderness literature. They take for their material—what Freud would call their "manifest content"—the world of nature and tradition of sublime discourse dating back to Burke; they reconstitute the energies already latent within this genre to create a history of the individual in the process of identity formation. The laws by which this investment occurs correspond roughly to the process of "dream-work," the procedures by which the unconscious inscribes its own concerns onto the materials of everyday life. This complex and self-censoring process, hiding even from itself desires it cannot directly express, extends far beyond the boundaries of simple "wish fulfillment." It penetrates to the very heart of the subject's identity, and transforms the canvas, or the written page, into a document recording through its fragile and evasive textuality the complex layering of desire and denial which constitute in their interactions the history of the individual.

Cole's wilderness accounts, which range in length from one to several pages, vary like his sublime paintings in their degrees of naturalistic precision while remaining constant to a specific narrative formula. Each account begins in the late afternoon on a day that commences in bright sunlight and high spirits but soon turns unexpectedly dark, whether from the sudden passing of an ill-blowing storm or the advance of evening twilight at a pace quicker than anticipated. In each narrative the speaker is alone, and experiences the advent of darkness with "an indescribable feeling of melancholy." The narrator's forebodings are associated with an attempted mountain ascent or the desire for a prospect vision, and soon translate into a series of unusual and dramatic adventures at once frightening and exhilarating. These misadventures constitute the bulk of the narrative, are usually threatening to the narrator's survival or health, and are surcharged with sexual energy and language. They culminate in a great and climactic moment of release, often associated with water, floods, and storms, and return the speaker at the denouement of his story to a world of renewed light described in pastoral and maternal imagery. The process of conflict and resolution may occur several times within the same narrative before the final resolution and the dawning of a pastoral vision at the end.

The entire sequence is summarized and condensed into a single paragraph in Cole's journal entry for 8 October 1826, labeled by Noble "Trip to Windham":

> At an hour and a half before sunset, I had a steep and lofty mountain before me, heavily wooded, and infested with wolves and bears, and, as I had been informed, no house for six miles. But I determined, in spite of all difficulties and an indescribable feeling of melancholy, to attain my object: so, pressing my portfolios to my side, I dashed up the dark and woody height. After climbing some three miles of steep and broken road, I found my self near the summit of the mountain, with (thanks to some fire of past times) a wide prospect. Above me jutted out some bare rocks; to these I clambered up, and sat upon my mountain throne, the monarch of the scene. The sun was now clearly setting, and the shadows veiled in dim obscurity the quiet valley. Here and there a stream faintly sparkled; clouds, flaming in the last glories of day, hung on the points of the highest peaks like torches lifted by the earth to kindle the lamps of heaven. Summit rose above summit, mountain rolled beyond mountain,—a fixed, a stupendous tumult. The prospect was sublime. A hasty sketch or two, and I commenced my descent. After a hurried walk of two or three miles, I came to a log-house .... A scene of neatness here presented itself that I had not yet expected. After a plain supper of cheese, rye-bread and butter, I was entertained by an old hunter with a recital of feats of the chase .... I slept soundly, and rose early, ate a good breakfast, and desired of my host what was to pay .... I then took my way back, "over hills, over dales, thorough brush, thorough briar."[42]

The passage contains all the elements of the Colean sublime arranged in a narrative sequence: the clash of light and dark; the aspiration toward visionary heights; the feelings of melancholy, fear, and danger along the way; the sense of exaltation accompanying a visionary relation to the landscape; and the conclusion of prospect and quest with an intimate and secure interlude within a domestic setting. The serial quality to Cole's account reflects the temporal structure underlying the sublime. Psychological states are mapped out in narrative fashion, their relations providing the temporal coordinates for Cole's story in a manner parallel to the use of spatial relations in the sublime paintings to articulate the underlying linguistic pathways.

The journey begins in an unsettling and unexpected act of interruption: the narrator is caught almost unawares by darkness or storms, and faces in the ensuing crisis a test of his independence and resolve. In "The Bewilderment," the third of Cole's sublime passages, the sense of surprise is reinforced by the narrator's feelings of isolation and presentiment of evil:

> The sun hung low in the sky and to me seemed to haste down with unaccustomed speed; for I was alone and a stranger in the wilderness. The nearest habitation I knew to be on the other side of a mountain that rose before me, whose tangled woods were well known to the Hunter as the favorite haunt of wild animals.[43]

Like the opening lines of many Poe short stories, Cole's passage commences with a state of defamiliarization.[44] The landscape is disengaged from its normal associations, and rendered frightening and uncanny. Time dilates into unaccustomed rhythms and the narrator encounters a world "whose tangled woods" cannot be sorted out or interpreted by conventional standards. The presence of "wild animals" (in "Trip to Windham" the forests are "heavily wooded, and infested with wolves and bears") reflects the narrator's fears of unknown but threatening forces, and suggests in its psychological underpinnings a probable projection and displacement onto the outer world of a deep-seated fear of the father's authority (Freud notes similar fears underlying the tales of the Wolf Man and the Rat Man, two of his most celebrated case histories).[45]

In both the "Windham" and "Bewilderment" passages, the journey into the forest world is accompanied by "an indescribable feeling of melancholy": "Though not quite so buoyant in spirit, as in the morning ... I could not but feel a tone of melancholy as I threaded the deepening shadows of the gloomy forest." The narrator's feelings have become disassociated. The unexplained origin of the melancholy betrays the repression and disguise masking the source of Cole's anxiety. Melancholia, Freud notes, arises from a state of narcissistic self-mourning,[46] and often reveals in narratives like Cole's an anger and frustration attached to the fear of punishment (castration). The self mourns the possibilities denied it, and hides its anger from itself by translating its frustration into a free-floating sadness that surfaces only when confronted with a symbolic representation of its own situation. To enter "tangled woods" inhabited "with wolves and bears" is to confront in disguised and symbolic fashion that moment in the individual's past when infantile pleasures were suddenly and unexpectedly shadowed by oedipal castration anxieties. The loss of innocence is associated with hostile forces external to the self. The freedom to express this originating state and to recapitulate its trauma is achieved by means of naturalization. The self transforms the original energy by redirecting it to the natural landscape, where it preserves its original patterns while remaining veiled enough to protect its origins and remain unnamed. Sunset becomes the governing metaphor for these transactions by providing a threshold region sufficiently dark to prevent either detection or naming of the original forces, and yet light enough to allow their engagement and reworking.

The defamiliarization of the landscape—its investment with the memory of a primal trauma too deep to be recognized and too painful to be ignored—leads the narrator upon a symbolic journey that reenacts the earlier childhood odyssey through the disguised imagery of the forest. This odyssey through childhood sexuality passes through three phases: the first a dialectic of bafflement, a state of sexual confusion and incomprehension associated with imagery of labyrinths and mazes. The narrator is gripped by a sense of his own powerlessness and finds the landscape surrounding him imbued with the characteristics of a punishing father, vengeful and threatening in its superior force. The second stage isolates the source of the narrator's guilt in an illicit mode of sexuality. The landscape is charged with a phallic energy in which narcissistic self-love expresses itself onanistically, attempting at times to disguise its desires through a use of feminine imagery. The final stage marks the conversion of the sexual struggle of the previous two states into the restored peace of a pastoral landscape. The narrator returns to a world of light and harmony through an act of deliverance that is both magical and inexplicable in its effects.

The dialectic of bafflement is most fully developed in "The Bewilderment," the most overtly fictional and dramatic of Cole's sublime passages. The "dark and woody height" of "Windham" in which the narrator ascends "some three miles of steep and broken road" is here elaborated as an epistemological quagmire:

> My path was fast descending into a deep valley and the shades
> deepened at every step and rendered its windings more and more

obscure—several times I hesitated in doubt of its course; for the fallen leaves were heaped upon it—I at length lost it entirely . . . long I struggled through the entangled roots and branches; but they seemed interminable—I became perplexed and bewildered and was utterly ignorant in what direction the nearest human habitation lay.[47]

The Dantesque quality of Cole's prose—its translation of baffled self-assessment into a forested journey of the soul—combines antique associations with labyrinthine imagery. The "ancient burthen of woods" conspires to isolate the narrator in a "glorious" solitude that soon devolves through "windings," obscurity, and "doubt" into "interminable" entanglements. Moments of clarity and illumination dissolve into the black "twilight" from which they emerge, false harbingers of security and peace:

> It was a perilous labour—I climbed,—stooped, was struck by the limbs of trees; and several times fell among the crashing branches—At length to infinite satisfaction I beheld the starry sky unbroken by the branches of trees—I advanced into the clear space; but stood again for the earth [ground] before me was a pitchy blackness; and yet I imagined that I could discern objects lying upon it and the rough outline of the mountain rose a short distance beyond—I ventured a little further and again stood in hesitation . . . .[48]

Cole's alternating states of vision and blindness carry with them great affective power. He is not only isolated geographically, but lost morally:

> a Tornado had recently passed in this direction and had laid prostrate every tree in its track of desolation . . . . Fatigued and disheartened; supperless and unsheltered as I was I sat down with the resolution of waiting patiently the coming of the day—This was a transient resolution—the air grew cold—wild clouds hurried across the sky and the wind moaned fitfully through the forest—I could bear inaction no longer—Again I endeavored to extricate myself from the Windfall.[49]

Cole's efforts to "extricate myself from the Windfall" not only draw upon popular conventions of wilderness adventures, but echo in their language of bewilderment and release the rhetoric of contemporary revivalist sermons.[50] The passage takes its tone and imagery from the language of evangelical Protestantism and betrays a sense of the narrator, like an Edwardsian sinner, lost in the darkness of his sin, "prostrate" before his God and fearful of His avenging power ("a Tornado had . . . laid prostrate every tree in its track of desolation"). Cole defines "Windfall" in a footnote to his own text as a "term given to heaps of trunks that have been thrown down by the wind"; he reveals through his definition the child's fear of an act of wrongdoing punishable as sin by a power of

awesome strength. Nature possesses for the narrator a terrifying energy
that looms in the face of his infantile anxieties as a displaced surrogate for
the father. In the "Windham" passage a "fire of past times" scars the
helpless landscape, while in "Storm in the Catskills" a "thunder storm"
and "unburthening . . . tempest" menaces the narrator. In each instance,
the speaker reexperiences the child's sense of helplessness before a force
that is not only superior in might, but paradoxically threatening and
inviting in its appeal. Powerlessness and punishment are linked in a dialectic that both excites the child and elicits a paralyzing sense of guilt.

In the phallic or second phase, the punishing energies of nature are
erotically invested with sexual imagery and serve as both the source for
and mirror of the child's own narcissistic desires. The text moves through
a series of veiled sexual encounters, each repeating with varying nuances
an experience of masturbatory sexuality that focuses on the isolation of
the subject, his preejaculatory bewilderment, and his ensuing feelings of
guilt, pleasure, and release at the moment of climax.

> The ground before me was a pitchy blackness . . . I ventured a little
> further and again stood in hesitation; but not long—The earth beneath
> my feet broke away and I was precipitated down a shelving steep—I
> clung to roots and shrubs as I descended but they failed me—Swiftly I
> shot down the steep accompanied by loose earth and stone; coming to a
> more precipitous place I was plunged and How far I feel I know not—a
> deep water received me—Emerging from the depth in my struggle I
> caught hold of a rock that rose above the surface and dragging myself
> upon it lay for some [time] exhausted and motionless.[51]

The narrator's inability to see ("the ground before me was a pitchy blackness") reveals the passive quality of his sexuality. He is alone with his
thoughts, and in a moment of "hesitation" undergoes a surge of preejaculatory power that climaxes "swiftly" and suddenly in an explosion of
"loose earth and stones." These latter provide in their fluid movement an
image of the ejaculate, culminating in a pool of "deep water" in which the
narrator lies "exhausted and motionless."

The phallic nature of the landscape in which he wanders—its composition of trees, "roots and branches," "craggy" rock formations, and fallen
"limbs"—reinforces the autoerotic quality of the situation. The child discovers in the landscape echoes of his own aroused and uncertain state.

> I remained extended on the rock for sometime in total inaction until
> my limbs began to ache with cold—The lonely star that I had seen in
> the sky was extinguished, and there was utter darkness—I heard the
> winds howling in the woody crags far above me and the nearer trees
> moaned as the[y] chafed each other—a large drop of rain fell in my

face—My situation was one of painful uncertainty—I thought if the
rain falls as it threatens to do, the torrents from the precipices will
descend into the gulf, and sweep me from this low rack [rock?]—
Nothing is so painful as suspense and inaction in situations of danger,
and I found it impossible long to remain quiescent.[52]

The interlude of sullenly moaning trees chafing against "each other" is
followed by a sensation of moisture ("a large drop of rainfall in my
face"), a sequence that repeats the child's own autoerotic experiences
and provokes a feeling of fear. "My situation was one of painful uncertainty ... and I found it impossible to remain quiescent." The pain,
restlessness, and "uncertainty" are all linked to the "torrents" of "rain,"
which "will descend into the gulf, and sweep me from this low" rock. The
narrator's inability to remain "quiescent," like his earlier encounter with
the "loose earth and stones" that "precipitated" him into wetness, reveals
both the strength of his unconscious arousal and his dread of being swept
away.

The autoerotic fantasies undergirding Cole's narrative, whether directed toward the self or toward the parent, place the speaker in situations of repeated peril. The infant's autoerotic activities are acts of self-
assertion as well as love, and the pride engendered in his own power
becomes confused with the illicit nature of his deeds. The guilt and fear
of punishment that the child experiences translates narratively into a
series of hazardous adventures, each climaxing with a need of rescue. *His
identity is associated with a forbidden act.* What commences in freedom and
sexual innocence develops into a state of acute anxiety, the source of
which appears to be the child's fear of castration. In an extraordinary
passage from "Storm in the Catskills," Cole progresses from the innocent
delight of a bystander at his own sexual arousal to a state of profound
despair and feelings of castration anxiety. Retreating to the shelter of an
"overhanging rock," the speaker watches the gathering of an oncoming
storm "with a proud joyousness of feeling such as we sometimes experience when some fearful event is expected, and know ourselves to be
beyond the reach of danger."

I thought as I strode over the hard floor of my temporary [shelter],
"here I can watch unscathed the battling of the elements"—The storm
came on in its majesty—Like a hoarse trumpet sounding to the charge,
a mighty blast roared through the mountains.... Then succeeded a
dead calm—the leaves hung drowsily upon the branches—the gloom
deepened—the valley below me blackened like an abyss—wild clouds
suspended from a leadened canopy encurtained it around—This was a
moment of sublime expectation—a forked stream of fire kindled the
gloom.

Then came a crash as of a riven world, and echo hurled the sound from crag to crag—then rose a whispering—the rain drops fell as though they might be counted—but anon the gush of torrents sounded on the ear.[53]

Like a dream sequence in which the sleeper knows himself to be dreaming, the narrator here observes from a distance the erotic motions of a storm: its state of gathering energy, the stillness and "expectation" that surrounds its discharge, the tensed explosion of "a forked stream of fire [that] kindled the gloom" (a phrase that combines natural and ejaculatory energies), and the succeeding spasms of liquid that empty onto the landscape with "sublime expectation."

The child responds to the libidinal energies of the storm through onanistic activities of his own. He recapitulates the violence and ecstasy of the scene he has witnessed in an imaginative interlude that begins in a moment of release but concludes in terror:

The scene was changed, I no longer saw the distant mountain . . . I was amidst the clouds—I saw no sky—no earth—my imagination took wing—I thought myself far from the earth careering through a permeable waste into some outer void, beyond the grasp of gravitation or attraction. With no law but my own will, I guided my chariot of rock through trackless regions—I rode over vast mountains of rolling vapour—I descended like a falling meteor into the lower depths of the fathomless obscure—I winged my flight over illimitable plains—and my fleet shadow was cast dimly on the sullen waves of shoreless oceans. My speed out[st]ripped the lightnings'—I left the struggling winds far behind . . . it was a chaos like the primeval one. . . . At length my wearied fancy alighted from its airy voyage, and I found myself standing on the firm-set rock[.] The storm had not abated; the roaring of the tempest was awful[.] The howling blast, the frequent thunder peal—the crash of falling trees and the hoarse bray of cataracts were comingled [*sic*]—Sometimes I feared the rocks were loosed from mountain summits and were rolling down the steps impetuously. The lightnings played around my tenement with a fearful sound, as of a broad flame struck by the wind and I could not but feel the weakness of humanity—My situation now became precariously romantic; on each side of my rock . . . descended a headlong torrent . . . I was made captive by the floods: all egress from my prison was impossible. . . . My lodging indeed, now promised anything but comfort, for the wind as if to punish me for former vauntings of security drove the chill vapour into my dwelling; and the water from the neighbouring cataracts flowd [*sic*] over the floor; and the soft couch of moss that I had looked upon as my resting place; was flooded.[54]

Cole's language functions here with extraordinary psychological precision. The sexuality of the father, when displaced onto the martial activities of nature, arouses the child's scoptophiliac tendencies (it is important that he witness the storm "unscathed" from a distance) and produces in him a state of sexual excitement that both sublimates and reveals its origins. The child sees in the father an extension of himself, and his onanistic behavior combines love for the Other with a more narcissistic love for himself consistent with the mirror phase. The narcissism attaches itself to autoerotic modes of sexuality, and produces in the child a state of exhilaration and release that forms the basis for all later sublime experiences. To career in a "chariot of rock through trackless regions . . . beyond the grasp of gravitation" with "no law but my own will," is to subvert the laws of nature, and ultimately the father, through an imagined superiority that elevates "fancy" into "law" and guides the self according to principles of its "own will." The vehicle for these desires, a "chariot of rock," is an oxymoronic construction, a weighted and phallic projection that penetrates the "fathomless obscure" and asserts the paradoxical superiority of the child's phallic freedom to that of the father by virtue of the child's ability, through fantasies of masturbation, to overreach the latter ("I thought myself . . . beyond the grasp of gravitation . . . I rode over vast mountains of rolling vapour.")[55]

Masturbatory sexuality becomes for the speaker the means by which externally imposed prohibitions are violated and secondariness redeemed. Like the swerving valley route that bypasses the authority of the central mountain in *Sunrise in the Catskills*, achieving by displacement what it cannot possess or defeat through direct engagement, masturbatory fantasies offer the child an imaginative power over the law of the Other. Such fantasies not only render the child the equal or superior of the Other, but provide him with a sense of power commensurate with his expectations from the mirror stage. The narcissistic self defeats the inevitable discovery of his own inferiority by a mode of sexuality that ratifies illusion, navigating the shoals of oedipal anxiety through reversion to an onanistic state. The mirror-stage self comes to substitute its own projected image for the reality of the helpless child, resolving its oedipal conflicts not by a shattering of its desires and sublimation of its love for the mother, but by redirecting the child's love-antagonism with the father into autoerotic forms of self-love.

The illusion of power that arises from the reversion to mirror-stage modes of sexuality cannot be sustained, and there follows in its aftermath a sense of "chaos" and loss of power. "At length my wearied fancy alighted from its airy voyage . . . I was made captive by the floods: all egress from my prison was impossible." The speaker's exhilaration fades with the onset of guilt and the possibility of punishment. The imagery shifts from the ecstasy of flight to the fear of castration ("the crash of falling trees"), and the child's love of his own phallus yields before a deeper fear of the avenging power of the father ("I feared the rocks were loosed from mountain summits and were rolling down the steps impetuously"). The impetuous rain of rocks serves two contradictory functions: it repeats the ejaculatory joy of the "careering" fancy at the same time as it turns that joy into a source of punishment and potential annihilation. Like the young Wordsworth of the *Prelude*, fleeing in panic from the anthropomorphic peak that pursues him in his "troubled pleasure" one "summer evening" in a "little boat" (1.357–400), Cole finds in the surrounding landscape an avenging presence, summarized in the effort of the "wind . . . to punish me for former vauntings of security." The very rock-phallus that had once offered the narrator refuge ("It was time to seek a place of shelter, and a ledge of overhanging rock invited to its covering") turns into an agent of retribution and renders the speaker a helpless child once more: "I could not but feel the weakness of humanity." The romanticization of the speaker's state—his discovery that his "situation now became precariously romantic"—reveals not only his ambivalence toward his erotic history, but the sadomasochistic inclinations underlying his punishment. With the breakdown of his mirror-stage defenses, the child's aggressive self-assertion turns back upon itself as masochistic behavior, and the passive arousal of childhood masturbation acquires a violent and self-destructive energy.

The cycle of phallic misadventures, we may speculate, runs thus: the speaker's mirror-state narcissism spills over into his oedipal struggles. The desire to make love with the father establishes a habit of masturbatory sexuality that satisfies both the infant's desire for filial love and his demands for narcissistic satisfaction. The latter, in turn, produces feelings of guilt and anxiety that fuel the infant's need to defeat the father's punitive wrath. At this point an impasse arises. The parent's superior power threatens the child's oedipal need either to triumph over the father or identify with him, while the threat of castration blocks the flow of narcissistic libido and precipitates a crisis of identity. Classical Freudian theory at this stage requires a renunciation of the child's impossible desires and the development in their place of modes of identification and sublimation that assist the child in his adjustments to the realities of an adult heterosexual world.[56] In Cole's sublime narratives, the child's response to his impossible desire—his love both for his own phallus and that of the father—is to revert to mirror-state modes of sexuality, preferring autoerotic fantasies to the demands of renunciation. This reversion dooms the child to an endless circuit of repetition, his ability to sustain his narcissistic and Imaginary self unequal to the intrusions of guilt and fear that mark the presence of the Other. The labyrinthine quality of Cole's narratives, the continual defeat of vision by darkness in adventure after adventure, is Cole's means of recording within his tales the larger insufficiency that characterizes his mirror-state illusions. Each adventure in Cole's picaresque narrative culminates, like the climactic ending of a Saturday matinee film serial, in a new misadventure posing novel difficulties for the hapless but ingenious hero. The cycle of misadventure continues unbroken until an event outside the chain of circumstance releases the narrator, as if by magic, to safety and a new day.

There is a moral to be inferred from Cole's tales. Salvation is impossible within a phallocentric world: the phallus by itself, cannot effect its own redemption. Left to its own Imaginary devices, it prefers the illusion and narcissistic satisfactions of the mirror stage to the sublimation and rewriting of desire that characterizes all genuine change.[57] The history of the subject unfolds in endless repetitions until an enabling power, like an act of grace, allows the individual to reroute desire along a new set of pathways. Cole's phallocentric subject, like his sinning counterpart within Protestant evangelicalism, inhabits a world defined as secondary and fallen. He measures his current (e)state against an idealized standard that he expresses as an impossible desire, while his powerlessness dooms him to perpetual defeat at its hands.[58] The gap between possibility and desire is filled for the Protestant imagination by grace, a power conceived as originating outside the circle of discourse and unmerited by the sinner. Its efficacy is tied to its semiotic newness: it is a foreign term introduced into the equation of human affairs, a signifier from a divine semiology, effective precisely because it is not reducible to the terms of the old. For Cole the failure of the phallus to redeem its world unassisted (a failure called by Christianity "pride") creates a rupture in the governing discourse and leads to the creation, as if by magic, of an alternative mode of understanding. Grace is a structural need within the bifurcated language systems of Protestant evangelicalism, and Cole, who shares with Protestantism the need for an outside term, an x to redeem the phallic self, effects his freedom through acts of sublimation, the closest that he comes during the sublime years to a Protestant experience of conversion. The language of masturbation, as a rhetorical and sexual strategy, is reformed and recast by an act of sublimation, and the circuit of misadventure is broken.

Sublimation, which marks the third stage of the Colean sublime narrative, occurs in moments of epiphany at the conclusion of the text. Unlike earlier experiences of vision or influxes of power punctuating the narrative, the epiphantic moment sunders the train of masturbatory imagery and replaces it with a pastoral conceit allied to heterosexual desire and associated with imagery of light and royalty. Twice in the sublime narratives the speaker hovers on the brink of preejaculatory climax when suddenly the pattern of release and reversion collapses into a new, and magically assumed, conversion. Here at last is epiphany: the emergence of light in a world of darkness, and the transformation of old desires into new, and now licit, demands. In the "Trip to Windham" passage quoted previously, the narrator emerges from the "wooded and infested" forest to discover the "wide prospect" of the mountain summit:

> Above me jutted some bare rocks; to these I clambered up, and sat upon my mountain throne, the monarch of the scene.... Here and there a stream faintly sparkled; clouds, flaming in the last glories of day, hung on the points of the highest peaks like torches lifted by the earth to kindle the lamps of heaven.... The prospect was sublime.[59]

The speaker's attainment of a prospect point is framed by the autoerotic opening of the passage. The jutting "bare rocks" house the narrator in a state that is phallic and solitary. The onanistic potential of the scene, however, fails to develop to an ejaculatory climax. Scoptophilia replaces masturbation as the primary mode of sexual activity, and the erotic energies of the passage are channeled into visionary ends. The inundating liquid characteristic of Cole's response to the landscape is sublimated into imagery of light: sparkling streams, flaming clouds, and "torches...to kindle the lamps of heaven." The passage turns on a moment of sublimation and reversal in which an ejaculatory outpouring of the speaker is experienced as an epiphantic influx of light. The narrator suddenly finds himself "the monarch of the scene," his jeweled kingdom a testament to the capacity of sublimation to convert masturbatory impulses into epiphantic power.

Though the epiphany of "Windham" marks a break from the autoerotic language of the sublime narratives, the passage remains largely masculine in its imagery of monarchs and thrones. A domestic interlude follows Cole's descent from the mountain, pastoral in its associations but lacking the heterosexual overtones that distinguish the conclusions of "Storm in the Catskills" and the "Bewilderment." The former, like the "Windham" story, hinges on an epiphantic "flood of light" that consummates the onanistic potential of the prose:

> I knew the sun had not set; yet scarce a ray that seemed to emanate from him, cheered the gloom—Suddenly a thicker darkness came on, a fierce blast shrieked through the woods, and instan[tan]eously tore the gray scud from the mountains, and rolled the cloudy curtains from before the golden sky—A flood of light burst on the darkness—the grim mountains lifted their heads rejoicingly—the leaves played in the gentle breeze like living gems,—the birds raised their sweet voices—the torrents failed in their courses—the blue smoke curled gracefully

from a secluded habitation in a neighboring valley, and I pursued my way down the mountains side with a heart filled with delight.[60]

The tempest menacing the narrator throughout the narrative arrives finally at a moment of crisis: "Suddenly a thicker darkness came on, a fierce blast shrieked through the woods . . . and rolled the cloudy curtains from before the golden sky." The language of the storm is translated into the language of sunshine ("A *flood* of light burst on the darkness"), while the oedipal fury of the father composes into the "sweet voices" of the dell and "the blue smoke curled gracefully from a secluded habitation." The colors and standards of the sky are now domesticated to the dimensions of the hearth, and ejaculatory energy sublimated into rustic prospects. Even the wind and "leaves," which once threatened the speaker with retribution, wear "living gems" in their now "gentle" frolic. The cycle of ejaculatory adventures has been broken, like the storm itself, through the magical transformation of phallic strategies into epiphantic clearings. Cole has restored his narrative to the daylight world lost in the story's opening lines, and has achieved in the process a capacity for language and the rewriting of desire. Sublimation in Cole is expressed as the capacity to substitute one name for another in the semiotic of desire, preserving the force of the original impulse while altering its pathways and ends.

The sublime narratives teach us the self-defeating nature of Cole's masturbatory strategies, their inability to break the cycle of mirror-state and oedipal struggle from within. What they lack, however, is an ability to account for the experience of sublimation they undergo. The narratives mystify sublimation by presenting it as a state of grace and magic, and fail to explore, as the paintings do so profoundly, the origins of sublimation and displacement in the fictional tendencies of the mirror state. Cole's prose, as opposed to his paintings, cannot explain that moment of reversal when the subject redeems his anonymity by an act of signification. His narratives describe the transition from neurotic repetition (onanism) to the rewriting of desire (sublimation) as a magical and unaccountable event, an occasion as mysterious as the historical intrusion baffling the figures in Irving's fiction. At its best, Cole's prose can re-create the experience of the subject in a world of change; it cannot, however, elucidate and explain it. To do that one must turn to the world of the paintings, where sublimation occurs not as a moment of intervention from an outside force (whether religious or magical), but as a strategy generated internally from the child's ability to substitute fictional pathways for its repressed and disguised desires. The irony of Cole's oeuvre is that the written works, for all their dream-like accuracy, cannot explain the source of their own linguistic power, while the visual works, those that the casual viewer would assume to be the most mute, pursue with indefatigable energy and precision the hidden origins of the language of the self.

VIII

The essential drama of the sublime is achieved in Cole through the painting's composition: the arrangement of space, the massing of forms, the play of light, and the pattern of movement directing the viewer through the landscape—all create an experience of sublime epiphany independent of the narrative subject that Cole tends on occasion to introduce. Unlike Benjamin West or even Washington Allston, each of whom found history an appropriate vehicle for the expression of his concerns, Cole subordinates historical narrative to the experience of the landscape, and uses his historical proclivities not to elevate landscape to a higher level, but to thematize and reinforce the vision already present in the composition.[61] History becomes in Cole's hands a key for unlocking the secret code of the mountains. It explicates at a thematic level the tensions and disjunctions implicit in the painting's structure. Hence in a work like *Gelyna* of 1826, reproduced and published as an illustration to the story of the same name in the Christmas annual *Talisman* (1830), Cole chooses as his point of departure a legend concerning the death of a hero from the French and Indian Wars. The dead soldier is found by his brother-in-law upon a promontory overlooking Lake George, scene of the battle in which the hero received his mortal wounds. Cole's painting romanticizes the past both in the sense of imbuing the American landscape with storied associations equivalent to those of Europe, and in the more traditional meaning of romanticization as a revision of the past by rendering it fictional, i.e., romanticizing it.

Cole paints the fallen Major Rutledge upon a ledge overlooking a deep canyon, a rugged mountain slope rising to the left and a vertical rock formation bounding the canyon at the right (fig. 57). The advancing figure of Herman Cuyler gestures toward the supine Rutledge, while in the distant background a passing storm leaves behind it a vista of Lake George on a clear summer day. Whereas the story places Rutledge upon a "rock [that] commanded a view of Lake George and its creeks and islets, and the opposite shore," Cole relegates the lake to a distant surface in the background and emphasizes instead the intervening peaks and valley.[62] Lake George exists in Cole's painting as a realm of beauty at the other end of a visionary prospect marked by all the signs and hazards of the sublime: the sense of exposure and secondariness, the abyss between asymmetrically matched rock outcroppings, and the movement of a passing storm. Fran-

57. THOMAS COLE, *Gelyna*, 1826. Courtesy of the Fort Ticonderoga Museum.

cis Herbert's story provides Cole with a narrative encompassing at a thematic level elements of the Colean sublime implicit in the composition. The death of Rutledge thematizes both the threat implicit in all sublime paintings and the visionary release linked to the moment of annihilation. Like the conflation of death with vision that so often concludes the short stories of Edgar Allan Poe, the fallen presence of Major Rutledge suggests an ecstatic quality to death, an apocalypse of self in which the subject is both ravished and destroyed at the moment of visionary consummation.[63]

In works like *Gelyna*, together with Cole's two versions of *The Last of the Mohicans* (Hartford, Connecticut, Wadsworth Atheneum, 1827, and Cooperstown, New York, New York State Historical Association, 1827), Cole employs narrative as a means of literalizing his own themes. The vertiginous quality of the chasms and rock outcroppings is translated into a *narrative* of death, sacrifice, and suspense. Narrative functions for Cole as a form of thematic self-accounting, explicating in temporal fashion an experience otherwise accessible only in the spatial structure of the work.[64] When skillfully developed, the narrative elements in Cole's paintings not only focus the viewer's attention on that aspect of the sublime landscape which they represent in condensed and anecdotal form, but advance through their narrative structure the premises of the painting itself. In *Landscape, Composition, St. John in the Wilderness* (1827; fig. 58) Cole creates a wilderness scene structured according to the visual imperatives of the sublime. A foreground outcropping of rock that retains the block-like proportions of the altar-boulder of *Sunny Morning on the Hudson* protrudes from the left-hand margin of the canvas over a vacant desert ravine. Below it sits a valley with a small stand of palm trees and two tiny figures dwarfed by the immense emptiness of the surrounding space. Across the valley rises a towering column of rock, its dark walls draped with desert vegetation. A barren pinnacle surges skyward across the upper right center of the canvas. To the right of the thrusting pinnacle a slender body of water courses down the deep valley walls and disappears into darkness. Above it and to the right a narrow line of birds spans the partially visible valley on the far side of the central rock formation, their height paralleling the base of the pinnacle to the left. The central valley and surrounding cliffs occupy the bottom two-thirds of the canvas. The low values that predominate cast the foreground and center of the canvas in darkness, the visual equivalent of a passing storm, punctuated only by the dramatically highlighted promontory, the intensely lit valley floor, and the rising arc of mist that curls along the left border of the canvas, sweeps behind the central pinnacle, and merges in the brilliant burst of white cumulus clouds filling the upper right frame of the painting. A gray pyramidal mountain hovers in the visionary distance of the upper left.

St. John in the Wilderness abounds with oedipal imagery. The juxtaposition of foreground promontory and central pinnacle, the former squat and rectangular, the latter erect and elongated, echoes the struggle of parent with child that resonates throughout Cole's sublime canvases. As in Cole's other works, the painting straddles a fine line between its narcissistic impulses and mirror-stage identifications on the one hand and its more overtly oedipal struggles on the other. The central pinnacle seems to project and fulfill the rocky and penile aspirations of the foreground promontory, the abyss that separates them marking the distance and ultimately the illusion dividing the fragmented and powerless self from the unified and alienating image it seeks. The difference in the respective conditions of pinnacle and promontory—the latter massively weighted and planted firmly upon the earth, the former suspended precariously in space, its apparent solidity belied by its susceptibility to collapse—transforms the narcissistic identifications of the two into an oedipal contest for supremacy. The foreground promontory, smaller in size and

58. THOMAS COLE, *Landscape, Composition, St. John in the Wilderness,* 1827. Wadsworth Atheneum, Hartford, Connecticut.

lower in elevation than the central pinnacle, challenges the pinnacle to no avail. Like the blighted trees on the right or the dwarfed and insignificant figures in the valley below, its physical presence remains inferior relative to the dominating strength of the pinnacle. Even the string of birds in the distant valley to the right, emblems of flight in their fragile ascent, cannot surmount the towering presence of the central mountain.

Only the valley mist, Cole's repeated image of sublimating energies, rises from the valley floor to form a fragile S-curve that circumvents the threatening power of the pinnacle and blossoms into the white serenity of light and air. The vulnerability of the promontory is redeemed not by physical prowess but by the quiet subversion of the mist that gnaws at the mountain's peripheries, carving out a pathway of alternative energies that restate the pinnacle's sky-reaching majesty as a cloud of vapor and light. Secondariness is redeemed through an act of language, the capacity to subvert the world of hand and history by translating their facticity and givenness, figured by Cole as sheer physical presence, into a different system of discourse that disguises the old while maintaining its underlying patterns. Language reshapes reality by resignifying it, binding it into an imaginative discourse that reverses the threat of the given by usurping its power. The subject substitutes its own (linguistic) authority for the discourse of the Other, at once incorporating the power of the Other while disguising and defeating its Otherness.

The lessons of the sublime are all present in prenarrative fashion in *St. John in the Wilderness*. Space is deployed formulaically according to the imperatives of the Colean sublime: the naturalization of the landscape, the reversal of the signifying moment, and the revisionary strategy of the beautiful. The introduction of figures and anecdotal elements, however, accomplishes more than a thematization and recapitulation of an experience already inscribed into the landscape. Cole's figures function as a critical subtext, revising by their presence the shape and nuancing of the original wilderness manuscript. Their appearance within the painting, like a play within a play, condenses the significance of the whole into a limited form and allows Cole the freedom of an editorial comment upon his own work. The result, as we shall see, is a renewed emphasis upon *signification* as the heart of the sublime experience. The drama Saint John enacts before his followers contains all the elements of a sublime epiphany, but privileges from among those elements the signifying moment as an experience redemptive of the subject's threatened state.

Cole silhouettes the figure of Saint John against the dark canyon wall opposite him (fig. 59). Girded only by a loincloth, Saint John fronts the elements as an emblem of humanity stripped to its essential dimensions. A plain wooden cross stands at his side and echoes in its simplicity the ges-

59. THOMAS COLE, detail of fig. 58, *Landscape, Composition, St. John in the Wilderness* (St. John the Baptist and figures).

turing cruciform figure of the Baptist. Both cross and figure form diminutive points of light against the black abyss of the valley. Their vulnerability derives from the process of naturalization within the painting. When reduced to terms of a lowest common denominator, their meager presence is no match against the authority of rock and stone. The two slender sticks of the cross can scarcely compete with the massive vertical thrust of the pinnacle, while the frail figure of the Baptist seems no more than a foil for the sheer physical presence of the natural landscape. The powers of nature and all that is naturalized (de-signified) into the anonymous mass of rock dwarf the silhouetted forms of Baptist and cross into impotent emblems of flesh and bone.

There is a difference, however, between the pointed intersection of the Baptist's cross and the wooden forms of the gnarled trees that straddle the promontory at the extreme right. Though cross and trees are both elemental in shape and linked through their mutual juxtaposition against the valley wall, they are distinguished from each other by the symbolic function that separates cross from trees. The trees possess no semiotic significance. Though they augur in their shape the lineaments of the cross, they remain natural objects in a mute world. They possess no intrinsic meaning until marshaled in the service of a symbolic system. The perpendicular intersection of slabs of wood means nothing as an expression of organic nature. The wood remains wood until its rearrangement serves larger symbolic ends, at which point it is suddenly transformed from two sticks, nature merely, into the image of a power that renders nature the servant and instrument of its own ends. *The difference between the bare simplicity of two sticks and the remarkable complexity of the cross is the difference described by the act of signification.* The powers of nature, awesome and threatening in their own terms, are rendered the passive tools of the human imagination when subjected to the individual's capacity as a symbol-maker. The sublime thus transforms paintings about nature into paintings about metaphor.

Language functions for Cole as the concept of the *eschaton* did for the early Christian community he depicts. It marks with its advent the introduction of a new power, a kingdom come, irrupting with eschatological power upon the scene and bringing in its wake a new dispensation. The signifying moment, by releasing the subject from his thralldom to the Other, corresponds to what theologians call "realized eschatology," the imminence of divine governance within the world of men. Signification is Cole's secularized rewriting of an eschatological theology. It reverses the course of nature by the introduction of a new power, an action of grace upon the temporal world. Christianity provides Cole with a drama of spirit over matter antedating his own, and it offers him in the figure of the cross an image of the paradoxical reversal by which the most natural and pedestrian of objects becomes the bearer of transcendent meaning. The naturalization that reduces all existence to two sticks of wood discovers itself suddenly the agent of energies larger than itself in that moment of sublime apocalypse, that influx of power, when image becomes symbol and the subject is redeemed from his anonymity by an act of language.

The process of signification, as an event of eschatological significance, unfolds in a manner paralleling the Kantian sublime. As recounted by Weiskel, the mind substitutes its own infinity for the apparent phenomenal infinity before it; we have seen that this substitution is essentially metaphorical because the two kinds of infinity are logically incommensurable—they belong to separate discourses. . . . How, we may ask, if "our power of resistance" is of "quite another kind" than nature's power—how is a comparison between these two categorically incommensurable powers meaningful? We are answered by an act of metaphor. Thus we perceive again that the intentional structure of the negative [or Kantian] sublime as a whole implies the conversion of the outer world into a symbol for the mind's relation to itself.[65]

The mind bridges the "incommensurable" gap between itself and nature, the abyss that always separates the subject from the desired/despised Other in Cole, by an act of metaphoric substitution. The "apparent phenomenal infinity before it" is replaced by "its own infinity," and the power of the Other is defeated by Cole's remarkable version of the *eschaton*, the self as Signifier. That finally is Cole's definition of human nature, and his resolution of the quest for identity running throughout the sublime canvases. The subject ceases to be the signified, another term in the discourse of the Other, and appropriates for itself the power of Signifier. The sublime is more than a strategy for aggrandizing the powers of the past or ratifying the discontinuity that makes the aggrandizement possible. It is an act of the deepest hubris, an alteration in the discourse of desire in which the subject substitutes his own signifying power for that of the Other. Saint John's importance, both to Cole and to traditional Christianity, is as Signifier. To Christian theology, he announces the coming of one who is greater than himself. Saint John is the harbinger of the Godhead. In Cole's more secular version of theophany, the Baptist is witness to his own powers of signification. His cruciform shape testifies to his status as *homo symbolicus*. Like the cross beside him, he summarizes in his very appearance the paradox of all questing humanity: that fragile flesh and bone can harbor within itself the Kingdom of God. That kingdom is the power of metaphor itself, an appropriation of the strategies of language understood as the heart of the subject's quest for identity.

The genius of Cole's resolution lies in his capacity to create a myth of the Romantic self as signifying subject. *St. John in the Wilderness* is a study in the power of signification as it first presents the paradox of its insufficiency and then redeems its insufficiency through a metaphoric leap by which it both evades and appropriates the Other. What is figured here is the very process of signification, sublime because of the state of incommensurability with which its starts, and subversive because in its act of incorporation of an alien power into its own creative process it inverts the ostensible order of relation with which it started. With double-edged precision the sublime records the paradoxical states of guilt and liberation associated with the exhilarating hubris of its achievement.

The Colean sublime commences as an effort of Romantic identity formation and concludes in a moment of signification that parallels the larger patterns of metaphor itself. When divested of its peculiar and private intensity, Cole's sublime resembles nothing so much as the paradoxical movement of all metaphors animated by that tension between tenor and vehicle that renders meaning a fragile compromise between discovery and disguise. In the transition from naturalization to signification, Cole reenacts for us the drama of the vehicle, negating itself in its reach toward larger meanings (naturalization) while nonetheless signifying, through its own contours, the shape of the world it images. What begins as an act of autobiography—a sublime experiment in self-origination—concludes in its maturity as an effort of language. The subject has not only generated a grammar equal to its desire, but created for itself a mode of expression, a vocabulary and *topos*, that embodies within its structure the negations and assertions intrinsic to all symbolic discourse. Cole's blocking peaks provide a prototype for the symbolic process as it passes around and through an opaque object (the vehicle) on the way to vision. The capacity of metaphors to subvert at least partially their own vehicles—a form of displacement that is the essence of metaphoric activity—lies at the heart of Cole's sublime, a discourse defined by its ability to resist the literal in a desublimated world. The sublime rescues the individual from his own anonymity, investing him with a power of metaphor, a capacity to signify, that completes the subject's quest for autonomy.[66] It provides a myth of the subject that is at the same time an investigation into the nature and functioning of metaphors. The sublime becomes a palimpsest of the self, and the self a figure of the profoundest textuality. The quest for identity is resolved through the advent of language. This myth of the subject as Signifier represents Cole's remarkable contribution to Romantic re-visionary activity.

Part Four

Epilogue:
From Allston to
Luminism

*A*merican Romanticism has been regarded until recently as a movement preeminently of words. The achievement of the American Renaissance was to press language—a language shaped by the collision of two centuries of Protestant experience with an aboriginal landscape—into the service of a vision making extravagant claims for itself. Those claims have included the radical divinity of the individual, the capacity of the self to generate an entire cosmos from its own private history, and the power of language to function as a surrogate for grace in a modern world. It is this last claim that is most significant, for it tends to elevate the artist to the status of a secular priest whose power extends only as far as his word.

No wonder, then, the effort by writers of the American Renaissance to render their own language an audible echo of the divine Word. Emerson's equivalent of the Word made flesh, his version of incarnation, is the sentence. It is here that subject meets object, the ME encounters the NOT ME. From the tumult of letters, syllables, and phrases conjoined in an ever new and original relation arises that miracle of visionary creation, the living text. And here too the verbal self discovers its visual possibilities. I take this to be the heart of the "transparent eyeball" passage in *Nature* (a passage as dear to art historians as to literary critics). The loss of "all mean egotism" ("I become a transparent eyeball; I am nothing; I see all; the currents of the Universal Being circulate through me; I am part or parcel of God") requires more than a mystical congruence of self and world. True power occurs only in a moment of *representation* when vision and language are conjoined and the self is at its "ocular" best ("I *see* all"). The ego is not so much dissolved as concentrated in a state of heightened awareness, its perceptual possibilities intensified (why else be a transparent eyeball?) rather than transcended. What Emerson provides us with, then, is not a metalinguistic event, an experience of contact outside language and time, but a moment of epiphany informed by the possibilities of perception. In the beginning was vision and the word, or as Emerson phrases it in "Experience," "As I am, so I see."

Given this bias toward perception in American Romanticism, an "I" shaped to the contours of the "eye," it should come as no surprise that there exists a second American Romanticism, a visual tradition of painters and artists better known today by art historians than literary critics. Though less familiar than their literary counterparts of the period, these painters of Romanticism were committed to the figurative possibilities of the landscape with an intensity paralleling that of the writers. Fully a generation before Emerson, Washington Allston was projecting the concerns of a nascent Romantic self implicitly modernist onto the forms of European academic art. In the decades following the appearance of *Nature*—during the same period in which Hawthorne, Melville, Thoreau, Whitman, and Dickinson were virtually creating an American literature—a group of second- and third-generation Hudson River School painters were experimenting with a radically new mode of painting that has since been labeled "luminist."[1] What unites each of these painters to a larger tradition of American Romantic writing is a concern for consciousness and language as the organizing centers of reality. Whether expressed through an attention to narrative shape, to formal composition, or to the power of light, the Romantic text (verbal or visual) generates itself primarily in relation to other texts and records within itself a history of its origins, suppressions, and achievements.

If we may tidy up history into biography, then we may say with only minor qualification that American Romantic painting begins with Washington Allston. His oeuvre provides us with a remarkable visual history of the origins and predispositions of early Romantic art. It also sets us irrevocably upon the road that leads to Thomas Cole and the flowering of an American landscape tradition. For what Allston shares with the landscapists that follow him is an insistence on the symbolic—the textual— value of the world as perceived. His canvases arrange reality according to the imperatives of the mind: portraits of family and intimate friends become studies in inner illumination; landscapes created according to classical formula subject the world of experience and emotion to the regulating principles of consciousness; and biblical subjects return the viewer repeatedly, almost obsessively, to moments of divine intervention when reason confronts supernal powers outside the boundaries of normal social intercourse.

As previous commentators have noted, Allston's work turns upon an uneasy alliance between the classical technique of Raphael, Poussin, Titian, and Veronese and the more subjective concerns of early Romanticism. Allston rejects the hard outlines and opaque colors of neoclassicism and substitutes for their angular rationality the softer contours, diffuse light, and transparent color implicit in the Venetian tradition of glazing. His remarkable *Self Portrait* of 1805 (fig. 60) demonstrates, as William Gerdts has noted, an altogether original mode of painting that breaks both with the "Copleyesque realism" of the previous century and the more "painterly, idealistic elegance" of his fellow expatriate, Gilbert Stuart.[2] In the *Self Portrait*'s distended shadows, mysterious architectural spaces, and curious manipulation of the human body (the virtual absence of shoulders seems to float the head upon a white collar and red cravat), the painting announces its pleasure with a world more mannered than classical, a world still governed by the priorities of the mind, but one in which imagination rather than reason predominates. Indeed, Allston's art provides a record of the imagination in its historical evolution from an enabling power recapitulating the creative process of the gods (Coleridge's primary and secondary imagination), to a potential source of terror and estrangement that compels the artist into activity that finds no parallel or correlative in the natural world.

Allston tends, then, especially in his earlier work, to manipulate the forms of classical art in essentially unclassical directions. Both his landscape and history paintings place their subjects within geometrically arranged spaces, binding the restless movement of their diagonal forms within vistas or architectural settings composed upon a stable axis of vertical and horizontal lines. Yet within each work or series of works Allston creates alternative dispositions of space that challenge the priority of the classical conventions or introduce themes subversive of its harmony and balance. To move, for instance, from the circular integration of forms in *The Dead Man Restored to Life by Touching the Bones of the Prophet Elisha* (1811–14; fig. 61) to the radical disruption of space in the off-centered and diagonally composed *Saul and the Witch of Endor* (ca. 1820; fig. 21) is to discover with Allston the incapacity of classical forms to assimilate the visionary powers claimed by the Romantic artist. Both paintings focus upon moments when supernatural powers, mediated by artists and prophet figures, irrupt into the realm of daily existence, shattering the ability of a classical world to contain the energies it would communicate.

From this crisis of Romantic vision and classical form, a question of new wine in old vessels, Allston arrives at two rather different resolutions. The first and more affirmative leads to works founded on the paradox of formal ambiguity, paintings like *Moonlit Landscape* (1819; fig. 17) and *Coast Scene on the Mediterranean* (1811; fig. 16), which turn mystery into poetry and play with the magic of their own inscrutable spaces. Here one senses in Allston categories later articulated by Emerson: a world of Reason that is intuitive and beyond the grasp of the slow and material Understanding; a

60. WASHINGTON ALLSTON, *Self Portrait,* 1805. Courtesy, Museum of Fine Arts, Boston. Bequest of Miss Alice Hooper.

growing self-consciousness and self-referentiality (all the later landscapes allude in their imagery of the earlier ones); and a substitution of private and contemplative states for the more traditional concerns of history painting. The second mode of resolution, the one that comes to predominate in the later works, places solitary singers or shepherds against a decayed classical background. Allston seems haunted in these elegiac canvases by his

61. WASHINGTON ALLSTON, *The Dead Man Restored to Life by Touching the Bones of the Prophet Elisha,* 1811–14. Courtesy of the Pennsylvania Academy of the Fine Arts, Philadelphia.

lack of an oracular self. The language of the old masters burdens the artist with forms incommensurate with his aspirations, and Allston winds up substituting memory for vision and elegy for prophecy.

Yet even in these haunting later works there is room for consolation. The very forms that betray the artist into retrospection also rescue him from the threat of an imagination untethered by social conventions. Though an ardent proponent of the imagination, Allston shares with his friend Coleridge a corresponding horror of its corrosive powers—its inability to be housed safely in the world in which we live. The nostalgia for classical forms in Allston's later works, together with his predilection for religious subjects, provide him with a system of checks and balances upon his own visionary impulses. What the Romantic artist has loosed upon the world by the powers of his mind he can reintegrate into the commerce of polite society through an act of conjuration, summoning the forces of the past to keep watch upon the impulses of the present.

Allston, in other words, concludes his career as a conservative Romantic modernist, incapable or unwilling to seize upon the possibilities of his world. He is joined in this regard by John Quidor, whose work inverts Irving's ironic vision of the radically fictional nature of our relation to reality. Quidor substitutes for Irving's narrative glee and "irresponsibility" an anxious and unhappy consciousness riven by potentially catastrophic psychic forces. Where Irving transforms the fate of the writer in a post-Kantian world into that of a labyrinth-maker and constructor of fictions, Quidor returns the burden of vision to a Miltonic tradition fearful of its visionary powers. The renunciation of self crucial to Miltonic vision lapses in Quidor's work into a gothic self-parody. The imagination comes to be associated with the horrors of the half-seen life, and the text rises to confront its maker with the crime of his own vision. However dissimilar in subject and form Quidor may be from Allston, he shares with the latter a hesitation—perhaps a humility—in the face of the modern world he conjures. Toward the end of their lives both artists create works of abjuration and denial. For each, the imagination has trespassed a boundary of its own creation: in Allston consciousness collapses under the burden of self-aware vision, and in Quidor a tendency to meddle in divine games results only in visionary narcissism.

It will take a subsequent generation of American painters, beginning with Cole (who in fact was born the same year as Quidor) and concluding with the luminists, to create an indigenous tradition of painting enamored of its own power and willing to accept the risks of provinciality (an American school of landscape painting)). The key term here is *landscape*, for what Cole and his successors possess, unlike Allston and Quidor, is a faith in the capacity of the landscape to provide an adequate visual correlative for the drama of the soul. Seen in this light, the Hudson River School and the luminists (the latter, as Ted Stebbins suggests, representing only a rearguard reformulation of the former) both share with Allston an unflinching faith in the power of visual metaphors.[3] Each figure or movement invests its material with significances beyond those of the pedestrian and ordinary. However ideal Allston's landscapes may be, they share with the most realistic luminist canvases a willingness to understand the world symbolically—as metaphor. Where Allston and the luminists differ is in the nature of their tropes, what subjects they choose to invest with meaning, not in the game of meaning-making itself.

Luminism, most broadly defined, is both a style and a metaphysic. As outlined by Barbara Novak, the term encompasses that body of mid-nineteenth-century American paintings noted for their glass-like surfaces and their rapt devotion to light.[4] Luminist classicism, as Novak calls it, stresses a horizontal format, a monochromatic palette, an attention to the surface plane, a down-playing of recessional depth, a strokeless application of paint, a tendency to quantify and formalize all aspects of the painting, and an alliance on occasion with the bold surface linearity of primitive art. It is best represented in the stilled and hermetically sealed spaces of Fitz Hugh Lane, John Kensett, Martin Johnson Heade, and, to a lesser extent, Sanford Gifford, although elements of the luminist style appear in selected canvases of virtually every major American painter from 1840 to the decades following the Civil War. Like all major movements, it tends to beget its own countervision, what Novak terms luminist anticlassicism, an impulse to explode the serenity of its space through a mannered use of diagonals and color. Above all luminism is a "conceptual" rather than "optical" mode of painting; it relies more on the artist's *idea* of the landscape than its actual presence to the perceiving subject.

Historically, luminism represents more than an obsessive concern with light by painters of the second- and third-generation Hudson River School. The fascination with light is itself only an extension of that deeper concern with meaning, with the symbolic potential of the landscape, that goes back to Cole, Quidor, and Allston. At the same time that the luminist painter is breaking out of the conventions of the picturesque inherited from the eighteenth century, he is reaffirming by redefining the underlying sublime possibilities of the American wilderness. For luminism is another form of the American sublime—not the sublime of Burke or even Cole, but the sublime of a generation uneasy with the grandiloquence of past painters and in search of a counter-rhetoric at once simple in its gestures and yet arresting in its power. For an age experiencing the rise of industrial capitalism, a loss of individual power within society, and

62. FITZ HUGH LANE, *Owl's Head, Penobscot Bay, Maine*, 1862. Courtesy, Museum of Fine Arts, Boston, M. and M. Karolik Collection.

a growing depersonalization of the work process, luminism provided an art that combated the mechanization of the period with its own subversive poetry of light and space. Where Cole and Frederic Church belong clearly to the era of prewar Jacksonian energies—exuberant, self-important, and possessed at moments with superhuman powers—the painters we identify most as luminists spring from a different set of social circumstances.

Not that the luminists present a uniform strategy of painting. The circular geometry of Lane's *Owl's Head, Penobscot Bay, Maine* (1862; fig. 62) together with his recurrent imagery of voyaging and his colors of early dawn, suggest a world secure in its traditional values, certain that the waters beyond its vision represent no more than an analogical extension of the microcosm already available to us. Kensett's *Shrewsbury River* (1859; fig. 63), on the other hand, eschews Lane's concern for cultural continuity and focuses instead upon the more abstract and formal possibilities of the landscape, looking forward in its asymmetric balance and its flattened forms to the work of Whistler, Sargent, and the generation of transitional painters that leads into post-Impressionist modernism. The most problematic figure associated with luminism is Frederic Church. As David Huntington has noted, Church's canvases roil in light that has

63. JOHN F. KENSETT, *Shrewsbury River*, 1859. Courtesy of the New-York Historical Society, New York City.

little to do with the monochromatic unity of the luminist world as defined by Novak.[5] Church's melodrama of pigment and impasto carries him back to his teacher Thomas Cole and to a religiously invested drama of American history that speaks more to the God of Armageddon and the passions of the Civil War than to the transparent eyeball of Emerson. Whether or not we term him luminist, Church, like his contemporaries, possesses an unquestioned place within that larger saga of landscape painting which marks the sublime with the stamp of American vistas.

Though the concern for light and the symbolic dimensions of the landscape continues well into the twentieth century, this study concludes with the triumph of the Romantic sublime in the early years of Cole's career. The mantle of the sublime will pass as a destiny and doom to other painters, most notably Church and the luminists. What links all these figures—however varied their individual concerns—to their literary counterparts is that combination of perceptual acuity and textual canniness which renders American Romantic art a continual effort of self-definition and cultural revision. "As I am, so I see."

Notes

Preface

1. Roger Stein, "Structure as Meaning: Towards a Cultural Interpretation of American Painting," *American Art Review* 3 (March–April 1976):66–78.

2. Dickinson's phrase has become the title of a recent study of her poetry. See Karl Keller, *The Only Kangaroo among the Beauty: Emily Dickinson and America* (Baltimore and London, 1979).

Chapter One

1. Born in South Carolina in 1779, Allston first traveled to England after his graduation from Harvard College in 1800. Before returning to America in 1808, Allston had studied at the Royal Academy in London and traveled extensively through Europe, including prolonged visits to Paris and Rome where he absorbed the masterpieces of Renaissance art, especially Raphael, Michelangelo, and the Venetian colorists. While in Rome from 1804 to 1808, he came into close contact with Coleridge, with whom he remained friendly throughout his life, composing an intriguing sonnet upon the poet's death about their mutual voyage on "some starless sea." There too he met Washington Irving and various literati who frequented Rome's Cafe Greco in the early years of the nineteenth century. In Boston from 1808 to 1811, Allston married Ann Channing, sister of Unitarian minister William Ellery Channing, and returned with her and the aspiring painter Samuel F. B. Morse to London in 1811. Allston's painting *The Dead Man Restored to Life by Touching the Bones of the Prophet Elisha,* exhibited at the British Institution in 1813, brought him a prize of 200 guineas and great acclaim within the British art world. The sudden death of his wife in 1815 followed Allston's own prolonged serious illness. He was confirmed later that year in the Episcopal Church. Allston's health remained fragile, and he died on 9 July 1843. He settled in Boston in 1818, never to return to Europe except, perhaps, in his art. See Edgar P. Richardson, *Washington Allston* (Chicago, 1948; New York, 1967), pp. 24–25, 97–98, 133–35; Doreen Hunter, "America's First Romantics: Richard Henry Dana, Sr. and Washington Allston," *New England Quarterly* 45 (March, 1972):21. The most recent critical and biographical account of Allston is to be found in William H. Gerdts and Theodore E. Stebbins, Jr., *"A Man of Genius": The Art of Washington Allston (1779–1843)* (Boston, 1979).

2. Allston coined the phrase in his *Lectures on Art* a century before T. S. Eliot introduced it to the modern critical vocabulary. Speaking of the need for a growing plant to have "predetermined correlatives, without which its existence could not be manifested," Allston continues:

> So, too, is the external world to the mind; which needs, also, as the condition of its manifestation, its objective correlative. Hence the presence of some outward object, predetermined to correspond to the preexisting data in its living power, is essential to the evolution of its proper end,—the pleasurable emotion.

Unlike Eliot, whose "objective correlative" is a literary device at the disposal of the artist,

Allston sees the objective correlative as a metaphysical expression of a prior harmony between mind and world. Allston is using his theory as a buttress or antidote against the solipsism implicit in his own work. See Washington Allston, *Lectures on Art* (New York, 1850), p. 16.

3. Washington Allston, *Monaldi, A Tale* (Boston, 1841; Gainesville, Fla., 1967), pp. 7–8.

4. William Butler Yeats, "Byzantium," in *The Collected Poems of W. B. Yeats* (New York, 1956), p. 243. The iconography of dolphins as potential vehicles of the imagination may be implicit in American painting in a work as early as John Singleton Copley's *Galatea*, copied from an engraving by Augustinus of Lazarini's *Galatea Triomphe Sur L'Onde*. See Jules David Prown, *John Singleton Copley*, vol. 1 (Cambridge, Mass., 1966), p. 19.

5. Only the distant, cold blue mountain rising from the flattened river valley, brown and silent, seems an image of genuine timelessness, repeating, in miniature, in its relation to the time-bound valley the larger relation between Williams and the background landscape that defines the picture.

6. See, for example, *The Genius of British Painting*, ed. David Piper (New York, 1975), p. 242.

7. As Ronald Paulson notes of George Stubbs in *Emblem and Expression: Meaning in English Art of the Eighteenth Century* (Cambridge, Mass., 1975), p. 169, "Man is not the center of Stubbs' universe, but only an element in the animal kingdom, a species to which no more attention is given than to the trees and plants."

8. One can sense the distance between Allston's sense of selfhood and that in the work of Lawrence, in an anecdote that Allston once recorded:

Lawrence had the bravura touch of the pencil—slap-dash—which always takes with novices. I was once at Mr. Angerstein's gallery with Walker and a young artist of genius who was much taken by a portrait of Angerstein by Lawrence. In the next room was a portrait by Vandyke, and a masterpiece. We were expressing our admiration of it when our young friend said:

"Yes, but I confess I like Sir Thomas better."

"Do you, sir?" said Walker. "Indeed! Well, sir, you won't think so long." And he was right.

There is something technically called "handling," which invariably surprises and delights the novice, but which is easily gotten and soon palls. A great picture has a simplicity about it, and is so true to reality that it seldom dazzles and surprises.

Recounted in Jared B. Flagg, *The Life and Letters of Washington Allston* (London, 1893), p. 374. Allston's metaphysical imagination apparently blinded him to the significance of the stylistic revolution effected by Lawrence and others; he could see it only as superficial show.

9. Robert R. Wark, *Ten British Pictures 1740–1840* (San Marino, Calif., 1971), p. 8.

10. Ibid., pp. 8, 47–48.

11. John Wilmerding, ed., *The Genius of American Painting* (New York, 1973), p. 42.

12. Jules D. Prown, *American Painting* (Cleveland, 1969), pp. 19–20.

13. In an effort to keep abreast of developments in England and to avail himself of professional advice from leading artists, Copley submitted *The Boy with the Squirrel*, a portrait of his stepbrother Henry Pelham, to be exhibited in London at the Society of Artists in 1766. Though the picture was greatly admired and Copley received friendly criticism from Benjamin West, who urged him to travel to England to study from masterpieces at first hand, he remained loyal to his "provincial" vision throughout his American career, emphasizing the linearity, bold and solid color planes, and starkly contrasting values that distinguished his work from the more softly modeled British art of the period. Ibid., pp. 47ff.

14. Quoted in James Thomas Flexner, *That Wilder Image* (New York, 1962, 1970), p. 42n. Cole's judgment has been repeated by many twentieth-century critics, most recently by John Lunsford in the "Introduction" to the Dallas Museum of Fine Arts catalogue *The Romantic Vision in America* (1971). "But all these works [Allston's landscapes] are still more

derivative than original. They are more European than American in feel; their muted orderliness is that of the Old World."

15. For an alternative account of Allston as a Romantic modernist painter, see Carter Ratcliff, "Allston and the Historical Landscape," *Art in America* 68 (Oct. 1980):97–104.

16. Suzi Gablik, *Magritte* (Greenwich, Conn., 1970), p. 76.

17. J. Hillis Miller, "The Interpretation of Lord Jim," in *The Interpretation of Narrative: Theory and Practice*, ed. Morton W. Bloomfield (Cambridge, Mass., 1970), p. 213. Miller is referring to Coleridge.

18. The ties between Friedrich and Allston are indirect rather than direct. The two painters never met each other, nor is there any evidence that they were aware of each other's work. Their circle of acquaintances may have overlapped in Rome, where a large number of German expatriate artists patronized the Caffé Greco during the years Allston, Coleridge, and Irving met there. The bonds linking Friedrich and Allston seem to rest instead on intellectual currents and sympathies common to their respective worlds rather than on any form of direct historical influence. Recent studies that link nineteenth-century German painting with British and American Romanticism include Robert Rosenblum, *Modern Painting and the Northern Romantic Tradition* (London, 1975); *The Natural Paradise: Painting in America, 1800–1950*, ed. Kynaston McShine [Museum of Modern Art] (New York, 1976); William Vaughn, *German Romanticism and English Art* (New Haven and London, 1979) and *German Romantic Painting* (New Haven, 1980); Kermit S. Champa, *German Painting of the Nineteenth Century* (New Haven, 1970); Jed Perl, "Mystics and Medievalists," *Art in America* 69 (October 1981):114–19 and Barbara Novak, "American and Europe: Influence and Affinity" in *Nature and Culture: American Landscape and Painting, 1825–1875* (New York, 1980, pp. 226–73.

19. The identification of the woman with Friedrich's wife is made by Helmut Borsch-Supan, *Caspar David Friedrich* (New York, 1974), p. 128. For a thoughtful review of the state of current Friedrich scholarship see Francoise Forster-Hahn, "Recent Scholarship on Caspar David Friedrich," *Art Bulletin* 58 (March 1976):113–16.

20. The dash of pink in the woman's ruffled collar serves to highlight an otherwise prim and self-contained body (note the tightly bound braids of hair) and reminds the viewer of that flair for freedom and color that even the most entrapped and self-contained individual possesses as if by right.

21. For an excellent discussion of Vermeer and the issue of framing, see Harry Berger, Jr., "Conspicuous Exclusion in Vermeer: An Essay in Renaissance Pastoral," *Yale French Studies* 47 (1972):243–65.

22. The analogy with Emerson runs deep: both figures initially invoked their Protestant heritage as a defense against a self defined by social processes. Emerson's cry for "transparency," for a moment outside history and the acculturated self, parallels Friedrich's efforts in *Chalk Cliffs* to create a space in which the self confronts without intervention or mediation the sources of its sustaining power. The play in *Chalk Cliffs* between the desire for unmediated vision and the knowledge of its impossibility is what animates the painting.

23. For a discussion of Romantic "inscription" poetry that has proven seminal for current scholarship, see Geoffrey Hartman's essay "Wordsworth, Inscriptions, and Romantic Nature Poetry" in *Beyond Formalism* (New Haven, 1970), pp. 206–30.

Chapter Two

1. The standard work on the origins of Unitarianism in America is Conrad Wright's *The Beginnings of Unitarianism* (Boston, 1955). For a more specific discussion of the relation between the rise of a middle-class ethos and Protestantism, the reader is referred to Max Weber, *The Protestant Ethic and the Spirit of Capitalism* (London, 1930), David Little, *Religion, Order, and Law: A Study in Pre-Revolutionary England* (New York, 1969), and Michael Walzer, *The Revolution of the Saints: A Study in the Origins of Radical Politics* (Cambridge,

Mass., 1965). Sydney Ahlstrom draws the connections between Unitarianism and a mercantile society in *A Religious History of the American People* (New Haven, 1972), pp. 38ff., as does Daniel Howe throughout *The Unitarian Conscience: Harvard Moral Philosophy, 1805–1861* (Cambridge, Mass., 1970).

2. Leo Marx, *The Machine in the Garden* (New York, 1964), pp. 56–57.

3. Ibid., pp. 69, 71–72.

4. Joseph Haroutunian, *Piety Versus Moralism: The Passing of the New England Theology* (New York, 1932, 1970), p. xxv. The phrase is a favorite one of Sydney Ahlstrom's, who has written an introduction to Haroutunian's book.

5. It is also Prospero's acknowledgment—to be reenacted many times in the nineteenth century—of the artist's fears of the magical powers he possesses.

6. Michel Foucault, *The Order of Things* (New York, 1970), p. 22.

7. In Sydney Ahlstrom, ed., *Theology in America* (New York, 1967), p. 204. Ahlstrom notes Channing's resemblances here to Emerson and Horace Bushnell.

8. Ibid., p. 208.

9. Ibid., p. 201.

10. Ibid., p. 208.

11. Ibid., pp. 199, 201.

12. Wright, *Unitarianism*, pp. 269ff. Despite opposition from conservatives led by Jedediah Morse, father of Samuel F. B. Morse, the Hollis Chair was eventually filled in 1805 by Henry Ware, Sr., a well-known liberal. The election in 1806 of Samuel Webber, another liberal, to the presidency of Harvard confirmed the shift in power from the moderate Calvinists to a new liberal hegemony. It might be noted that William Ware, son of Hollis Professor Henry Ware, would later write a series of lectures on Allston published posthumously in 1852 after William Ware's death. See William Ware, *Lectures on the Works and Genius of Washington Allston* (Boston, 1852).

13. Ahlstrom, *Religious History*, pp. 388–89, 393. In reference to King's Chapel, Ahlstrom notes that "the first Episcopal church in New England, became the first Unitarian church in America."

14. Ibid., pp. 389–92.

15. Edgar P. Richardson, *Washington Allston* (Chicago, 1948; New York, 1967), p. 29.

16. Deborah Howard, "Some Eighteenth Century Followers of Claude," *Burlington Magazine* 111 (1969):731–32. The appearance of classical ruins in Allston's landscapes occurs at a later point in his career and suggests important developments in his understanding that will be discussed further in the essay.

17. Jeannine Hensley, ed., *The Works of Anne Bradstreet* (Cambridge, Mass., 1967), pp. 204–14.

18. Ahlstrom, *Theology*, pp. 209, 204.

19. Ibid., p. 205.

20. Ahlstrom, *Religious History*, p. 391.

21. Perry Miller, *Errand Into the Wilderness* (New York, 1956, 1964), p. 185.

22. That Revere's relation to his teapot mirrors Copley's relation to his portrait of Revere was first noted by Jules Prown:

> Revere ponders the problem of design, one hand cradling the globular teapot, the thing created, and the other supporting his head, the source of mind and imagination. Copley ingeniously creates a compositional interplay between the two spherical forms, one in each hand, which echoes the significance of the moment portrayed. Copley's perceptive insight into his subject results from an understanding of a creative process that parallels his own.

Jules David Prown, *John Singleton Copley*, vol. 1 (Cambridge, Mass., 1966), p. 75.

23. Paul de Man, "The Rhetoric of Temporality," in *Interpretation: Theory and Practice*, ed. Charles S. Singleton (Baltimore, 1969).

24. Walter Friedlaender, *Poussin, A New Approach* (New York, 1965), p. 34.

25. Specific figures throughout Allston's ouevre seem to be direct quotations from Poussin. The running foreground figure in *Landscape with a Man Killed by a Snake* (1648,

London, National Gallery), for example, appears as the prototype for Allston's single pilgrim in *Landscape with a Lake* (1804, Boston, Museum of Fine Arts) and for the central pilgrim in *Italian Landscape* (1805–8). For a discussion of *Italian Landscape* in relation to Poussin and to nineteenth-century German painting, see William H. Gerdts and Theodore E. Stebbins, Jr., *"A Man of Genius": The Art of Washington Allston (1779–1843)* (Boston, 1979), p. 47.

26. Friedlaender, *Poussin*, p. 26. Friedlaender writes:

Poussin arrived at classicism only through strong-willed intention. He could achieve the simplicity, clarity, and spatial abstraction so prominent in Raphael's style only by subduing the impulsive vehemence and passion which his drawings show to be deeply ingrained in his artistic nature. This suppression of spontaneous feeling may be seen in his finished paintings, and for this reason Poussin's work has been called overcalculated and rigid. The conscious crystallization that takes place in Poussin's *modus operandi* explains the difference in spirit between the two matters, Poussin and Raphael.

27. Ibid., p. 24.

28. *Rising of a Thunderstorm at Sea* represents an anomaly in Allston's early art. The painting presents a foreground occupied by a low valley of water and cresting waves of foam near the viewer's eye level. The spectator is engaged emotionally at this level and brought through the water trough into the picture space, where he encounters, as if himself a participant, a beleaguered single-masted craft with its struggling occupants. No help seems available from the distant blue sky, which, like the sailing vessel on the horizon, is soon to be overtaken by the swirling masses of clouds from an advancing storm line. *Rising of a Thunderstorm* shares with the *Romantic Landscape* an emotive vocabulary designed to engage the sympathies of the viewer and draw him into the picture's composition. Unlike the earlier picture, however, the viewer is not carried along a line of ascending vision in a process of sociomoral transformation. Instead, as Roger Stein has noted, he is left alone to "face the power of the dark sublime sea . . . . Here there is no reassuring harbor view or umbrageous foliage, no saving power in either rescuing boat or dancing nymphs, no distancing in time or space." The sensuality implicit in the opening interlude of the *Romantic Landscape* has been translated in the *Rising of a Thunderstorm* into an elemental and tumultous nature, at the same time as the painting as a whole has been dispossessed of the hope that characterized the earlier work. See Roger B. Stein, *Seascape and the American Imagination* (New York, 1975), pp. 25–27, and Edgar P. Richardson, *Painting in America* (New York, 1956), p. 145.

29. Thomas Cole similarly employs an architectural imagination to express a visionary state in *The Voyage of Life: Youth* (1842, Utica, New York, Munson-Williams-Proctor Institute). The exotic castle that appears in a bubble of light in the upper left corner of the canvas is clearly visionary and, in relation to the following series of pictures, probably ironic. In Allston the distinction between visionary and real is purposefully blurred. For an excellent discussion of the ironic nature of Cole's series, see Joy S. Kasson, *"The Voyage of Life*: Thomas Cole and Romantic Disillusionment," *American Quarterly* 27 (1975):42–56.

30. Friedlaender, *Poussin*, p. 81.

31. Allston provides here an expression of that architectural imagination which will later run wild, empty, and labyrinthine in later pictures like *The Prophet Jeremiah Dictating to the Scribe Baruch* (1820, New Haven, Connecticut, Yale University Art Gallery), but which in the *Italian Landscape* still conveys a sense of vision as a form of construction, a mode of building and transforming a world.

32. This process of synecdochic transformation is not without its problems. The questions of power and its abuse that run throughout the play, together with Caliban's perseverant ineducability and Prospero's darker applications of his artistry, suggest the problematics of Shakespeare's analogical world. The coherence of the playwright's magical isle is as hard-won an order as it is a natural starting point. That a symmetrically balanced world is as much an end-product of the play as it is an initial structural assumption provides a demonstration of synecdoche's precariously achieved power of return.

33. Three landscapes noted by Richardson from the middle Boston period, *Landscape of American Scenery* (1810), *Sunrise* (1810), and *Landscape, Alpine Scenery* (1810), are to the best of my knowledge unlocated at present. The fourth, *Landscape* (Baltimore, Maryland, Baltimore Museum of Art), could well date from an earlier period, though Richardson originally notes it as 1810. For a brief discussion of the work, as much a genre scene as a landscape, see Howard S. Merritt, "American Landscape Paintings in the Museum Collection," *Baltimore Museum of Art News* 25 (1962):5–6. For a more general discussion of Allston's landscape interests during this period, see Gerdts, *Allston*, p. 58.

34. Erwin Panofsky, *Meaning in the Visual Arts* (New York, 1955), pp. 300, 304–5.

35. Ibid., p. 312.

36. Foucault, *The Order of Things*, p. 34.

37. Anthony Blunt, *Nicolas Poussin* (New York, 1967), p. 114. Panofsky acknowledges Blunt's contributions in an earlier article from *Art Bulletin* 20 (1938):96ff.

38. Panofsky links the grammatically correct Latin meaning "Even in Arcady, there am I" with the tone of medieval moralizing he perceives in the Chatsworth version of *The Arcadian Shepherds*. The phrase "I, too, lived in Arcady," though grammatically suspect, he identifies as interpretively correct for the later Louvre painting.

39. Jared B. Flagg, ed., *Life and Letters of Washington Allston* (London, 1893), pp. 319–20.

40. Though I speak of Allston's "awareness" here, I do not wish to be guilty of an "intentional fallacy" that claims that Allston actually *intended* to record in the Toledo *Italian Landscape* his artistic self-consciousness. On the contrary, it is possible that Allston's largely Claudian iconography allowed him to assume an already established pictorial vocabulary as a way of *hiding* his awareness even from himself. I wish to suggest only that, at a level perhaps deeper than conscious intentionality, Allston's compositional structures betray a sense of loss that, like a Freudian dream-text, can be analyzed as much for what they attempt to hide as what they openly express.

41. To return for a moment to the Unitarian origins of this pattern of nonreturn: one can see in Channing an understanding of "transcendence" as a process of spiritualization that denies its origins in the natural world. The analogical habit of mind that sees "natural beauty" as a "type of spiritual beauty" does not always resolve itself into the organic and culturally continual process of transformation and return present in a work like Shakespeare's *The Tempest*. Instead, Channing's thought tends to divide into a more rigid dualism of spirit and matter, wherein triumph of the former occurs as a suppression or abnegation of the latter. The rhetoric of transformation, divested of its sense of return, becomes a language of transcendence, in which origins are abandoned in the name of a higher spirituality. In Allston the process occurs by another name. Moral pilgrimage proceeds by a logic of displacement in which ethical concerns are subsumed into aesthetic categories, and the process of mediation into a mode of self-referential discourse.

42. David Hume, *An Enquiry Concerning Human Understanding*, 2nd ed. (London, 1750; reprinted New York, 1963), pp. 75, 79.

43. Ibid., p. 52.

44. For a different attempt to understand rhetorical tropes as patterns for, and expressions of, deeper habits of thought, the reader is referred to Paul de Man, "Action and Identity in Nietzsche," *Yale French Studies* no. 52 (1975), pp. 16–30. De Man states that "the illusion of thought as action is the result of an . . . illegitmate totalization from part to whole," that is to say, "synecdoche" as a "rhetorical structure . . . of consciousness." According to de Man's interpretation, the traditional Western habit of attributing to thought the properties of a continuous and enduring substance is for Nietzsche a "fiction, arrived at by singling out one element from the process and eliminating all the rest, an artificial arrangement for the purpose of intelligibility."

45. Late in his life Allston was to write, "I would observe, however, that to no other man whom I have known, do I owe so much *intellectually*, as to Mr. Coleridge, with whom I became acquainted in Rome, and who has honored me with his friendship for more than five and twenty years." Flagg, *Life and Letters*, p. 314. Allston might have substituted

"share" for "owe," for the intellectual discipleship seemed based upon the deeper bonds of a common sensibility. Coleridge's use of gothic and antinarrative devices (even within ostensibly narrative contexts) in a poetry of dislocation has abundant parallels in Allston's writing and art, as does his willingness to experiment with referentiality while acknowledging its fictiveness. The two are also bound by their interest in organized religion as a conservative force capable of balancing or containing an imagination run rampant, e.g., Washington Allston, *Monaldi, A Tale* (Boston, 1841; Gainesville, Fla., 1967), pp. 52, 176.

46. For a discussion of the relation between philosophy and plagiarism in Coleridge see Norman Fruman, *Coleridge, The Damaged Archangel* (New York, 1971). Fruman outlines the problem in the introduction and proceeds in a chapter titled "Coleridge as Critic and Aesthetician" to rescue Coleridge's enduring *historical* significance as a synthesizer and a disseminator of new ideas and a new critical idiom; Fruman concedes the unoriginality of Coleridge's ideas when taken individually. That the *Biographia Literaria* should be read primarily as literary text, rather than as a philosophical or critical study, is not sufficiently considered.

47. The ostensible letter writer responds to Coleridge's ideas as if he had been translated from "our light airy modern chapels of ease" to "one of our largest Gothic cathedrals in a gusty moonlight night of autumn." Though the images suggest a movement from shallow to profound thought, they also seem to progress from clarity to ambiguity.

48. Barbara Novak, *American Painting of the Nineteenth Century* (New York, 1969), p. 54.

49. Ibid., p. 55.

50. Charles Feidelson has suggested a somewhat different reading of the painting that parallels the one given here. Feidelson understands the picture to be defined by a tension between "potentially representable objects and the universal source of light, which either fails or blinds." The failure of the light lies in its refusal "to inform" the objects it illuminates, to place them in coherent and intelligible relationships. One might infer from such a reading Allston's sense of a world lacking a divine or ordering authority.

51. Ronald Paulson has explored the issue of the "readibility" of eighteenth-century British painting in *Emblem and Expression* (Cambridge, Mass., 1975). In the introduction he summarizes his concerns:

> If Hogarth . . . was in some sense making fun of traditional iconography, and subverting and fragmenting it to make a new meaning of his own, then the next stage may well be the questioning of any traditionally accepted visual significance adhering to an object. It may then lead to a search for a private language or for no language or meaning at all.

52. Robert Rosenblum, *Transformations in Late Eighteenth Century Art* (Princeton, N.J., 1967, 1969), p. 11. Rosenblum in turn attributes the phrase to a mimeographed catalog of the British Museum, *William Blake and His Circle* (1957), p. 20.

53. Rosenblum, *Transformations*, p. 12.

54. Friedlaender, *Poussin*, pp. 39ff.

55. Allston tends to choose for his historical canvases those moments when natural and supernatural worlds come into contact. In works like *The Dead Man Restored to Life by Touching the Bones of the Prophet Elisha* (1811–13, Philadelphia, the Pennsylvania Academy of the Fine Arts), the mystery of life and creation occurs as a divine and therefore accountable process. In later works like *Saul and the Witch of Endor* this accountability is lost. This pattern is literalized in Allston's portraits, which may be roughly divided into groups where inspiration comes from sources exterior to the self (*Uriel in the Sun, Jeremiah Dictating His Prophecy of the Destruction of Jerusalem to Baruch the Scribe*) and those paintings in which a more Eakins-like interior consciousness defines the subject (*William Ellery Channing, Mrs. William Channing, Isaac of York*). A middleground group of portraits seems to externalize the subject's interior state in the suggestive background architecture (*Samuel Taylor Coleridge*, 1814 version, *Samuel Williams*). In Allston's marvelous *Self Portrait* (1805, Boston, Museum of Fine Arts), Allston plays, not unlike Bronzino and other mannerist painters, with the ambiguity of the background architecture—its planar,

shadowed, and nonmeasurable space—to express the mysterious nature of that inner world only teasingly hinted in the boyish face. For an informative account of *The Dead Man Restored*, see Elizabeth Johns, "Washington Allston's *Dead Man Revived*," *Art Bulletin* 61 (1979):78–99.

56. Allston, *Monaldi*, pp. 93–94.

57. The concern for the personality as split into separate and irreconcilable halves appears in paintings like *Dido and Anna* (1805–8, Coral Gables, Florida, Lowe Art Gallery), *The Sisters* (before 1818, Cambridge, Fogg Art Museum), and *Lorenzo and Jessica* (1832, private collection), in which pairs of figures intertwine in a dialectic of unity and opposition.

58. *The Journals of Ralph Waldo Emerson*, ed. Alfred R. Ferguson (Cambridge, Mass., 1964), vol. 5, p. 195; vol. 7, p. 24.

59. For an excellent and suggestive account of the more oracular and prophetic aspects of Emerson's thought, especially in their relation to Blake, see Barbara Packer, "Uriel's Cloud: Emerson's Rhetoric," *Georgia Review* 31 (1977):322–42, as well as "Emerson's Apocalypse of Mind" (unpublished Ph.D. dissertation, Yale University, 1974).

60. Doreen Hunter, "America's First Romantics: Richard Henry Dana, Sr. and Washington Allston," *New England Quarterly* 45 (March 1972), pp. 22, 26, 27. Hunter's article is excellent not only for its account of an important conservative bias in Allston, but for the way in which it links Allston with Richard Henry Dana, Sr., in their common appreciation of religion for its value as a constraint upon the imagination.

61. The point is suggestively made, though in a somewhat different context, by Richardson, *Washington Allston*, p. 147:

Allston's art was an art of memory . . . . His images of the beauty of a tree against the sky, of a plant growing by the roadside, or of distant effects of light over mountain and sea are images distilled by time and affection and translated into the harmonies of art . . . . His work had the quality of reflection which meant so much to the spirit of that generation: the quality of experience seen through the veil of memory and transposed to another plane by having lived long within the mind.

62. For a variant reading of Coleridge that acknowledges the unintelligibility of his world while still taking his moral intentions a bit more seriously than I do, see Frances Ferguson, "Coleridge and the Deluded Reader: 'The Rime of the Ancient Mariner,'" *Georgia Review* 31 (1977):617–37.

63. Geoffrey Hartman, *Beyond Formalism* (New Haven, 1970), pp. 302, 299.

64. Ibid., p. 300.

65. The language is Allston's own, the concluding half-line of a "Sonnet, On Rembrandt; Occasioned by his Picture of Jacob's Dream," *Lectures on Art* (New York, 1850), p. 276.

Chapter Three

1. Richard W. B. Lewis, *The American Adam* (Chicago, 1955), p. 1.

2. Perry Miller, *Errand into the Wilderness* (Boston, 1956; New York, 1964), p. 214.

3. John Milton, *Complete Poems and Major Prose*, ed. Merritt Y. Hughes (New York, 1957). All references to *Paradise Lost* are from this edition.

4. Geoffrey Hartman, *Beyond Formalism* (New Haven, 1970), p. 134.

5. For a splendid account of the peculiarly masculine tradition of "naming" and its relation to a feminist aesthetics, see Margaret Homans, *Women Writers and Poetic Identity* (Princeton, 1980).

6. Stuart Ende, *Keats and the Sublime* (New Haven, 1976), p. 15.

7. Ibid., pp. 15–16. For a related treatment of Milton's poetry, the reader is referred to Leslie Brisman, *Milton's Poetry of Choice and Its Romantic Heirs* (Ithaca, N.Y., 1973).

8. Ende, *Keats*, p. 12.

9. The Bible, King James Version, Matthew 10:34–35.

10. Edwards goes on to note, in a manner that Milton probably would have approved of, that sin is not so much something "new" in the self, "but only the same self-love that necessarily belongs to the nature working and influencing, without regulation from that superior that primitively belongs to our nature, and that is necessary in order to the harmonious existing of it." (*Miscellanies*, no. 301, quoted in Sydney Ahlstrom, *Theology in America* [New York, 1967], p. 172.)

11. William Wordsworth, "The Recluse," in *The Poetical Works of William Wordsworth*, ed. E. de Selincourt and H. Darbishire, 5 vols. (London, 1940–49), vol. 5, pp. 4, 338.

12. Ahlstrom, *Theology*, p. 172.

13, *The Oxford English Dictionary*, compact edition, vol. 1 (Oxford, 1971), p. 294.

14. Meyer H. Abrams, "Structure and Style in the Greater Romantic Lyric," in *From Sensibility to Romanticism: Essays Presented to Frederick A. Pottle*, ed. Frederick W. Hilles and Harold Bloom (New York, 1965), pp. 527–57. See also Geoffrey Hartman, *The Unmediated Vision: An Interpretation of Wordsworth, Hopkins, Rilke, and Valery* (New Haven, 1954; New York, 1966), pp. 3–45.

15. Jonathan Edwards, *Five Discourses* (Boston, 1738), p. 145. This particular sermon of Edwards was brought to my attention by David Laurence, author of a forthcoming study on Edwards.

16. Wordsworth, *Poetical Works*, vol. 5, pp. 4, 338.

17. John Neal, one of American's first art critics, had written in 1824 that the country could boast only three good landscape painters: Joshua Shaw, Francis Guy, and Thomas Doughty. Though landscape painting existed in America prior to Trumbull's discovery of Cole, it lacked the scope and power that Cole would soon forge into a new visual idiom. See Matthew Baigell, *A History of American Painting* (New York, 1971), p. 107. For an account of Cole's first public recognition, see William Dunlap, *History of the Rise and Progress of the Arts of Design in the United States*, 2 vols. (New York, 1834; reprint New York, 1969), vol. 2, part 2, pp. 359–60.

18. William Feaver, *The Art of John Martin* (Oxford, 1975), pp. 107–10. For a larger study of Cole's relation to his English sources, see Earl A. Powell, "English Influences in the Art of Thomas Cole," unpublished Ph.D. dissertation, Harvard University, 1974.

19. It is interesting to note the series of waterfalls receding into the background on the *earth* side of the picture, all bodies of water on this side being torrential currents that fall continuously as they approach the picture plane, while contrasting it with the single prominent body of water found in Eden, a still lake with two swans. The only water in motion on the Edenic side is a quiet foreground stream whose water, curiously enough, appears to *rise* after falling from the bordering summits of Eden rather than continuing its downward plunge.

20. Herman Melville, *Moby-Dick, or, The Whale*, ed. Charles Feidelson, Jr. (New York, 1964), p. 634.

21. Like Ahab, Cole's Adam fends off the brightness of God's presence with his raised arm, while Milton's Adam cries to Eve, "those heav'nly shapes / will dazzle now this earthly, with their blaze / Insufferably bright" (9.1082–84).

22. Richard Brodhead, *Hawthorne, Melville, and the Novel* (Chicago, 1973), p. 11.

23. Ibid., p. 20.

24. Quoted from *Works, Letters and Journals*, vol. 3, p. 405, in Meyer H. Abrams, *The Mirror and the Lamp* (New York, 1953), p. 14.

25. Like Allston, Cope professed himself to be a believing Christian. His later religious allegories like *The Voyage of Life* (1840, Utica, New York, The Munson-Williams-Proctor Institute) suggest how Christianity provided him with a resolution to the dilemma of natural recurrence that nature itself could not provide. In *The Voyage of Life*, the doom and destruction that culminate life's journey appear to be circumvented by the promise of resurrection (or some process like it), which removes man from the scene of earthly strife and elevates him to an eternal reward. An earlier work like *The Expulsion from the Garden of Eden*, however, offers no such vision.

26. For an informative account of Peale's picture see Roger Stein, "Charles Willson Peale's Expressive Design: The Artist in His Museum," *Prospects* 6 (1981):139–85.

Chapter Four

1. Walter Benjamin, *Illuminations*, ed. and with an intro. by Hannah Arendt (Frankfort, 1977; New York, 1968), pp. 83–109. For a parallel account of folk narrative that centers on its linguistic rather than cultural patterns, see Tzvetan Todorov, *The Poetics of Prose*, trans. Richard Howard (Ithaca, N.Y., 1977), pp. 66–79.

2. Benjamin, *Illuminations*, p. 83.

3. Washington Irving, *Tales of a Traveller*, Knickerbocker Edition (New York, 1865), p. 456.

4. Ibid., p. 456.

5. Geoffrey Crayon is the fictional exception here, for he is not at Hell Gate, but, as he tells us in the book's preface, is writing instead of the forementioned events while indisposed in "the old frontier town of Mentz" on "the fair banks of the Rhine." Crayon's location may itself be presumed to be fictional. He concludes his preface "To the Reader" with lines suggesting the endless intertranslatability of fact with fiction:

> "*Dated from the* HOTEL DE DARMSTADT,
> *ci-devant* HOTEL DE PARIS,
> MENTZ, *otherwise called* MAYENCE."

6. The poignancy of Miles Coverdale's situation in *The Blithedale Romance* rests on just that distinction between fiction and fact which leaves him forever hovering, "Minor Poet" that he is, on the brink of everyday relations with the world, a poetic exile whose task is to perceive mankind from the periphery of life's bustle.

7. Irving, *Tales*, p. 431.

8. Henry Adams uses the image of an oyster in his *Education* as a metaphor for the historical imagination secreting patterns of order where it otherwise would find only chaos. The result is not a history that is true, so much as one that is beautiful. "Man knew it was true because he made it, and he loved it for the same reason." Notice the striking similarity between Adams's language and the closing affirmation of Keats's "Ode to a Nightingale" discussed below. See *The Education of Henry Adams* (Cambridge, Mass, 1961), p. 458.

9. Stuart Ende, *Keats and the Sublime* (New Haven, 1976), pp. 116–59. For a larger reading of Keats that centers upon the humanism of his verse, see Walter Jackson Bate, *John Keats* (New York, 1966).

10. Irving, *Tales*, pp. 9–10.

11. Ibid., p. 515.

12. John F. Lynen, *The Design of the Present* (New Haven, 1969), p. 154. Lynen's brilliant but brief account of Irving is perhaps the best single treatment available. For more extended and often helpful discussions, the reader is referred to Martin Roth, *Comedy and America: The Lost World of Washington Irving* (Port Washington, N.Y., 1976); William Hedges, *Washington Irving: An American Study* (Baltimore, Md., 1965); and Donald A. Ringe, *The Pictorial Mode: Space and Time in the Art of Bryant, Irving and Cooper* (Lexington, Ky., 1971).

13. Washington Irving, *A History of New York From the Beginning of the World to the End of the Dutch Dynasty*, Knickerbocker Edition (New York, 1864), p. 238.

14. Washington Irving, *The Sketch Book*, Knickerbocker Edition (New York, 1864), p. 51.

15. Ibid., pp. 49–50.

16. Irving, *Tales*, p. 462; emphasis mine.

17. Nathaniel Hawthorne, *The Centenary Edition*, ed. William Charvat et al. ([Columbus, Ohio], 1962–74), vol. 1, p. 10.

18. David M. Sokol, "John Quidor: His Life and Work" (unpublished Ph.D. dissertation, New York University, 1971), p. 24.

19. Sokol speculates that Irving probably knew of Quidor's "illustrations," which, though unsold, were exhibited regularly at The National Academy of Design as early as 1828. Ibid., pp. 54ff.

20. Irving, *Tales*, p. 513; emphasis mine.

21. Quidor's painting, with its necrophiliac undertones, puns with Irving's title. The term "Money Diggers" is converted by Quidor into the *grave* diggers, an insight first brought to my attention by Michele Cone of Yale University.

22. Christopher Wilson, "Engraved Sources for Quidor's Early Work," *American Art Journal* 8 (November 1976):17–25.

23. Charles Coleman Sellars, *Charles Willson Peale* (New York, 1969), p. 299. Emphasis mine. Barbara Novak notes a similar sense of a "second creation" among the "artist-explorers" of the American West half a century later. "But the most profound intentions of the artist-explorers coincided exactly with their role as curates of the natural church. They were rehearsing and reliving Genesis through the landscape, just as the geologists were attempting to do." Barbara Novak, *Nature and Culture: American Landscape and Painting 1825–1875* (New York, 1980), p. 152. For a discussion of the Peale painting in its historical context, see Lillian B. Miller, "Charles Willson Peale as History Painter: The Exhumation of the Mastodon," *American Art Journal* 13 (Winter 1981):47–68. For a discussion of *Watson and the Shark* in relation to visual conventions of the day, see Roger Stein, "Copley's *Watson and the Shark* and Aesthetics in the 1770s," in Calvin Israel ed., *Discoveries and Considerations: Essays on Early American Literature and Aesthetics Presented to Harold Jantz* (Albany, New York, 1976).

24. Sigmund Freud, *The Standard Edition of the Complete Psychological Works*, trans. and ed. James Strachey et al. (London, 1953–74), vol. 22, p. 80.

25. John Milton, *Complete Poems and Selected Prose*, ed. Merritt Y. Hughes (New York, 1957).

26. She tells Adam, "for I this Night ... have dream'd, / If dream'd, not as I oft am wont."

27. *The Journals of Søren A. Kierkegaard*, a selection edited by Alexander Dru (New York, 1938). See also *Concluding Unscientific Postscript*, trans. David F. Swenson, intro. and notes by Walter Lowrie (Princeton, 1941, 1961), pp. 74ff. For an excellent discussion of Kierkegaard as literary strategist, see Louis MacKey, *Kierkegaard, A Kind of Poet* (Philadelphia, 1971).

28. Irving, *History*, pp. 311–12.

29. Freud, *Standard Edition*, vol. 5, pp. 567–68.

30. The similarity of dress and stature between the two antagonists also suggests a countervailing habit of mind in Quidor, a cynicism about the ultimate nature of all change. Quidor seems to hint, like the old French adage, *"plus ça change, plus c'est la même chose."*

31. See Marvin Meyers, *The Jacksonian Persuasion: Politics and Belief* (Stanford, Calif., 1957), Michael Kammen, *People of Paradox: An Inquiry Concerning the Origins of American Civilization* (New York, 1972), and for a more overtly psychoanalytic approach Michael Rogin, *Fathers and Sons: Andrew Jackson and the Subjugation of the American Indian* (New York, 1975).

32. I am indebted for this observation to Christopher Wilson of Middlebury College.

33. Hawthorne, *Centenary Edition*, vol. 10, pp. 78–79.

34. Ibid., pp. 82–83. The reader might note the pun by which the cloud is described as a "black mass," together with the use of " be*wild*ered" to describe wretches lost in the "*wild*erness." Hawthorne is an avid and shameless punster.

35. Ibid., p. 88.

36. The tendency of the Puritan mind to seek after sin is described by Hawthorne in the speech delivered by the "sable form" to Goodman Brown and Faith:

By the sympathy of your human hearts for sin ye shall scent out all the places—whether in church, bedchamber, street, field, or forest—where crime has been committed, and shall exult to behold the whole earth one stain of guilt, one mighty blood spot .... It shall be yours to penetrate, in every bosom, the deep mystery of sin, the fountain of all wicked arts, and which inexhaustibly supplies more evil impulses than human power—than my power at its utmost—can make manifest in deeds. [Ibid., p. 87.]

37. Ralph Waldo Emerson, *Selections*, ed. Stephen E. Whicher (Boston, 1957), p. 53.

38. Ibid., p. 338.

39. Ibid., p. 169.

40. Ibid., p. 330.

41. Ibid., p. 331.

42. Ibid., p. 269.

43. Ibid., p. 338.

44. Ibid., p. 24.

45. Ibid., p. 272.

46. Ibid., p. 271.

47. Ibid., p. 269.

48. Hawthorne, *Centenary Edition*, vol. 9, p. 47.

49. Ibid., p. 37.

50. Ibid., pp. 40–41.

51. Martin Heidegger, *Being and Time*, trans. James Macquarrie and Edward Robinson (New York, 1962), pp. 294ff.

52. He notes on three separate occasions that the veil consisted of only "two folds of crape."

53. For a discussion of Coleridge's language games in the *Biographia Literaria*, see chapter 2, "The Collapse of Intelligibility: Allston's Classical Landscapes," pp. 000–00.

54. Hawthorne, *Centenary Edition*, vol. 3, p. 114.

55. Ibid., pp. 97, 161.

56. The historical relation between Quidor and Daumier is uncertain. Daumier started as an illustrator for Parisian journals, and his work might have found its way in journal form to America and Quidor's eyes. Quidor might also have seen lithographs or woodcuts of Daumier's.

57. Jules Prown points out the political overtones behind West's painting in its pictorial "call for a change in the values and standards of contemporary society." (Jules Prown, *American Painting From Its Beginnings to the Armory Show* [Cleveland, 1969], p. 40.)

58. Irving, *Sketch Book*, p. 68.

59. Wilmerding can find no concrete proof to support his belief that Quidor might be quoting from Michelangelo, though he does suggest that Quidor probably "knew earlier European art through copies or engravings circulating in New York galleries." John Wilmerding, ed., *The Genius of American Painting* (New York, 1973), p. 121.

60. Wilson, "Engraved Sources," pp. 21ff.

61. Harold Bloom, *The Anxiety of Influence* (New York, 1973), pp. 5–16. Bloom himself resists being called a Freudian critic. He notes in the introduction to *Poetry and Repression* (New Haven, 1976) that "on a strict Freudian view, a good poem is a sublimation, and not a repression . . . . By attempting to show the poetic ascendancy of 'repression' over 'sublimation' I . . . deny the usefuless of the Unconscious, as opposed to repression, as a literary term."

62. Hawthorne, *Centenary Edition*, vol. 1, p. 12.

63. Ibid., pp. 11–12; emphasis mine.

64. Ibid., p. 26; emphasis mine. The significance of puns in Hawthorne's works was first pointed out to me by Jerry Kleiner of Yale University.

65. Ibid., p. 93.

66. For a discussion of the alliance of artists, intellectuals, clergy, and women in mid-nineteenth century America, see Ann Douglas, *The Feminization of American Culture* (New York, 1977) and, alternatively, Nancy Cott, *The Bonds of Womanhood: "Woman's Sphere" in New England, 1780–1835* (New Haven, Connecticut, 1977).

67. Hawthorne, *Centenary Edition*, vol. 3, p. 97.

68. The tension between vision and action is explored as the key to an American literary tradition in David Minter's *The Interpreted Design as a Structural Principle in American Prose* (New Haven, 1969). Minter discusses Blithedale in the introduction and again in a separate chapter on Hawthorne's novel.

Chapter Five

1. For an account of Arachne's web as an image of modern art see J. Hillis Miller, "Ariachne's Broken Woof," *Georgia Review* 31 (1977):44–60, and along the same lines, "Ariadne's Thread: Repetition and the Narrative Line," *Critical Inquiry* 3 (1976):57–77.

2. Thomas Weiskel, *The Romantic Sublime: Studies in the Structure and Psychology of Transcendence* (Baltimore, 1976), pp. 10–11, 22–23. I am profoundly indebted throughout this essay to Weiskel's compelling work. Weiskel's book provides what may well be the single most significant account of the sublime since Edmund Burke, providing us, through its interest in psychoanalytic and semiotic categories, with a new and remarkably suggestive perspective for reconceiving the Romantic sublime. For studies which link the sublime to the works of Thomas Cole, the reader is referred in particular to Charles L. Sanford, "The Concept of the Sublime in the Works of Thomas Cole and William Cullen Bryant," *American Literature* 28 (January 1957):434–48; Earl A. Powell, "Luminism and the American Sublime" in *American Light: The Luminist Movement, 1850–1875*, ed. John Wilmerding (Washington, D.C., 1980), pp. 68–94, and "Thomas Cole and the American Landscape Tradition," *Arts Magazine* 52 (February 1978):114–23, (March 1978):110–17, (April 1978):113–17; Barbara Novak, *American Painting of the Nineteenth Century: Realism, Idealism and the American Experience* (New York, 1969) and *Nature and Culture: American Landscape and Painting, 1825–1875* (New York, 1980); and John C. Riordan, "Thomas Cole: A Case Study of the Painter-Poet Theory of Art in American Painting from 1825–1850," unpublished Ph.D. dissertation, Syracuse University, 1970.

3. Ralph Waldo Emerson, *Selections from Ralph Waldo Emerson*, ed. Stephen Whicher (Boston, 1957; 1960), p. 157.

4. Louis Legrand Noble, *The Life and Works of Thomas Cole* (New York, 1853; reprint Cambridge, Mass., 1964, with an introduction by Elliot S. Vesell), p. 33.

5. Ibid., p. 33.

6. Ibid., p. 24. Emphasis mine.

7. William Dunlap, *History of the Rise and Progress of the Arts of Design in the United States* (New York, 1834; reprint New York, 1969), vol. 2, part ii, pp. 359–60.

8. Barbara Novak, "The Double-Edged Axe," *Art in America* 64 (1976):44–50, and Nicholai Cikovsky, Jr., "'The Ravages of the Axe': The Meaning of the Tree Stump in Nineteenth Century American Art," *Art Bulletin* 61 (1979):611–26.

9. Edmund Burke, *A Philosophical Enquiry into the Origin of Our Ideas of the Sublime and Beautiful*, ed. with an introduction and notes by James T. Boulton (Notre Dame, Ind., 1958, 1968), pp. 39–40, 79–81, 145–49.

10. Sigmund Freud, *The Standard Edition of the Complete Psychological Works*, trans. and ed. James Strachey et al. (London, 1953–74), vol. 5, pp. 408–9.

11. Freud describes the origin of repression in those "traumatic moments, when the ego meets with an excessively great libidinal demand . . . which cannot be dealt with by the normal rules of the pleasure principle." Freud, *Standard Edition*, vol. 22, p. 94.

12. Weiskel, *Sublime*, pp. 10–11, 75–76, 91–94.

13. Freud, *Standard Edition*, vol. 19, pp. 24–29, 38–39. See also Silvano Arieti, ed., *American Handbook of Psychiatry, Second Edition*, vol. 1, *The Foundations of Psychiatry* (New York, 1974), pp. 310–11.

14. Esther Seaver, *Thomas Cole, 1801–1848: One Hundred Years Later*, exhibition catalogue, Wadsworth Athneum (Hartford, Conn., 1948).

15. For an alternative account of poetic identity formation as it relates to women, see Margaret Homans, *Women Writers and Poetic Identity* (Princeton, 1980).

16. For an introduction to Lacan's thought and the ideological values at stake in his reading of Freud, see Fredric Jameson, "Imaginary and Symbolic Action in Lacan: Marxism, Psychoanalytic Criticism, and the Problem of the Subject," *Yale French Studies. Literature and Psychoanalysis. The Question of Reading: Otherwise* 55/56 (1977):364. For a more general account of Lacan, see Anika Rifflet-Lemaire, *Jacques Lacan*, trans. David Macey (London and Boston, 1977).

17. Jacques Lacan, *Ecrits: A Selection*, trans. Alan Sheridan (New York, 1977), p. 4.

18. I borrow this description from Jean Roussel.

19. Lacan, *Ecrits*, p. 2.

20. Jameson, "Lacan," pp. 351, 353.

21. Barbara Novak, *American Painting of the Nineteenth Century: Realism, Idealism and the American Experience* (New York, 1969), p. 63. Novak returns to the theme of the real and the ideal in Cole in *Nature and Culture*, pp. 263–65.

22. Noble, *Cole*, p. 148. One also finds in Cole and others, most notably Irving, the opposite lament: a bemoaning of the lack of associative memories attached to the American landscape. Cole writes from Europe in 1841: "I remarked that, although American scenery was often so fine, we feel the want of associations such as cling to scenes in the old world. Simple nature is not quite sufficient. We want human interest, incident and action, to render the effect of landscape complete." (Ibid., p. 219.)

23. Weiskel, *Sublime*, p. 14. The history of the translation of divine attributes into the natural landscape has been traced, as Weiskel notes, in Ernest Tuveson, "Space, Deity and the 'Natural Sublime,'" *Modern Language Quarterly* 12 (1951):20–38, and Marjorie Nicolson, *Mountain Gloom and Mountain Glory: The Development of the Aesthetics of the Infinite* (Ithaca, N.Y., 1959).

24. Weiskel, *Sublime*, p. 13.

25. The phrase is borrowed from Norman Mailer, *Armies of the Night: History as a Novel, The Novel as History* (New York, 1968). Mailer is another twentieth-century Romantic engaged in the effort to recover the power of the mysterious and demonic for the revitalization of the American middle class.

26. For a suggestive account of the significance of "prospect views" in landscape painting, see Jay Appleton, *The Experience of Landscape* (London and New York, 1975).

27. I wish to stress here that my choice of paintings for individual examination is somewhat arbitrary. Any number of paintings from Cole's sublime period would produce variant but still closely related readings. The decision to focus on *Snow Squall*, *Sunrise in the Catskills*, and *Sunny Morning on the Hudson River* represents an effort to arrange and clarify a narrative that is implicit in a number of different works.

28. One might speculate that Cole's presumably unconscious allusion to Hogarth and the canons of eighteenth-century art provides a means for tracing his own intellectual relation to the age that preceded him. The failure of the S-curve to reappear as a basis for either narcissistic or oedipal identification—except perhaps in the distorted forms of the blasted trees—suggests that Cole's development of his own version of the Romantic sublime is his means of putting behind him the standards and authority of the eighteenth century. The high hopes associated with the S-curve in *Snow Squall*, together with the apparent bitterness of the blasted tree motif, might tell us something of the emotional intensity surrounding his struggle with eighteenth-century art. It is interesting to note along these lines Cole's comments to a remark of Hogarth's:

The first of Hogarth's pictures I saw were that series called Love a la Mode. In colour and handling they were far beyond my expectation. Objecting to the study of pictures, Hogarth says, "The most original mind, if habituated to these exercises, becomes inoculated with the style of others, and loses the power of stamping a spirit of its own on the canvass." There is truth in this remark. [Noble, *Cole*, p. 81]

Cole seems to be using Hogarth in Emersonian fashion as a guide for the smashing of all guides, an attempt to break loose from the authority of the past. All this, of course, is speculation.

29. The term "homosexual" is used here in its psychoanalytic rather than popular meaning. Freud employs the idea of homosexuality to denote an erotic object attachment toward a figure of the same sex. During the oedipal years the male child's desire to love or make love with the father is understood as homosexual; this attraction is complicated by the child's counter sense of rivalry and frustration. It forms a normal component of the oedipal crisis and should not be confused with post-adolescent and adult modes of sexuality. See, for example, Freud, *Standard Edition*, vol. 7, pp. 125–248.

30. Ibid., pp. 125ff.

31. Freud, *Standard Edition*, vol. 22, pp. 112, 135. For more recent accounts of psychoanalytic approaches to women, see Jean B. Miller, ed., *Psychoanalysis and Women* (New York, 1973), and Jean Strouse, ed., *Women and Analysis* (New York, 1974).

32. An alternative reading might note that maternal imagery is introduced into Cole's sublime work as early as *Sunrise*, in which the rounded central mountain appears to be as breast-shaped as it is phallic in form. The introduction of feminine imagery in *Sunrise* complicates the sense of ambivalence in the child's mode of relation to its desired object. It suggests either a feminization of the father or a confusion between masculine and feminine objects of desire. *Sunny Morning* then represents a clarification of the earlier confusion into an overt sense of opposition on the part of the father toward the son's (now objectified) desire for the mother. Whether the central mountain is understood as masculine, feminine, or both, however, does not affect the larger movement from male-male to male-female bonding that informs the progression from *Snow Squall* to *Sunny Morning*.

33. The ego's attempt at self-fulfillment carries with it a surcharge of libidinal energy in the form of anxiety. In its more narcissistic stages, this anxiety attaches itself to the subject in its efforts to achieve an "orthopaedic" unity, a state which fictionalizes the actual situation of the self, as Lacan notes, and is therefore experienced as a self-estrangement.

34. Or, as Lacan might phrase it, the subject translates its "needs" into "desires," the latter being the socialized products of organic impulses.

35. For a brief discussion of "belatedness" as a term introduced in contemporary criticism by Harold Bloom, see chapter 4, "Irving, Quidor and the Catastrophe of Imaginative Vision," pp. 000–00.

36. Weiskel discusses the peculiarly *oral* underpinnings of the sublime, the child's desire to ingest a larger or "excessive" force, in his (Weiskel's) effort to establish a preoedipal and largely maternal substructure underlying Kant's mathematical sublime. See Weiskel, *Sublime*, pp. 83–106. Neil Hertz discusses Weiskel's account in "The Notion of Blockage in the Literature of the Sublime," in *Psychoanalysis and the Question of the Text*, ed. Geoffrey Hartman (Baltimore, Md., 1978), pp. 62–85. Weiskel's emphasis on the maternal and oral stages of preoedipal behavior differs from my own reliance on Lacan's mirror state and the narcissistic and onanistic qualities of the preoedipal subject.

37. The secondariness associated with naturalization expresses not only the subject's sense of his own belatedness, his perception of his inferior power relative to the commanding and established presence of the Other, but suggests also his fear of punishment-castration for his desire for a forbidden object, whether that be an autoerotic extension of himself or the cathected image of the parent.

38. For Cole the origins of a visionary art, and, specifically, the visionary energy underlining the structure and apprehension of the beautiful, can be traced back to the child's sublimation of his narcissistic and homoerotic desires into charged states of scoptophilia.

39. The reader will find similar childhood fantasies in Freud's accounts of the Rat Man, the Wolf Man, and the "psychotic Dr. Schreber." See Freud, *Standard Edition*, vol. 10, pp. 153–320; vol. 17, pp. 3–122; and vol. 12, pp. 3–84, respectively.

40. Feminine is understood here to express a *cultural* perception implicit in Cole's paintings that links women with passivity, beauty, and similar socially determined attributes.

41. Noble, *Cole*, p. 46.

42. Ibid., pp. 42–43.

43. Thomas Cole, Journals and Manuscripts, the Archives of American Art, Microfilm ALC-3. In "Storm in the Catskills," the second of the three sublime narratives, the storms of oedipal crisis break upon the unexpectant narrator in a deluge of darkness and thunder. The reversion to a passive verb construction in the opening sentence underscores the surprise and helplessness of the speaker. The loss of infantile innocence is associated with hostile forces external to the self, threatening from a "distance" to disrupt a scene of prior harmony:

> In one of my mountain rambles I was overtaken by a thunderstorm—In the early part of the day the sky had been brilliant and unclouded; but as it advanced, huge masses of vapour were seen moving across the deep blue. Notwithstanding there was some reason to expect a storm, I contented myself with the hope that the clouds would pass over the mountains without unburthening themselves; but my hope proved a fallacious one—A sudden darkness enveloped the scene which a few moments before was beaming with sunlight, and there was a muttering of thunder. [Ibid., ALC-3.]

Noble's transcriptions of Cole's journals tend to vary from the letter—though not the spirit—of Cole's handwritten manuscripts. My analysis of the wilderness texts, therefore, follows Cole's writings rather than Noble's transcriptions (except for those few passages I have not been able to locate among the original manuscripts).

44. Cole's narratives resonate in a "perverse" and uncanny manner with the short stories of Edgar Allan Poe. In "The Fall of the House of Usher," the narrator enters a landscape whose "bitter" reality unfolds as "the hideous dropping off of the veil" experienced by the "reveller upon opium." This moment of alienation and estrangement implicit in the landscape parallels Cole's own narrative "defamiliarization": that moment when "everyday life" comes up against its most hidden and unacknowledged feelings.

45. Freud, *Standard Edition*, vol. 10, pp. 165ff.; vol. 17, pp. 32ff.

46. Ibid., vol. 14, pp. 237–58.

47. Cole, Journals, ALC-3.

48. Ibid.

49. Ibid.

50. A major series of revivals occurred in upstate New York during the period of Cole's sublime work. Charles Grandison Finney ignited powerful religious emotions in an area labeled the "burned over district," a sweep of communities in central and upper New York State where a series of religious revivals in the years 1825–30 were to spark a larger national revival that would continue intermittently until the Civil War. A fundamental force in the reform movements of the 1830s and 40s, and a central impetus behind the Abolitionist and antislavery crusades of the period, the revivalism of figures lke Finney and Lyman Beecher convinced people of the guilt that hung Damocles-like over their heads and of their own power to rid themselves of the burden. Cf. Whitney R. Cross, *The Burned-Over District: The Social and Intellectual History of Enthusiastic Religion in Western New York, 1800–1850* (Ithaca, N.Y., 1950); Timothy L. Smith, *Revivalism and Social Reform: American Protestantism on the Eve of the Civil War* (New York, 1957); Bernard A. Weisberger, *They Gathered at the River: The Story of the Great Revivalists and Their Impact upon Religion in America* (Boston, 1958); and Paul E. Johnson, *A Shopkeeper's Millenium: Society and Revivals in Rochester, New York, 1815–1837* (New York, 1978).

51. Cole, Journals, ALC-3.

52. Ibid.

53. Ibid.

54. Ibid.

55. The choice of the word "careering" in this instance is significant, suggesting as it does not only the wild and liberating motion of the "chariot," but the possibilities of *vocation* linked implicitly to the artist's release from the wrath of the father.

56. The rhetoric of mid-nineteenth-century American culture drew attention to the "sphere of women" and the "home" as an alternative to values of a male-dominated

market society. Cole's language may reflect this larger cultural division between male and female roles. Cf. Nancy Cott, *The Bonds of Womanhood* (New Haven, 1977), and Ann Douglas, *The Feminization of American Culture* (New York, 1977).

57. In all but one incident, the evidences of female sexuality are overshadowed by the speaker's prior concern for phallic power.

58. Cole notes twice in his writings of the period that his sketches were often mistaken for the work of a mapmaker rather than an artist. See Noble, *Cole,* pp. 43, 68.

59. Ibid., p. 42.

60. Cole, Journals, ALC-3.

61. For a suggestive study of the retention of narrative elements in the landscape works of J. M. W. Turner, see Ronald Paulson, "Turner's Graffiti: The Sun and Its Glosses," in *Images of Romanticism: Verbal and Visual Affinities*, ed. Karl Kroeber and William Walling (New Haven, 1978), pp. 167–88.

62. The story in fact plays down the visionary qualities attached to Rutledge's moment of death and emphasizes instead the practical difficulties confronting him. The stress on a visionary space is Cole's own.

63. Cf. "MS Found in a Bottle," "The Narrative of A. Gordon Pym," "Berenice," "William Wilson," and a host of other Poe stories in which death and vision combine in a moment of perverse and lyric beauty.

64. Again the reader is referred for comparative purposes to a study of the relation of narrative elements to landscape art in Ronald Paulson, "Constable and the Suppression of Literary Landscape," in *Literary Landscape: Turner and Constable* (New Haven, 1982).

65. Weiskel, *Sublime*, p. 85.

66. In a Lacanian view of things, we might say that the subject positions himself within the signifying chain at a point *prior to* the discourse of the Other. For Lacan such a possibility is illusory—Imaginary—for it suggests a mode of selfhood unfettered by the language of the Other. For Cole, as perhaps for Romanticism in general, the possibility of the subject as Signifier (rather than as signified) lies at the heart of Romantic identity formation.

Epilogue

1. The term "luminist" was originally applied to painters of the mid-nineteenth century in America by John I. H. Baur, in "American Luminism: A Neglected Aspect of the Realist Movement in Nineteenth-Century American Painting," *Perspectives USA 9* (Autumn 1954):90. The most recent and comprehensive account of luminism is *American Light: The Luminist Movement, 1850–1875*, ed. John Wilmerding (Washington, D.C., 1980).

2. William H. Gerdts and Theodore E. Stebbins, Jr., *"A Man of Genius": The Art of Washington Allston (1779–1843)* (Boston, 1979), pp. 49–50.

3. Theodore E. Stebbins, Jr., "Luminism in Context: A New View," in Wilmerding, *Luminism*, pp. 211–34.

4. Novak discusses luminism at length in both *American Painting of the Nineteenth Century: Realism, Idealism and the American Experience* (New York, 1969) and *Nature and Culture: American Landscape and Painting, 1825–1875* (New York, 1980). Her most succinct effort at defining luminism formally may be found in "On Defining Luminism" in Wilmerding, *Luminism*, pp. 23–29.

5. David Huntington, "Church and Luminism: Light for America's Elect" in Wilmerding, *Luminism*, pp. 155–90. For a somewhat earlier account of Church's career, especially in relation to that of Cole, see also David Huntington, *The Landscapes of Frederic Edwin Church: Vision of an American Era* (New York, 1966). Barbara Novak provides a parallel account in *Nature and Culture*, pp. 67ff.

Index